Handbook
of
AMERICAN IDIOMS
and
Idiomatic Usage

NEW EDITION

by

HAROLD C. WHITFORD
Lecturer in English, Columbia University

and

ROBERT J. DIXSON

This Handbook lists and defines more than 5000 idioms of the American language and illustrates their use in sentences.

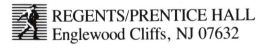 REGENTS/PRENTICE HALL
Englewood Cliffs, NJ 07632

© 1973 by Harold C. Whitford and R. J. Dixson Associates

 Published by Prentice Hall
A Simon & Schuster Company
Englewood Cliffs, New Jersey 07632

Printed in the United States of America

10   9   8   7   6

ISBN   0-13-372566-9

Prentice-Hall International (UK) Limited, *London*
Prentice-Hall of Australia Pty. Limited, *Sydney*
Prentice-Hall Canada Inc., *Toronto*
Prentice-Hall Hispanoamericana, S.A., *Mexico*
Prentice-Hall of India Private Limited, *New Delhi*
Prentice-Hall of Japan, Inc., *Tokyo*
Simon & Schuster Asia Pte. Ltd., *Singapore*
Editora Prentice-Hall do Brasil, Ltda., *Rio de Janeiro*

PREFACE

Experienced teachers of English have long recognized the importance of the idiom in introducing color and adding grace and precision to speech and writing.

Students of English as a second language lack confidence in their ability to use idiomatic expressions. Even those fluent in English are often puzzled by the idiomatic structure of the language. And if they steer clear of idiomatic usage, their speech and writing tend to become formal and stilted.

To meet this situation the authors offer this handbook which covers idiomatic usage of American English. More than 5,000 of the most common idiomatic phrases and constructions of American English are included here. Each idiom is defined and its use illustrated in a sentence.

No effort has been spared to make the book as practical as possible. Thus, particular stress has been given to the basic idiomatic constructions deriving from such common verbs as *bring, take, go, come, get, do, let, leave, make, put, find*, etc. Specialized or esoteric phrases, which are often colorful but which are of low frequency, have not been included. Only those slang expressions have been listed which are firmly established in the language.

The intention at all times has been to make the book a working manual and a textbook for advanced students of American English.

As a work of reference, it is hoped that this handbook may serve all those, both here and in foreign countries, who need definition and explanation of the idiomatic phrases they come across in their reading or in daily conversation on the streets of American cities, in American motion pictures, or in current literature.

Students of language are no doubt aware of the different words used to describe similar things in Britain and the United States, such as British *petrol* for American gasoline, *cinema* for movie, *lift* for elevator, etc.

In the case of idiomatic usage, the difference is even greater and much more subtle. Thus, a phrase like *to put one's foot into it*, meaning to commit a social blunder, is expressed in Britain by the phrase to *drop a brick*, which would not be generally understood in the United States. This book therefore should prove useful to scholars and to the many Europeans accustomed to British terminology and who are, therefore, at a loss to understand strictly "American" English.

Particular attention is directed to the system of alphabetizing in this book. In a dictionary, where only one word is involved, the problem is simple. An idiom, however, consists of more than one word; the problem is where to place the idiom so that the reader can readily locate it.

The following logical system has been used: All idioms have been alphabetized according to the key or strong word in the idiom. Thus, *make out* is found under *make; up to par* is listed under *par; on the heels of* under *heels*. In addition, extensive groupings have been made under such basic verbs as *go, get, do, make, take,* etc. In this way, the fundamental importance of these verbs in the English language and their use in American idioms has been made obvious.

HAROLD C. WHITFORD
ROBERT J. DIXSON

A

about face a sudden change of course, or to an opposite decision:—His choice of that house was an about face from his original intention.

about, be about something (1) engaged in, doing:—What is he about now? (2) consist of, subject-matter:—What is that novel about?

about, be about to ready, on the point of doing something:—We were just about to leave when you telephoned.

about, going about being circulated, told:—There is a story going about concerning the impending divorce of the President's daughter.

about, what about information requested concerning, regarding: — What about those books you were going to bring me?

about See also **bring** about, **come** about.

above all most importantly:—You must, above all, be loyal to your country.

above board straightforward, honest, open, sometimes expressed "open and above board":—All his business dealings were above board.

abreast, keep abreast of be informed as to the latest developments:—It is difficult to keep abreast of the international situation these days.

absent-minded forgetful:—He is the typical absent-minded professor, always leaving his umbrella and other possessions on the bus or streetcar.

accident, by accident accidentally, unexpectedly:—I met him quite by accident on Fifth Avenue.

accord, of one accord in agreement:—We were of one accord in placing the blame on Helen.

accord, of one's own accord of one's own wish, voluntarily:—He went to the police and confessed of his own accord.

account, on account of because of:—He was discharged from the army on account of poor health.

account, on no account under no circumstances, definitely not:—On no account are you to touch an electrical appliance with wet hands.

account See **call** to account, **no** account, **square** accounts, **take** into account, **turn** to account.

ace, within an ace of within a very short distance of:—The car came within an ace of hitting the child.

acid test a thorough, conclusive trial:—Misfortune is an acid test of friendship.

act of God something beyond human control:—Some insurance policies do not protect the insured against acts of God.

act upon follow, proceed in accordance with:—The committee acted upon the suggestions the experts made.

act up act badly, have tantrums, etc.:—Every time Susan takes her baby to the supermarket he acts up.

ad lib improvise, interpolate while speaking:—When the actor forgot his lines, he ad libbed convincingly.

advance, in advance beforehand:—It is necessary to pay in advance for the lessons.

advanced in years no longer young:—Parsons was well advanced in years when he started his new business.

advantage, take advantage of (1) impose upon, gain at the expense of another:—Taking advantage of John's ignorance, the dealer sold him a worthless car. (2) to utilize, make use of a particular opportunity:—Many veterans have taken advantage of the opportunity offered them to attend school at government expense.

affair, have an affair have extramarital relations with someone of the opposite sex:—It is rumored that he is having an affair with her.

after all despite earlier views, nevertheless:—It has turned out to be a nice day after all.

after, be after someone pursue, seek to obtain:—He is always after me to go into business with him.

after, get after someone scold, criticize:—When Jill failed in three courses, her father got after her.

after, go after something strive for, try to obtain:—Now that he has graduated from college he wants to go after a master's degree.

after one's own heart to like someone because of kindred interests:—With his love for the great outdoors he is a man after my own heart.

again and again repeatedly:—He makes the same mistakes again and again.

again, as much again twice as much, double:—These shoes cost me as much again as the last pair I bought.

again, now and again occasionally:—Now and again I see Chris walking along Broadway.

against the grain irritating, contrary to one's natural inclinations:—It goes against the grain to have to pay him for such poor work.

age, of age be 21 years old, or older:—When Harry becomes of age he will inherit a great deal of money.

age, overage beyond a specified age:—He was not eligible for the examination because he was overage.

ager, underage too young, under a certain age requirement:—John was rejected by the army because he was underage.

age See also **awkward** age; **teen** age.

ahead of time before an appointed or agreed time:—Whenever I have an appointment I always like to arrive a little ahead of time.

ahead, go ahead begin, proceed, move forward:—We are going ahead with our plans to move to Florida.

air-minded advocating travel by air:—America became air-minded after the end of World War II.

air, by air in an airplane:—When I travel, I prefer to travel by air.

air, give someone the air dismiss a person you are tired of:—Herb wanted to marry Janet, but she gave him the air.

air, hot air exaggerated talk, without substance or foundation:—Don't pay any attention to him; what he told us was a lot of hot air.

air, in the air rumored, suspected but not definitely known:—What changes they will make nobody knows, but there is something in the air.

air, on the air on the radio or TV, engaging in some radio or TV program:—They say that the President will go on the air tonight at ten o'clock.

air, up in the air (1) confused, undecided:—Our plans for a vacation are still up in the air. (2) angry, excited:—He is all up in the air because he had to wait for her a few minutes.

airs, give oneself airs act in a superior or conceited manner:—Ever since her husband was elected mayor, Mrs. Allen's neighbors resent the way she gives herself airs. See also **put** on airs.

air See also **castles** in the air; **clear** the air; **take** the air; **walk** on air.

alert, on the alert watchful, cautious;—They must be constantly on the alert for enemy planes.

alive with full of, infested with:—When we opened our picnic basket, our lunch was alive with ants.

all along during the past interval, from the beginning:—Even though she had changed very much in those years, I knew all along that it was Joan.

all at once suddenly:—All at once it began to rain.

all at sea completely confused:—When I try to compute my income tax, I am all at sea.

all ears curious, attentive:—When John heard his name mentioned, he was all ears.

all in exhausted:—Bea was all in after her climb up the steep mountain.

all in all in general, considering all the facts:—He has his faults, but all in all he is a valuable employee.

all of a sudden suddenly:—We were sitting peacefully at dinner when all of a sudden the lights went out.

all-out thorough, complete:—The strike proved to be an all-out battle between management and labor.

all over (1) finished, completed:—By the time we arrived, the party was all over. (2) everywhere:—The news of the catastrophe was broadcast **all over the world**.

all set ready, prepared:—Our plans for the new corporation are all set.

all the better even better:—If we plant early, it will be all the better for our garden.

all the same (1) the same, equal, of complete indifference:—It's all the same to me whether we meet on Tuesday or on Thursday. (2) despite the fact, nevertheless:—All the same, I would enter the contest if I were you.

all there sane, rational:—Ever since he suffered that injury to his head, he has not been quite all there.

all to the good See **good**, to the good.

all told, counting everything:—He owns fifteen horses all told.

all up with said of a dying person:—It's all up with that hospital patient. They say she'll not live through the night.

all See also **above** all; **after** all; **at** all; **once** and for all; **one** and all; **piece**, all of a piece; **rage**, all the rage; **time**, all in good time.

alley, up one's alley something with which one is familiar or in which one is skilled:—With your knowledge of sports, that football question should be right up your alley.

allow for take into consideration, provide for:—In working with this cloth, be sure to allow for shrinkage.

allowance, make allowance for take into consideration:—In judging his work, we must make allowance for his lack of experience.

American plan referring to hotels which include meals as well as the room in the price quoted, as contrasted to the European plan, which is on the basis of charging for the room only, the guest paying separately for meals:—Most American hotels are on the European plan rather than on the American plan.

amount to add up, signify:—His total sales didn't amount to more than a few hundred dollars.

and how! an expression meaning "of course," "to a great degree":—You say that he is popular with the girls. And how!

answer for be liable for, responsible for:—If you don't tell the truth now, you may have to answer for it later.

answer (serve) the purpose suit or serve a particular need:—This room will answer the purpose until we can find something better.

answer to be named, reply to:—He answers to the name of Charles.

answer, what's the answer? what is the solution?:—One doctor tells me not to eat fats; the other wants me to go on a cream diet. What's the answer?

ante up to pay—usually unwillingly:—When his wife was awarded alimony by the court, Kerr had to ante up.

any, in any case nevertheless, come what may:—In any case, we must help all we can.

appearances, keep up appearances to maintain an outward show of prosperity despite financial reverses:—After Mr. Darrell failed in business, his family had great difficulty keeping up appearances.

appearance, make an appearance appear, arrive:—It was ten o'clock when he finally made an appearance.

apple, be the apple of another's eye to be greatly treasured, valued highly:—She is the apple of her mother's eye.

applecart, upset the applecart spoil through clumsiness, cause to fail:—When he referred to that incident of last summer, he upset the applecart and the whole deal fell through.

apple-pie order in neat and perfect condition:—Before her guests arrived, the hostess had put her house in apple-pie order.

applesauce pretense, not to be believed, hot air:—A lot of those campaign promises to lower taxes were just so much applesauce.

approval, on approval returnable, said of merchandise that can be returned within a short time:—We bought that picture on approval.

arm, give one's right arm to sacrifice, give something of great value:—During the long sermon I would have given my right arm for a cigarette.

arm, put the arm on (sl.) coerce, request, demand:—Jack's mother put the arm on him for a new fur coat.

arm's length, keep at arm's length keep at a distance, away from one:—She kept him at arm's length, thinking that he might try to kiss her.

arms, bear arms carry weapons:—Every able-bodied man was expected to bear arms against the enemy.

arms, take up arms prepare to fight:— When the Germans invaded Belgium, the Belgians immediately took up arms against them.

arms, up in arms angry, annoyed, ready to fight:—Everyone was up in arms about the new parking restrictions.

arms, with open arms with a hearty welcome:—He was received with open arms when he returned to his family.

arms See also **lay** down one's arms.

around, to have been around to be experienced, sophisticated, well-traveled, etc.: —The sex in that play didn't bother my uncle. He's been around.

around See also **stick** around.

as a matter of fact in fact, to speak the truth, actually:—As a matter of fact, there are as many oranges grown in California as in Florida.

as far as to the extent that:—As far as I am concerned, we can leave on either Saturday or Sunday.

as is in its present condition, said of a marked-down piece of merchandise:— That twenty-dollar dress is reduced to twelve dollars as is.

as it were in other words, so to speak:— He became, as it were, a kind of hero from a strange land.

as long as provided:—As long as they don't annoy us, we cannot take any legal action.

as one united, in agreement:—We were as one in our opinion of the way the matter had been handled.

as to with regard to, regarding:—As to his lack of education, there is nothing he can do about it now.

as yet up to the present:—As yet we have not heard a word from him.

aside from excepting, apart from, besides: —Aside from his meager savings, he has no resources to fall back on.

ask for it provoke it:—Why do you complain about being fired? You asked for it when you called the boss a crook.

at all in the least, to the smallest degree: —I doubt whether he knows any English at all.

at best at the maximum, under the most favorable circumstances:—At best, this car will go only fifty miles an hour.

at large (1) in general, not confined to a particular locality:—He has been elected as a delegate-at-large. (2) free, escaped:—The prisoner who escaped is still at large.

at most maximum:—They will give you, at most, four or five dollars for the watch.

at once immediately:—She told him to leave the room at once.

at one united, in agreement:—We were at one in our opinion of the way the matter had been handled.

at that nevertheless, despite the fact:— Helen's assertion that Tom and she are strangers is absurd; but at that, I doubt whether he has known her for more than a few weeks.

at times occasionally:—At times he prepares his lessons well; at other times he does very poor work.

attached, to be attached to have much affection for:—He seems more attached to his dog than to his wife.

awkward age physical and social immaturity of adolescence:—Although she is at the awkward age now, she will probably become a beautiful, graceful young woman.

AWOL absent without leave or permission—an army term:—Don was demoted from corporal to private because he had been AWOL.

axe, get the axe be discharged from one's job:—Henry got the axe when he arrived late for work three days in succession

axe, have an axe to grind have an interested or selfish motive:—In suggesting the sale of the building he had an axe to grind, because it meant a big commission for him.

B

babes in the woods innocent and inexperienced persons:—In that difficult and competitive business the Hunts are like two babes in the woods.

baby, be one's baby be one's preserve, belong to one, entrusted to one:—Your job is to answer complaints. Don't try to sell our product. That's Tom's baby.

baby grand a small grand piano:—If we can sell our old upright piano, we shall buy a new baby grand.

back away to draw back, move away from:—He backed away from the window as though it were the edge of a precipice.

back down to retreat, withdraw from one's previous position:—Don't back down on what you said to them.

back number something out of date, out of fashion:—Among so many young people on the dance floor he certainly felt like a back number.

back off retreat:—When Jim offered to fight, his detractor backed off.

back out desert a cause, fail to fulfill a promise or obligation:—Although he tried to back out of the agreement, the court finally made him fulfill all its terms.

back-seat driver a passenger in an automobile who is constantly telling the driver how to drive:—Mother is a back-seat driver and drives Father nuts.

back talk impertinence, an impudent reply:—She told the man that she would tolerate no back talk from him.

back the wrong horse support one who ultimately loses:—In voting for Smith for mayor, you certainly backed the wrong horse, since he lost by 10,000 votes.

back up (1) support:—The President backed up the statements made by his assistant. (2) go toward the rear, put a car in reverse:—She put the car in reverse instead of in drive and backed up over the curb.

back, be back return:—I'll be back in an hour.

back, get one's back up cause another person to become obstinate and resist or refuse to cooperate:—Unreasonable demands on that employee got his back up.

back, have one's back to the wall be hard-pressed, on the defensive:—Because of the enemy's superior numbers our troops found themselves with their backs to the wall.

back, turn one's back on ignore, refuse to help, desert:—Being a good Christian, she did not turn her back on her neighbors when they needed help.

back See also **behind** one's back; **get** back; **go** back on; **hang** back; **hold** back; **pay** back; **set** back; **take** a back seat; **take** back; **water** off a duck's back.

backfire to misfire, have a reverse effect from that intended:—The candidate's plan to discredit his opponent backfired, and his own reputation suffered greatly.

backing and filling indecision, state of being unable to decide:—After weeks of backing and filling, Henry accepted the offer of a job.

bad blood hostility, bad feeling:—The slavery issue stirred up bad blood between the North and the South.

bad off seriously ill:—Ames is in the hospital and is pretty bad off.

bad, be too bad be unfortunate, a pity:—It is too bad he doesn't know English better.

bad, go bad spoil:—The pudding went bad so we had no dessert with our dinner.

bad, in bad in disgrace, disfavor:—John is in bad with his boss for coming to work late every day.

bad, too bad unfortunate (a sympathetic remark):—So your wife's still in the hospital. That's too bad.

bag, a mixed bag a set of varied or oddly assorted components or parts, said of objects, qualities, etc.:—That new play was a mixed bag of wit and broad farce.

bag and baggage with all one's portable belongings:—They arrived at our house, bag and baggage, at one o'clock in the morning.

bag, be one's bag something one is interested in, possibly competent at:—Why did you suggest that I work in a restaurant? That's not my bag, I want to be a lawyer.

bag, in the bag successfully settled or arranged:—Judging by the enthusiastic reception given him everywhere, they felt that the election was in the bag.

bag See also **cat**, let the cat out of the bag; **hold** the bag.

bail out (1) to parachute from a plane:—When the plane's motor failed, the whole crew bailed out. (2) to remove water from a boat:—While John rowed, his wife bailed out the water from the leaky boat.

bail, go bail advance the necessary money as security in order to release an accused person until trial:—The driver who had been arrested had no trouble in finding someone to go bail for him.

bail, put up bail (same as **go bail**).

baker's dozen thirteen rather than twelve: —When we opened the package of doughnuts, we found that he had given us a baker's dozen.

ball up confuse:—We got balled up in our directions and drove miles out of the way.

ball, have a ball have a very good time, thoroughly enjoy oneself:—Last Saturday we went to a county fair and had a ball.

ball, have a lot on the ball capable, skilled—like a good baseball pitcher:—He will do well in that work because he has a lot on the ball.

ball, keep the ball rolling prevent a lull or cessation of activity:—Although we were strangers, the dinner was successful because our hostess, a good conversationalist, easily kept the ball rolling.

ball, on the ball alert, attentive:—If we want to finish this on time, we must keep on the ball.

baloney nonsense, worthless promises (sl.):—His talk about helping the working man is a lot of baloney.

band together form a group, unite:—The citizens banded together to protest the closing of the highway.

bandwagon, get on the bandwagon join up with the majority:—All the delegates to the convention began to desert Smith in order to get on Parker's bandwagon.

bang, get a bang out of enjoy, be thrilled by:—I always get a bang out of children at Christmas time.

bang, with a bang successfully, enthusiastically—literally with a loud noise:—The new movie went over with a bang.

bank on something or **someone** rely upon, depend upon:—You can always bank on Collins if you need help.

bankroll subsidize, support:—That new play has been bankrolled by a prominent publisher.

bar, call to the bar admit a law-school graduate to practice:—After he passed the bar exams, Frost was called to the bar.

bargain for expect, anticipate:—She got more than she bargained for when she undertook to care for the kittens.

bargain on expect:—When John bought a car, he hadn't bargained on the cost of gasoline and garage rent.

bargain See also **drive** a bargain; **strike** a bargain.

barge in enter, interfere—especially rudely or clumsily:—We were sitting there minding our own business when Evans barged in.

bark up the wrong tree be on the wrong trail or track:—If he expects to borrow money from me, he is barking up the wrong tree.

barrel, have someone over a barrel have someone in an embarrassing position, at one's mercy:—We had no other alternative but admit defeat; they had us over a barrel.

base, get to first base make a decent beginning or some progress:—I couldn't get to first base with that girl.

basket case a victim without arms or legs: —Some soldiers injured in the war became basket cases.

bat, go to bat for defend, sponsor, help:—In an emergency we can always depend upon Smith to go to bat for us.

bat, not to bat an eye remain unconcerned, calm:—When the jury pronounced him guilty of murder, he did not bat an eye.

bat, right off the bat immediately:—He told us, right off the bat, that he intended to leave her.

batting average degree of accomplishment—originally a baseball term:—With his long record of victories, that lawyer has a high batting average in that particular type of lawsuit.

bawl out scold, reprimand:—Ralph's boss bawled him out for being lazy.

bay, at bay cornered, trapped:—When held at bay, cowards will often fight.

bay window protruding stomach of a fat man:—That old banker has quite a bay window.

beads, tell one's beads said of a holy person who says a prayer for each bead in his necklace or rosary:—That nun is telling her beads.

beam, off (on) the beam in the wrong direction, functioning inaccurately (sl.):—Judging by his confused remarks, I would say that he is slightly off the beam.

beans, full of beans (1) active, alert, ambitious, energetic:—That new employee is full of beans and gets things done. (2) incorrect, misinformed:—John is full of beans and doesn't know what he's talking about.

beans, not to know beans about to know absolutely nothing about:—Don't ask Jim. He doesn't know beans about forestry.

beans, spill the beans disclose a secret:—The trip was supposed to be a secret, but Fred spilled the beans when he mentioned buying plane tickets.

bear a grudge continue or nurse ill feeling toward another:—Mary won't speak to John because she still bears a grudge against him for his rudeness last year.

bear down upon approach, draw constantly nearer—especially with speed or force:—From all sides, the crowd bore down upon the street from where the flames were coming.

bear in mind remember:—Bear in mind that I am not as young as I used to be.

bear off turn aside or away from gradually: At the river the road bears off toward the left.

bear out confirm, corroborate:—Those facts bear out what I told you yesterday.

bear up endure suffering:—Amy is bearing up well after the loss of her brother.

bear with tolerate, endure, be patient with:—If you will bear with me a little longer, I am sure I can locate those papers.

bear, be a bear for be enthusiastic, vigorous about doing something:—William is a bear for work.

bearing, have bearing upon related to, have connection with:—What he said has absolutely no bearing upon the subject under discussion.

beat a hasty retreat:—fly, run away from some uncomfortable or threatening situation:—When a passerby approached the thief who was robbing a girl, the thief beat a hasty retreat.

beat about the bush delay coming directly to the point, be indirect in manner:—Instead of answering my question about his marks, he began to beat about the bush and tell me all about the different courses he was taking.

beat generation term applied to those of our post-war youth who seem to be unable to relate to conventional mores:—Some members of the beat generation avoid work, neatness, cleanliness, and all self-control.

beat it leave, go away (sl.):—He kept bothering me so I told him to beat it.

beat one to it arrive or get ahead of another person:—Fred applied for the job, but someone else had heard about the vacancy and beat him to it.

beat one to the draw originally, pull out one's gun first; also win over another, snatch the victory:—Both Tom and Jerry wanted to marry Rosalie, but Tom beat his rival to the draw.

beat one's brains out think and work at energetically, desperately:—The poor author beat his brains out trying to find someone to publish his novel.

beat one's head against a stone wall struggle against insurmountable difficulties: —It is useless for him to seek work in that company; he is just beating his head against a stone wall.

beat the band tremendously:—That singer can sing to beat the band.

beat the rap escape the legal penalty, be acquitted (sl.):—Despite the strong evidence against him, the prisoner beat the rap and went free.

beat time mark or otherwise follow the rhythm of a piece of music:—He beat time with his foot.

beat up attack and assault bodily:—The thieves not only took his money but beat him up badly.

beat, to beat one puzzle:—It beats me how my uncle can still play tennis at the age of eighty.

beat See also **deadbeat, pound** a beat.

beaten path the usual route established by custom or convention·—He is a conservative person who can be counted upon to follow the beaten path.

beaten track Same as **beaten path.**

become of happen to:—What will become of the children now that both parents are dead?

becoming, be becoming to suit, look well on—said of clothes:—That hat is very becoming to you.

bed of roses a place of beauty, ease, and comfort:—Anyone who thinks that the job of being President of the United States is a bed of roses is quite mistaken.

bed See also **take** to one's bed; **get** up on the wrong side of the bed.

bee, have a bee in one's bonnet have some set, foolish or exaggerated notion:—He has a bee in his bonnet about reforming the world.

beef about complain (sl.):—He is always beefing about the amount of work he has to do.

beef up increase in size or amount or in strength, spend more money on:—That sales manager told his salesmen to beef up their sales.

beeline, make a beeline for take or follow the shortest possible route:—At exactly twelve o'clock everyone made a beeline for the dining room.

before long soon:—We'll be seeing you again before long.

beg the question to assume the validity of a point in dispute before it is proved: —To refer to the accused as a "thief" at the outset of the trial is to beg the question.

begin with in the first place, as a preliminary statement:—To begin with, John is too young for that kind of job.

behind bars in prison:—The judge will put him behind bars for at least five years.

behind one's back speak or act treacherously, outside the victim's hearing, or without his knowledge:—Jean seems very fond of her friend Ellen, but she loves to gossip about her behind her back.

behind the eight ball unlucky, in a very awkward or disadvantageous position (sl.):—Because of his handicap, it is very difficult for him to obtain work, so that if he loses his present job he will certainly be behind the eight ball.

behind the scenes at the rear, where the inner mechanism of something is revealed:—That documentary film took us behind the scenes and showed us how the Department of Justice really operates.

behind the times out of date:—Their courses in physics are very much behind the times.

behind, get behind support, help:—Let's all get behind his drive for a new hospital and contribute generously to the fund.

believe in have faith in the existence of: —Atheists do not believe in God.

bellyache to complain (sl.):—He's always bellyaching about the amount of traveling he has to do.

below par below standard:—His health has been below par recently.

belt, below the belt unfairly, in an unsportsmanlike manner, an unjustified remark, foul blow:—When Sam's boss said to him: "You have not only made a mess of your job but also of your marriage," he was hitting below the belt.

belt, under one's belt acquired, taken care of, provided for:—With the necessary capital under my belt, I can open the bookstore I have always wanted.

bend over backwards make a supreme or exaggerated effort:—She bent over backwards to show that she had overlooked the incident.

bend see **ear, bend one's ear.**

beneath one below one's dignity or ideals:—He felt it would be beneath him to accept such a menial job.

benefit, give someone the benefit of the doubt assume a person to be innocent rather than guilty:—The money had been stolen and John was in the house at the time, but we gave him the benefit of the doubt and assumed that some burglar had taken it.

bent on determined, decided upon a certain act:—He is bent on becoming a lawyer.

berth, give a wide berth to avoid:—He disliked his uncle and always gave him a wide berth.

beside oneself angry, frantic:—She was beside herself with grief at the news of her son's accident.

beside the point not pertinent, away from the subject being discussed:—We were discussing political parties, and his remarks about high prices were completely beside the point.

best man the groom's aide at a wedding:—Who will be your best man when you get married?

best-seller a popular book, notable for the large number of copies sold:—**Gone with the Wind** was a famous best-seller.

best, all for the best for the ultimate good:—He has decided to continue at the university, and I am sure that it is all for the best.

best, have the best of win, gain supremacy:—Although Carl put up a good fight, his opponent had the best of him.

best, make the best of something do as well as one can in an undesirable situation:—Since we can't find a bigger apartment, we'll have to make the best of what we have.

best See also **level best.**

bet, you bet! an exclamation meaning "certainly," "surely"—something so sure that one can bet on it:—You ask whether he is a good tennis player. You bet he is!

better half one's wife (humorous):—I'll go with you if my better half lets me.

better off in a better condition, richer, happier:—You will be better off living nearer to your job.

better, get the better of get the advantage of, win over:—He always gets the better of anyone he deals with.

better, had better it would be wise or advisable for one:—He had better go to a doctor at once before infection sets in.

better, so much the better even more advantageous:—If he sells more goods it will be so much the better for his company.

better, think better of reconsider, decide prudently on a different course:—He was going to leave school, but later he thought better of it.

bid fair to looks as if, be likely to:—With such strong voter-support, the political candidate bids fair to win the governorship.

big brother an all-seeing dictator in a police state:—In the novel **1984** Big Brother could watch the interior of everybody's home through a television receiver.

big shot an important person (sl.):—He is a big shot in the State Department.

big, in the big time (sl.) in a position of importance, at the top of one's business or profession:—Since the war he has always associated with a lot of big-time lawyers and politicians.

big, make it big become very successful:—Although he left his village a poor boy, Ellis made it big in New York.

big, talk big exaggerate, give oneself importance:—He talks big, but don't pay any attention to what he says.

bind, in a bind circumscribed, imprisoned, unable to get loose:—We can't issue any more stock in our company because the government has us in a bind.

bird in hand something that one already has as opposed to something one may possibly obtain:—A bird in hand is worth two in the bush.

birds of a feather those belonging to the same group or class:—If he associates with criminals then he himself must be a criminal, because birds of a feather flock together.

birds, for the birds said of something not valued, or worthless:—Hot dogs? They're for the birds. Give me a steak.

bird, give someone the bird tease, annoy, jeer at (sl.):—Every time the speaker referred to all he had done for the organization they gave him the bird.

bird See also **early** bird; **kill** two birds with one stone.

bit, do one's bit do one's share or duty:—In wartime everyone should do his bit, either at the front or at home.

bit, not a bit not in the least:—When I asked whether he was afraid, he answered, "Not a bit!"

bit, take the bit into one's mouth assert oneself, revolt:—He took the bit into his mouth and warned us that henceforth we would be answerable to him only.

bite off more than one can chew undertake something which is beyond one's capacity or power:—In trying to swim across that river he bit off more than he could chew and had to be rescued when only halfway across.

bite one's head off answer someone angrily:—You don't have to bite my head off just because I asked you a simple question.

bite, I'll bite an expression suggesting that one agrees to serve as the victim or butt of a joke:—When I asked him whether he knew the difference between a woman and an umbrella, he said: "All right! I'll bite. What is the difference?"

bite, put the bite on solicit funds:—Jerry's church, his relatives, and his club all put the bite on him.

bits, two bits See **two.**

black and blue badly bruised:—Her ankle was black and blue from the fall.

black eye a bruised eye:—Enraged, he swung at his companion and gave him a black eye.

black eye, give a black eye discredit:—His subversive action will give a black eye to the whole liberal movement.

black out (1) make dark:—The city was blacked out during the air raid. (2) faint, lose consciousness temporarily The pilot blacked out for a moment upon reaching such a high altitude.

blackout darkening of a city during an air raid:—During the last war New York had many blackouts.

black power movement to increase the political and economic strength of black Americans:—Black power was one of the reasons responsible for the election of a black mayor.

black sheep a ne'er-do-well, a good-for-nothing member of a family:—All the brothers except James were honest men; James was always the black sheep of the family.

black, in black and white in writing, clearly and unequivocally expressed:—He wants everything put in black and white before he enters the business.

blame, be to blame have the responsibility, be at fault:—Who is to blame for all this damage?

blank, draw a blank get no results, get nothing:—Our English teacher tried to get the principal's job, but she drew a blank.

blanket, wet blanket someone who spoils an idea or situation by his pessimism or lack of cooperation:—Don't invite him again. Remember what a wet blanket he was on the last picnic.

blast, full blast at full capacity:—With all those government orders, that factory is running full blast.

blast, give one a blast telephone:—After you have decided which suit you want, just give me a blast and I'll proceed with the alterations.

blind alley an alley or a street closed at one end, a dead end, impasse:—Such a routine job would only lead him into a blind alley.

blind date an engagement or "date" arranged by mutual friends for a young man and woman who have not previously met:—Bill says he definitely refuses to go on any more blind dates.

blind, have a blind spot be unable or unwilling to see defects in another:—Though Elsa's mother can see faults in her daughter, Elsa's father has a blind spot where his daughter's shortcomings are concerned.

blink, on the blink not working, out of order:—Our refrigerator went on the blink and much of our food was spoiled.

block, chip off the old block a copy of or close resemblance to one's father:—His father was quite an athlete, and with his interest in sports Jack appears to be a chip off the old block.

blockbuster something tremendous in size and explosive impact, something that shocks:—The sudden failure of that large corporation was a blockbuster to investors.

blood, in cold blood mercilessly, ruthlessly:—They say he murdered her in cold blood.

blot out cover, obscure, obstruct:—The fog blots out the view of the river.

blow away carry away into the distance:—The wind blew away the clothes that were hanging on the line.

blow down throw or blow to the ground:—The strong wind blew down a number of trees on our block.

blow hot and cold vacillate, change completely from one point of view to another:—The administration has blown hot and cold on the question of certain import duties.

blow in, come in, return:—What time did Mark blow in last night?

blow off steam gain relief through venting one's anger:—Don't discuss that touchy matter with him now; after he blows off a little steam he will be more reasonable.

blow one's lines forget his part, said of an actor:—It was her first appearance on television, and the nervous actress blew her lines.

blow one's own horn boast, praise oneself:—He likes to blow his own horn about what he accomplished during the war years.

blow one's stack be furious, lose control of oneself, berate:—When Mr. Green found that his wife had crumpled two fenders of the car, he blew his stack.

blow one's top become very angry or excited, hysterical (sl.):—He got so upset over what she said that I thought he was going to blow his top.

blow out (1) fail, cease to function, explode—said particularly of tires and fuses:—The accident occurred when his front tire blew out. (2) to extinguish:—She blew out the candle and went to bed. (3) a big party:—At the end of the campaign we celebrated with a big blowout at the Hotel Waldorf.

blow over subside, become less serious:—All this publicity about his accepting bribes will blow over in a few months.

blow taps sound the final bugle call of the evening:—After taps is blown, the young campers have to turn out their lights and go to sleep.

blow-up a greatly enlarged photograph or drawing:—That theater posted a blow-up of a favorable review of the play in front of its box office.

blow up (v.) (1) explode and destroy:—The retreating troops blew up the bridges behind them. (2) lose one's temper:—When his secretary asked for the day off, Mr. Smith, with so much work piled up in front of him, blew up. (3) inflate:—I have to get my front tires blown up.

blue depressed, melancholy:—She has been blue ever since her boy friend left for Europe.

blue-collar worker a manual worker in contrast to a white-collar or office worker:—Many blue-collar workers are effectively supported in their demands by powerful labor unions.

blue moon, once in a blue moon seldom, almost never:—He visits us once in a blue moon.

blue-pencil to edit:—The author complained that his manuscript had been heavily blue-penciled by the publishers.

blue-ribbon jury a special jury recruited to try a complex or particularly important case:—When the bank president was on trial for embezzlement, a blue-ribbon jury was chosen.

blues, have the blues be sad, gloomy in spirits:—I don't know why, but I have had the blues all day.

board, across-the-board for all employees in a company or union:—The union arranged an across-the-board raise of five percent.

board, go by the board be neglected or left unattended to, undone:—Those children have lots of spending money, but their clothes go by the board.

board, on board in or on a ship, train, etc.:—The ocean liner stopped in the harbor to take the pilot on board.

board See also **above board.**

boat, in the same boat sharing the same experience or destiny:—We wage earners are all in the same boat during these inflationary times.

boat, miss the boat fail at something:—That publicity agent could have had the mayor endorse his client's product, but he missed the boat.

bob up appear suddenly and unexpectedly:—She is always bobbing up at the most inopportune moment.

bobby soxers young girls in their teens, so called from their use of short socks instead of stockings:—The theater was full of bobby-soxers yelling and screaming for their favorite singer.

body, in a body in a group, collectively:—The whole committee of seventeen arrived in a body.

body, keep body and soul together keep alive, sustain oneself:—In these days of rising prices it is difficult for many poor people to keep body and soul together.

bog down slow down, be so entangled that further progress is impossible:—The truce negotiations have bogged down for the third time.

boil away disappear through the process of boiling:—When I finally remembered to look at the coffee, it had all boiled away.

boil down condense, reduce:—That 500-page manuscript must be boiled down to 200 pages.

boil over (1) rise through boiling, and overflow the sides of a pan or pot:—Take that milk off the stove before it boils over. (2) become enraged:—When Max learned that they had not included him in their plans, he boiled over.

boil, make one's blood boil make one very angry:—His unkind remarks about Helen made my blood boil.

bold, make bold have the temerity to, be rash enough to say:—May I make bold to suggest that our President spend a little less time on the golf links and more time in his office?

bolt from the blue a sudden surprise stroke or blow, a catastrophe:—The news of the attack on Pearl Harbor came like a bolt from the blue.

bolt upright in a rigid, upright position:—The doctor's warning made me sit bolt upright in my chair.

bolt See also **shoot** one's bolt.

bone of contention cause or matter in disagreement:—The real bone of contention between the owners and the strikers is not higher wages but better working conditions.

bone up on study, review:—Before taking his exams, John had to bone up on several subjects which he hadn't studied for years.

bone, have a bone to pick with someone have an unpleasant matter to settle or discuss with someone:—I have a bone to pick with you. Why didn't you return those reports to me as you promised to do?

bone See also **feel** in one's bones; **funny** bone; **make** no bones about.

boner, pull a boner make a bad error or social blunder:—You pulled a boner when you spoke so disparagingly of that country; Jack's wife comes from there.

booboo, make a booboo make a glaring mistake:—When I invited Dick and his ex-wife to the same party I made a real booboo.

book (v.) (1) register in a police docket, put in jail:—He was taken to the police station and booked on a charge of assault. (2) employed, hired under contract:—The popular star was booked for six weeks on Broadway.

book, in one's book in one's opinion:—In my book, Harry isn't fit to hold the job he has.

book, keep books maintain an accounting system:—It's a small company and as yet they have not started keeping books.

book, one for the book said of something remarkable that ought to be remembered:—So that miser married a spendthrift widow. That's one for the book.

book, take a leaf out of someone's book follow the example of another:—I am going to take a leaf out of your book and have a nice long vacation this year.

book See also **throw** the book at; **crack** a book.

boot, to boot something extra, in addition, also:—I paid him what he asked for and gave him two dollars to boot.

border on adjoin, come close to:—His actions border on irresponsibility.

born with a silver spoon in one's mouth born into a family of wealth and position:—He was born with a silver spoon in his mouth and has never had to work a day in his whole life.

born yesterday, simple, inexperienced, credulous, easily duped:—Don't try to sell me that beat-up old car as a bargain. I wasn't born yesterday.

borrow trouble get into difficulties unnecessarily:—Let's not borrow trouble by giving preferred treatment and discounts to favored customers.

bosom friends close, intimate friends:—They have been bosom friends since their high-school days.

bottleneck a narrow passage preventing free and easy movement:—The worst bottleneck is at 79th Street where three principal streets converge at one point; traffic is always congested there.

bottle up to trap, enclose:—The enemy bottled up a whole army division in the narrow valley.

bottom dollar one's last dollar:—I'll bet my bottom dollar that he won't arrive on time.

bottom, get to the bottom of investigate thoroughly, find the basic reasons for:—He tried unsuccessfully to get to the bottom of the strikers' demands.

bottom, touch bottom reach the lowest point:—Prices touched bottom during the depression years.

bottom See also **rock** bottom.

bounce (v.) (1) to discharge, fire:—He has been bounced out of one good job after another. (2) eject forcibly, throw out:—The drunk was bounced out of the bar by the official bouncer.

bound, be bound for be going in the direction of:—Where are you bound for? We're all bound for Dick's house.

bound, be bound to (1) be sure to:—With so little time to prepare, he is bound to fail his examinations. (2) obligated:—Henry is bound to support his wife. (3) determined:—Maria is bound to go to Europe this next summer.

bound, be bound up with be involved with, connected:—The housing problem is bound up with the problem of rent controls.

bow out (rhymes with how) withdraw, retire, disappear gracefully:—He bowed out of the whole affair without giving anyone an explanation.

bow, take a bow (rhymes with cow) bow one's head in recognition of applause:—After the premiere of the drama, the author took a bow.

bow See also **strings,** have two strings to one's bow (rhymes with low).

bowing acquaintance a casual acquaintance whom one knows only well enough to nod or bow to:—I have never spoken to Mr. Harris. He and I have only a bowing acquaintance.

bowl over knock over, overturn by force or a sudden blow, surprise greatly:—We were simply bowled over by the news of Jack's marriage.

box one's ears slap, chastise:—If he does that again I'll box his ears.

box See also **soap box.**

brace up take courage, recover one's morale:—His doctor cautioned him to stop drinking and to brace up if he wanted to lead a normal life.

brain trust a group of highly intelligent specially equipped associates:—President Roosevelt's brain trust helped him to plan many of his political moves.

brain, have something on the brain have a fixed idea, be obsessed by:—That fellow has sports on the brain. He talks of nothing else.

brain See also **rack** one's brains.

brainstorm a clever idea:—I have just had a brainstorm. Let's economize by selling our car and buying a motorcycle.

brainstorming said of a meeting or conference where ideas are freely offered:—We had a brainstorming session last night on drug use by minors.

branch out expand:—That firm is branching out all through the West.

brand new completely new:—He is driving a brand new Cadillac.

brass, get down to brass tacks go directly to the basic facts of a matter:—After some preliminary small talk the committee got down to brass tacks and voted a large appropriation.

brass, high or top brass the top executives in the army, in business, etc.:—The decision of whether to merge or not lies with the top brass.

bread-and-butter letter a written acknowledgment of hospitality received:—We spent the weekend at my cousin's in the country, and I must remember to write her a bread-and-butter letter this week.

bread, know on which side one's bread is buttered to understand what action or attitude is personally most advantageous:—He is wise to treat his old aunt so affectionately. She is rich and may soon die; he knows on which side his bread is buttered.

bread, take the bread out of someone's mouth deprive another of a living or means of support:—The invention of the spinning jenny took the bread out of the hand weavers' mouths.

break away leave, free oneself from:—Fortunately, he broke away from that lawless group years ago.

break down (1) fail to function or operate:—Our car broke down and had to be towed to a garage. (2) divide into parts or subdivisions for greater clarity:—Please break down those income tax totals by age groups. (3) relent, confess:—The prisoner finally broke down and revealed all the facts of the crime. (4) weep:—The speaker's words were so moving that Mrs. Smith broke down and had to leave the room.

break even gain or lose nothing in a business transaction:—Since I sold the car for exactly what I paid for it, I broke even on the deal.

break forth erupt, occur suddenly:—The crowd broke forth in cheers when Senator Reese appeared.

break ground start to excavate for the foundation of a new building:—They will break ground on the new housing project next week.

break in (1) begin to use, initiate, train, tame:—I never like to break in a new pair of shoes or a new employee. (2) interrupt:—I could tell the story much more easily if you didn't break in so often. (3) see break into.

break into (1) burglarize:—Thieves broke into our apartment and stole my wife's fur coat. (2) enter a new profession or trade:—It is difficult to break into the field of advertising.

break loose become free, escape:—The boat broke loose from its mooring.

break off terminate abruptly:—As the result of the incident, the government broke off diplomatic relations with that country.

break one's heart hurt another's feelings deeply:—Her refusal ever to see him again almost broke his heart.

break one's word (promise) fail to fulfill a promise or obligation:—You can trust him; he is not the kind of person who will easily break his word.

break out (1) happen suddenly:—Last night fire broke out in Smith's barn. (2) to have a skin rash, erupt:—During the hot weather the baby's skin broke out.

break the bank win so heavily at gambling as to cause the "banker" to suspend the play:—If you keep on winning at this rate you will soon break the bank.

break the ice promote cordiality within a group, put an end to an awkward situation:—Our hostess broke the ice the moment she began to serve the refreshments.

break through penetrate:—Our troops had little difficulty in breaking through the enemy's lines.

break up (1) break into small pieces:—I broke up the candy and gave each child a small piece. (2) terminate:—The meeting didn't break up until twelve o'clock. (3) scatter, separate:—"Come on!" said the policeman. "Move along. Break it up!"

break with quarrel with, sever relations with:—One by one he broke with all of his old friends.

break, a clean break a complete separation:—After the death of his wife he made a clean break with all his old associations and left for South America.

break, a good (bad) break good (bad) luck:—He certainly got a good break when he began to work in that firm; yet he deserved it because previously he had had a series of bad breaks.

break, give another person a break give one a chance, excuse one for a misdeed, etc.:—Officer, please give me a break. I've never driven faster than the speed limit before. Don't give me a ticket.

breaks, get the breaks have luck, be fortunate:—That fellow gets all the breaks. He has been working there only six months and already has been promoted to the position of vice-president.

break See also **make** or **break**; **record,** break the record; **take** a break.

breath, save one's breath refrain from useless talk or discussion:—You can save your breath; there is no use talking to him about his drinking.

breath, take one's breath away overwhelm, astonish with surprise:—The Grand Canyon is a sight so beautiful that it fairly takes one's breath away.

breath, under one's breath inaudibly, softly, in a whisper:—He muttered something under his breath which I did not hear.

breath See also **catch** one's breath; **out** of breath.

breathe freely feel relief, relax:—Only after we received the news that they had arrived safely did we begin to breathe freely.

breather, take a breather take a break, take a brief time off a job for relaxation:—After two hours of intense discussion, we decided to take a breather.

breathing spell a period of rest:—After working steadily for three hours we decided to take a breathing spell.

breeches, wear the breeches dominate, have authority within a family group:—It is Mrs. Smith, not Mr. Smith, who wears the breeches in that family.

breeze in arrive suddenly and airily, nonchalantly:—Helen breezed in about four o'clock after we had waited two hours for her.

breeze See **shoot** the breeze.

bridge, toll bridge a bridge that charges cars a fee:—New York's George Washington Bridge is a toll bridge and charges fifty cents each time a car is driven across.

brief one give one directions, information and orders:—Before that new ambassador leaves for his embassy he will be briefed by the State Department.

brief, hold a brief for endorse or approve:
—I hold no brief for those who are disloyal to their employer.

bring about cause to happen:—What brought about his illness?

bring around (1) help, cure:—I am sure the doctor's new medicine will bring him around in no time. (2) influence, bring to a point through a circuitous route, secure acceptance:—If we show him these figures I am sure that we can bring him around to our point of view. (3) bring to visit:—Why don't you bring your wife around to see us sometime?

bring down reduce, make lower:—It will take more than speeches to bring prices down these days.

bring down the house amuse or please an audience greatly:—The comedian's last few jokes brought down the house.

bring forward introduce, suggest:—Finally Mr. Hunt brought forward his plan for the new building.

bring home the bacon succeed in some project, be triumphant:—Our team, which was greatly superior to the others in the tournament, had little trouble in bringing home the bacon.

bring home to emphasize, make very vivid and clear:—His description of several battle scenes brought home to the audience the suffering which our soldiers must have endured.

bring in produce, yield income:—How much does that garage business bring in each month?

bring on cause:—His illness was brought on by worry over his business losses.

bring one to revive, restore to consciousness:—When Charlotte nearly drowned, we brought her to by artificial respiration.

bring out (1) emphasize, underline:—In his rendition the pianist brought out the bass melody very clearly. (2) reveal:—The lawyer brought out the fact that Smith had not been near the scene of the crime at the time. (3) elicit, extract:—His wife always brings out the best in him.

bring round Same as **bring around.**

bring something off succeed, accomplish some particular plan:—The performers didn't quite bring off the main idea of the play.

bring to a close terminate, cause to end:—The meeting was brought to a sudden close when the chairman became ill.

bring to bear place pressure upon, concentrate upon with some special end in view:—They brought to bear upon him all the political influence they had at their disposal.

bring to light reveal, unearth:—The archaeologist, through his investigations, brought to light several interesting facts.

bring to mind remind, cause one to recall:—Your story brings to mind a similar experience which I had some time ago.

bring to pass cause to happen:—It was our careful planning that brought to pass our great superhighways.

bring to reason convince through logical argument:—It was not difficult to bring him to reason when we pointed out to him the dangers involved in picking up hitchhikers.

bring up (1) to rear, nurture:—He was born in Ohio but brought up in Texas. (2) introduce, present:—Stevens brought up the question of finances at the family dinner table.

bring up the rear follow at the rear of a parade or procession:—A group of mounted policemen brought up the rear.

bring See also **head,** bring to a head; **play,** bring into play; **terms,** bring to terms.

broad, as broad as it is long equal:—Either of two alternatives will have the same result:—Since the cost is the same, and the distances are equal, whether we take the bridge or the tunnel is about as broad as it is long.

broke (also **dead** broke, **flat** broke, **stone** broke) completely without money:—She is so extravagant that two days after payday she is always dead broke.

broke, go for broke spend all one's money lavishly, speculate, invest all of one's resources on a single deal:—Don't put everything you have in that speculative stock. You are going for broke.

broke See also **heart,** broken-hearted; **housebroken.**

broken English incorrect and imperfect English:—When I heard him speaking such broken English, I knew he was not a native American.

Bronx cheer a derisive, jeering sound:— The audience gave the incompetent entertainer a Bronx cheer.

brown, in a brown study completely absorbed in thought:—I tried to attract Claudia's attention, but she was in a brown study.

brush aside ignore, push aside:—Brushing aside the adverse reports of his scouts, the general ordered the attack at dawn.

brush off (v. & n.) ignore, disregard in a brusque manner, reject:—When he invited Jane to go out with him, she gave him the brush-off.

brush up on review:—Before I go to Paris I must brush up on my French.

buck for work for, seek to obtain:—Vice-President Moore is bucking for the presidency when the incumbent steps down.

buck up hearten, encourage:—Can't someone try to buck up our secretary? She's been in the dumps ever since her boyfriend went into the army.

buck, pass the buck evade responsibility by passing it to another:—When I asked Henry why the merchandise had not been sent, he passed the buck by saying that it was William's job to get the packages ready.

buckle down pay attention to, concentrate upon:—I told him to stop fooling around and to buckle down to work.

bug, to bug one (1) annoy, irritate, bother:—This ill-fitting dress bugs me. I think I'll give it away. (2) wiretap:—All the rooms in that embassy were bugged.

build up increase, strengthen:—We first have to build up our reserves of manpower.

bull session a discussion by several participants often covering a variety of trivial topics:—Last night at our fraternity house we had a bull session which lasted until three o'clock.

bull, sling (throw) the bull (sl.) exaggerate, brag:—Don't pay much attention to what he says. He likes to sling the bull.

bull See also **cock** and bull story; **horns,** take the bull by the horns.

bum a ride, a cigarette, a dollar, etc. beg, ask for something free:—John bummed rides all the way from Chicago to New York.

bum around wander, go without particular direction more or less in the manner of a vagabond:—Instead of looking for work he prefers to bum around with the boys in his club.

bum, give a bum steer misdirect or mislead (sl.):—You certainly gave me a bum steer on that last investment I made; two days after I bought it the stock dropped ten points.

bump into meet unexpectedly:—On my way downtown I bumped into an old friend whom I hadn't seen for years.

bump off kill, murder (sl.):—The police think the racketeer was bumped off by a member of a rival gang.

bumps and grinds wiggles that a show-girl makes when performing:—The striptease artist did many bumps and grinds.

bundle one off hustle another off:—Right after supper the children were bundled off to bed.

bundle up dress warmly, protect oneself against the cold:—It's pretty cold outside. You'd better bundle up well.

burn a hole in one's pocket having a great desire to spend the money in one's possession:—I knew that he would go out and buy everything he saw, because the money was burning a hole in his pocket.

burn down burn to the ground:—Before the firemen were able to arrive, both buildings burned down.

burn one's bridges behind one cut off one's means of retreat, or return to a former position:—The thing to do is to write your letter of resignation and thus burn your bridges behind you.

burn out become useless, go out of order —said particularly of electrical appliances:—We need some new electric light bulbs. These two are burned out.

burn the candle at both ends overdo, exhaust oneself:—To work all day and go out to parties every night is simply burning the candle at both ends; he can only end up by having a nervous breakdown.

burn up (1) burn completely:—We gathered up all the old newspapers and burned them up. (2) anger, infuriate:—The way he talks to some of his employees burns me up.

burst forth escape suddenly, break out:—The crowd burst forth into loud cheering at the daring feats of the trapeze artists.

burst into enter suddenly and violently:—Without even stopping to knock, Bill burst into the conference room.

burst into flames begin to burn suddenly:—When a spark flew into the gasoline, the whole tank burst into flames.

burst into tears begin to cry suddenly:—When her father told her she could not go, Helen burst into tears.

burst out crying, burst out laughing begin to cry or to laugh suddenly:— The idea seemed so ridiculous to her that she burst out laughing.

bury one's head in the sand refuse to recognize the real facts of a situation:—He is losing money constantly, but instead of doing something about it he buries his head in the sand and just waits for better times.

bush league said of less prominent teams, businesses, or persons in general:—Why don't you leave the bush league and work for our vast international corporation?

business, get down to business begin to work seriously:—If he wants to make a success in life, it's about time he got down to business and applied himself more diligently to his work.

business, give one the business (sl.) attack, scold:—When Mrs. Brown's young son insulted her, she gave him the business.

business, go about one's business mind one's own affairs:—He kept bothering me, and so I finally told him to go about his business.

business, have no business have no right:—He has no business saying such things about me.

business, mean business have a serious purpose or intent:—I thought at first that he was joking, but when I saw that he really meant business I became quite concerned.

business See also **land** office business; **mind** one's own business; **send** someone about his business.

bust up terminate—especially a marriage partnership or similar association (sl.):—I am sorry that they busted up after so many years of such close cooperation.

butt in interfere, intrude:—Don't butt into other people's business

butter up seek to ingratiate oneself:—How Alice butters up her supervisor!

button, on the button alert, active, efficient:—We're going to give our young accountant a raise because we've found he is always on the button.

buttonhole approach, accost another person in order to speak privately:—After waiting several hours I managed to buttonhole him just as he was leaving his office.

buy (v.) adopt, accept a plan, a reason, an explanation:—I like your suggesting that our company open an employees cafeteria, and I'm sure the President will buy it.

buy off bribe:—The gambler bought off the police and thus was able to operate freely.

buy out purchase the entire rights of:—When Jones decided to retire from business, his partner bought him out.

buy up purchase the entire stock of:—The government is trying to buy up all the available tungsten.

buzz, give one a buzz telephone:—When you get home give me a buzz.

by and large in general:—By and large the brighter students are more attentive in class.

by oneself alone:—She now works at a desk by herself, and I work at another desk by myself.

by the way incidentally:— By the way, have you seen anything of Carter lately?

by, not by a long shot by no means:— When I asked him whether he expected Holmes to be elected president, he answered, "Not by a long shot!"

by See **hook by hook** or by crook; **skin, by the skin of one's teeth.**

bygones, let bygones be bygones let the the past be forgotten:—Though we had really quarreled bitterly we decided to let bygones be bygones and resume our former business relationship.

bypass evade, fail to consult or consider:—They bypassed Senator Hill's recommendations and presented an entirely new bill.

byword, become a byword become well-known, notorious:—His lack of tact has become a byword in our office.

C

cake, have one's cake and eat it too enjoy two opposed advantages from the same thing:—You can either spend your money on a trip to Europe or save it to buy a car, but you can't do both; that would be having your cake and eating it too.

cake See also **take the cake.**

call a halt terminate:—As it was getting late we decided to call a halt to our game.

call a spade a spade call something by its actual name, use plain, direct speech:—He is one politician who tells the truth. In his speeches he can be depended upon to call a spade a spade.

call away summon from:—The doctor was called away from the meeting to attend an emergency case.

call-back a telephoned request for an absent person to phone the party calling:—When the boss returned from lunch, he asked his secretary if she had received any call-backs.

call down reprimand, scold:—John's boss called him down for coming late to work.

call for (1) go to pick up someone or something:—We will call for you at about eight o'clock. (2) ask for, summon:—He called for his car and suddenly left the meeting. (3) require, demand:—That kind of lawless rioting calls for stern action.

call forth summon, elicit:—It was a situation that called forth all his initiative and courage.

call-girl a prostitute who can be reached by phone for an assignation:—Detectives found that married man in a hotel room with a call-girl.

call in (1) summon for consultation:—I think we ought to call in a specialist at this point. (2) recall something that has been issued previously:— The government is calling in all the ten-year Series F bonds.

call into play bring into action:—The skill of his opponent caused Jones to call into play all the tricks he knew.

call it a day quit for the day:—I think we have accomplished a great deal. Let's call it a day.

call it quits retire, retreat, give up:—After arguing back and forth about the matter, the committee decided to call it quits and adjourn.

call off cancel:—The game was called off on account of rain.

call on (1) visit:—Yesterday the salesman called on three prospects. (2) summon, ask to participate or contribute:—The chairman called on Mr. Brown to make a few remarks.

call one names swear at another, address him by ugly names:—When he began to call me names, I got mad and hit him.

call one's bluff challenge, defy—particularly when it is suspected that the other person is bluffing:—As long as he thought Henry was afraid of him he acted very pugnaciously, but when Henry stepped up to him and called his bluff, he became very meek.

call one's own possess, have:—He is so poor he doesn't have one good suit of clothes to call his own.

call out (1) summon:—If the rioting continues they will have to call out the state militia. (2) speak loudly, shout:—He called out my name several times, but somehow I failed to hear him.

call the roll call out the names on a certain list, take attendance:—Each day before class begins the teacher always calls the roll.

call to account criticize, censure, ask for an explanation:—I am not surprised he was called to account for his actions. They were inexcusable.

call to arms summon into the army:—Every able-bodied man was called to arms at once when news of the attack was announced.

call to mind recall, cause one to remember:—Your story calls to mind something similar which happened to me some time ago.

call to order start a meeting:—The chairman called the meeting to order.

call up (1) telephone:—I'll call you up about seven o'clock. (2) See **call** to arms.

call, close call a narrow escape:—Did you see how close that bus came to hitting that man? That was really a close call.

call See also **bar,** call to the bar; **pay** a call; **shots,** call the shots; **square,** call it square; **toll call.**

calm down become quiet:—Since there was no need to become excited, I told him to calm down and wait his turn with the others.

camp (n.) or campy (adj.) commonplace, unsophisticated decor or writing, theater, or movies:—That western movie was pure camp.

camp out live outdoors as in a camp:—There is nothing I like better than to go up into the mountains and camp out for a few days.

can, in the can (1) completed, said of film:—All of that new movie has now been shot and is in the can. (2) (sl. and vulg.) in the toilet:—Al can't come to the phone now. He's in the can.

candle, hold a candle to compare favorably with:—As regards intelligence, Helen can't hold a candle to her sister.

candle See also **burn** the candle at both ends.

canned music recorded music:—Let's go to a concert and hear some real music. I'm tired of listening to canned music all the time.

cap the climax exceed what is already a high point:—The story which you told was funny enough, but Bill's tale capped the climax.

cap See also **feather** in one's cap; **night** cap; **redcap; set** one's cap for.

card an amusing fellow:—After a couple of drinks at a party Milton is certainly a card.

card, have another card up one's sleeve have something in reserve:—Ross wasn't ruined by his business failure; he had another card up his sleeve—his wife's fortune.

card, in the cards destined, fated:—He had always felt that his marriage to Helen was in the cards.

cards, put one's cards on the table be absolutely truthful, reveal all the facts:—I told him that I would put all my cards on the table but that he would have to do the same if he expected me to invest any money in the scheme.

card See also **drawing** card; **trump** card.

care, in care of in charge of, to the direction of—used especially in addressing articles through the mail:—He wants it sent to him in care of the American Embassy in Paris.

care See also **rap,** not to care a rap about; **take** care of.

carpet, on the carpet under censure, called in by one's superior and reprimanded:—John's boss called him on the carpet this morning for his failure to cooperate with his fellow employees.

carpet See **red** carpet.

carry arms be armed, carry weapons on one's person:—No one is permitted to carry arms without a special license.

carry away inspire, transport:—The audience was carried away by the speaker's eloquence.

carry coals to Newcastle supply something to a place which already has an abundance of it:–Selling refrigerators to the Eskimos seems like carrying coals to Newcastle.

carry off (1) abduct, steal:–After destroying the village the enemy carried off all the cattle. (2) execute, perform:– I must say that father carried off his role of Santa Claus very well.

carry on (1) misbehave, be indiscreet:– They say that he has been carrying on with his friend's wife for some time. (2) continue, keep up:–We have carried on a correspondence for years. (3) weep, become hysterical:–She carried on terribly at the news of her daughter's elopement. (4) keep on doing one's job or duty:–"Carry on," cried the sergeant to his squad of rookies.

carry out perform, complete an assigned task:–He promised that he would carry out every one of her wishes.

carry something too far go to extremes, overdo:–I like to be amused, but Leon sometimes carries his jokes too far.

carry the day win a contest or fight:– The superior artillery of the enemy carried the day.

carry weight impress, have significance: –Any recommendation of the President carries great weight.

carry See also **chip,** carry a chip on one's shoulder; **feet,** carry one off one's feet; **tune,** carry a tune.

carrying charge cost of buying merchandise on time or on a charge account:– There is a carrying charge of one per cent a month on those charge accounts.

cart, put the cart before the horse be illogical, place something which is second in importance before that which logically comes first:–To learn to dive before learning to swim well seems to me to be putting the cart before the horse.

case the joint study secretly the location and activities at a certain address:– Before we go to that restaurant let's case the joint to see how many diners there are and if they have any room.

case, as the case may be whichever of two or more things happens to result:–We shall let you know whether the experiment proves to be a success or a failure, as the case may be.

case, in case if:–In case he arrives before I get back, please ask him to wait.

case, in case of in the event of:–In case of fire, break the glass and push the red button.

cash in on exploit, take advantage of:– The movie actress cashed in on her sudden popularity and signed up for several television appearances at a fabulous salary.

cash, petty cash small amounts of money kept in an office for incidental expenses: –Please make out a petty cash slip for the two dollars you spent for stamps.

cash See also **spot** cash.

cast about for search for, look about for:– Being without funds, Owen cast about for some means of obtaining financial help.

cast down depressed, sad, dejected:–He seemed cast down as a result of his failure to find work.

cast light upon make clear, throw light upon:–Their findings cast much light upon the burial customs of the Indian tribes of that area.

cast off leave, untie the moorings of a boat:–The ship cast off from Boston early the next morning.

cast up thrown upward to the surface:– The bodies of the two drowned men were finally cast up by the sea.

cast, put in a cast placed in a plaster form—as in the case of a broken arm, leg, etc.:–The doctor said that he would have to put Richard's arm in a cast for at least a month.

castles in the air daydreams of grandeur: –Instead of working hard at her lessons, Mary spends her time building castles in the air.

cat, let the cat out of the bag reveal a secret:–John and Edith planned to keep their engagement a secret, but Edith's sister let the cat out of the bag when she mentioned Edith's new engagement ring.

cat, see which way the cat jumps determine how the leaders or the majority will decide, gauge the result of some situation:—He is a clever politician and will wait until he sees which way the cat jumps before he declares his position on that new proposal.

catch (1) a trick, something designed to deceive:—They cannot sell a well-made television set at such a low price; there must be a catch somewhere. (2) a person much sought after and highly desirable as a matrimonial prospect:— With his good looks and his great personal fortune he is considered the catch of the town.

catch cold become sick with a cold:—If I sit in a draft I always catch cold.

catch fire begin to burn:—Be careful with that match. That straw catches fire easily.

catch hold of grasp:—The police threw him a rope which he caught hold of; they then drew him up from the river.

catch it receive a scolding or punishment: —Anne will catch it for breaking that vase.

catch on (1) understand, grasp the point of:—Being a foreigner, Carl did not catch on to the joke. (2) become popular:—The songs from that new show are beginning to catch on.

catch one napping discover someone asleep or off his guard:—Carl's opponent at chess caught him napping and defeated him in several quick moves.

catch one's breath rest, regain one's normal breathing:—This hill is very steep. Let's sit down and catch our breath.

catch one's eye attract the attention of another:—When I finally caught Jim's eye, he came over at once to talk with me.

catch sight of see, obtain a view of:— I turned around and caught sight of Helen getting into a taxi.

catch up with reach, gain the same level as:—After being out of school so long, Helen had to work hard in order to catch up with the rest of the class.

cater-cornered diagonally opposite:—They lived cater-cornered from the post office.

catty gossipy, slanderous, malicious—particularly with reference to remarks made by one woman about another:— When she says that Mrs. Smith certainly looks her age she is being catty, because there is no one in our group more youthful looking than Mrs. Smith.

cave in collapse, fall in:—During the earthquake many buildings caved in.

cease fire stop firing of guns:—As soon as news of the armistice arrived, the order was given to cease fire.

chain gang a group of convicts chained together:—Penologists condemn the practice of using chain gangs.

chain smoker a heavy smoker—one who lights each fresh cigarette from one just finished:—Henry is a chain smoker, smoking almost three packs of cigarettes each day.

chain stores a series of stores in different locations joined together under one ownership and management:—Prices in chain grocery stores are generally lower than those in independent stores.

chance, by chance accidentally:—I met him by chance on Fifth Avenue.

chance See also **fat** chance; **fighting** chance; **ghost** of a chance; **stand a** chance; **take a chance.**

change hands transfer ownership:—The building changed hands twice within one month.

change of life the menopause:—Most women undergo a change of life in their forties.

change one's mind alter one's opinion or plan:—I have changed my mind about going to Florida for my vacation.

change one's tune alter one's attitude, change from one fixed opinion to another:—He used to criticize the Democrats constantly, but lately he has changed his tune.

change-over said of the introduction of new products:—The current new cars have not been much affected by the long-range change-over policies.

change, for a change for variety:—I am tired of looking at television every night. Let's go to a movie for a change.

channels, go through proper channels in wanting something done in an organization one goes to the appropriate department first:—When John asked the company president if he could have the day off, his immediate superior chided him for not going through channels.

character, out of character inconsistent, out of keeping:—The actor's Southern accent was out of character with his role as Hamlet.

charge-a-plate a small plastic card entitling the bearer to charge bills at restaurants, airlines, stores, etc. Also called credit card:—If you lose your charge-a-plate, report the loss at once to the issuing company.

charge with accuse in a court of law:—The teller was charged with embezzlement of the bank's funds.

charge, be in charge of have the management of:—He is in charge of the accounting department.

charge, get a charge out of find exciting, enjoyable, attractive:—I get a charge out of camping in the deep forest.

charge, have charge of Same as **be in charge of.**

charge See also **carrying** charge, **take** charge of.

cheap, feel cheap feel inferior, humiliated:—When everyone except me offered to contribute to the fund, I felt very cheap.

cheap, get off cheap pay less than the normal price:—If you had your motor repaired for only ten dollars, you got off cheap.

cheapskate a reluctant spender of money, a miserly person:—He is a cheapskate; when he takes his girl out he takes her for a walk in the park so as not to spend any money.

cheat on be secretly unfaithful to:—Mr. Frost cheats on his wife. He has a mistress.

check in sign when reporting for work or duty—also register in a hotel:—Everyone has to check in at the factory by nine o'clock.

check out leave a hotel:—The record shows that he checked in at the hotel on Monday, and checked out Tuesday night.

check up on examine, investigate, verify:—Two detectives have been assigned to check up on the prisoner's statements.

check with (1) agree with:—Do these figures check with the bank statement? (2) consult:—I want to check with Ames before I sign the papers.

check See also **draw** a check; **spot** check.

cheer up console, make more cheerful:—He was so depressed that nothing we said served to cheer him up.

chew the rag (the fat) chat, converse endlessly:—We sat there chewing the rag about old times.

chicken feed small amounts of money:—What Brown earns at the postoffice is just chicken feed. It's his other job as a plumber that really brings in the dough.

chicken-hearted timid, lacking courage:—I can't imagine Albert becoming a police officer; as a boy he was always so chicken-hearted.

chicken out avoid doing something that requires courage or foolhardiness:—The three brothers planned to go bear hunting, but one of them chickened out.

chickens, count one's chickens before they are hatched depend on the advantages or the profits from some transaction, the results of which are not yet certain:—Let's find a buyer for the building first, before we decide how we are going to spend the money. Otherwise we shall be counting our chickens before they are hatched.

child's play something easy to perform:—That simple game is child's play for Bill, who is an expert in all forms of athletics.

child, with child pregnant:—Three months after her marriage Mrs. Long found that she was with child.

chime in with agree with, echo:—Most of the nation's editorial writers chimed in with the President when he expressed his views on national defense.

chin, keep one's chin up be brave, courageous:—Your wife's going to get well. Keep your chin up.

chin, take it on the chin suffer, lose:—What with heavy hospital expenses and an extravagant family, Jim is certainly taking it on the chin these days.

chip in contribute:—Everyone in the office chipped in a dollar to buy Mary a wedding present.

chip, carry a chip on one's shoulder be of a quarrelsome nature:—He is a difficult man to get along with; he always carries a chip on his shoulder.

chip See also **block**, a chip off the old block.

chips are down there is hard luck, ill fortune:—Roger can smile even when the chips are down.

chips, in the chips well-off, wealthy:—Ever since Henry inherited that property from his father, he has been in the chips.

chisel in on penetrate, work one's way into insidiously, appropriate, seize:—He has a good sales territory but is always afraid that someone else may chisel in on it.

chum around with be close friends with, travel around with:—He chums around with Charles.

clam up be silent, refuse to talk or give desired information:—When the police started to question the suspect, he clammed up.

class, have class have refinement and good breeding:—Martin married a girl who had class.

clean bill of health complete approval, sanction—actually a document certifying that there exists no trace of disease or infection:—The committee, after examining Holmes for his views on communism, gave him a clean bill of health.

clean house empty, remove personnel, etc.:—When that new President joined the Company, he decided to clean house and fired a number of minor executives.

clean out remove everything from within a place, clean completely:—Before Saul quit his job, he cleaned out his desk.

clean slate something absolutely clean, an unblemished record or reputation:—After paying off all his old debts, he was able to start his new business with a clean slate.

clean sweep a complete, or preponderantly complete victory:—He won the last election by a clean sweep.

clean up (1) wash and make oneself presentable:—Give me just a few minutes to clean up and put on a different suit. (2) finish, terminate:—I promised my boss I would clean up all this work before I left on my vacation. (3) make a large profit:—That investor cleaned up on Wall Street last month.

clean, make a clean breast of confess:—The police urged the criminal to make a clean breast of everything.

clean See also **break**, a clean break.

clear away remove, clean from a shelf, table or other flat surface:—The waitress will clear away these dishes in a moment.

clear-cut definite:—His new policy of aggressiveness is a clear-cut departure from his old methods of appeasement.

clear off remove objects from a table, shelf, or other flat surface:—If we clear off that shelf you can leave your books there.

clear out (1) remove, empty a closed area, tidy up:—I'll clear out that closet and then you can hang your clothes in there. (2) leave, depart suddenly and unceremoniously:—He finally told his mother-in-law to clear out and let them live their own lives.

clear the air calm or compose a tense situation:—Roger's friendly remarks seemed to clear the air and put an end to what was becoming a very difficult situation.

clear the decks put everything in readiness for a major activity, eliminate unessentials:—The President urged Congress to clear the decks of all but the most important legislative matters.

clear the table remove the dishes from a table:—Mother does the cooking, but Doris always clears the table and washes the dishes.

clear the way remove all obstructions:—The passage of this law will clear the way for further monetary reform.

clear up (1) become clear or fair—said particularly of the weather:—Although it is still raining, it looks as though it might clear up. (2) make plain, solve:—The detective cleared up the mystery when he forced one of the servants to tell what she knew of the crime.

clear, in the clear relieved of all guilt or responsibility, free:—As a result of the new evidence Smith is now in the clear, although Williams is still being held by the police for questioning.

clear See also **see** one's way clear; **coast** is clear; **steer** clear of.

clip one's wings limit, restrict the power or authority of:—The best way to clip his wings is to cut down drastically on his spending allowance.

clip-joint a disreputable cabaret or night club where the patrons are exploited and often robbed:—Jack got into a fight in a clip-joint and finally landed in the police station.

clock watcher a bored employee who works with his eye on the clock while waiting for the time to go home:—The employer told the job applicant that he didn't want to hire any clock watchers.

clock, around the clock continuously for twenty-four hours:—That patient has nurses around the clock.

close call See **call**, close call.

close in on surround, approach from several directions:—The enemy closed in on our troops from three different directions.

close-mouthed uncommunicative, reticent:—You'll never get much news from Harris; he's very close-mouthed about his personal affairs.

close out eliminate, liquidate—used especially with reference to store merchandise on sale:—The advertisement says that Macy's is closing out their entire supply of men's summer suits at a great bargain.

close quarters limited, cramped space:—With six soldiers to each tent we were living in very close quarters.

close shave Same as **close call.**

closed shop a plant or factory employing only union workers:—The Ford Company fought against the closed shop for many years.

close-up a photograph taken at very close range:—The movies frequently show close-ups of their stars.

cloth, make something out of whole cloth manufacture a plausible fact with no basis or foundation:—Ernest never cheated on his wife. Elly made up that charge out of whole cloth.

cloud over (up) become cloudy:—The newspaper predicted that we would have sunny weather, but it is already beginning to cloud up.

cloud, be under a cloud be in disfavor, under suspicion:—Kellogg will be under a cloud until he is definitely judged free of any communist leanings.

clouds, in the clouds absent-minded, given to day-dreaming:—Gloria has been in the clouds ever since John asked her to marry him.

clover, in clover in luxury:—With the sale of his new novel to the movies, Holmes can live in clover for several years.

clue one in give information to, advise of some action:—The President clued his new assistant in on the impending tax suit.

coals, haul (rake) over the coals censure, rigorously examine:—When his company discovers that Evans was responsible for the loss of that important account, they will certainly rake him over the coals.

coals See also **carry** coals to Newcastle.

coast along take it easy, expend little or no effort:—In that job Ellis just coasts along and hardly lifts a finger.

coast is clear a complete absence of danger, of being detected or apprehended:—The thieves waited until they saw that the coast was clear before entering the house.

cock-and-bull story an incredible story:—The jury did not believe the witness' cock-and-bull story.

cocked, go off half-cocked act before adequate preparation is made, act prematurely:—His editor warned him not to go off half-cocked and write about the scandal until he was sure of all the facts.

cocked, knock into a cocked hat disprove completely, discredit: — The lawyer knocked his opponent's story into a cocked hat.

cockeyed drunk (sl.):—He had been drinking all afternoon, and when I met him he was so cockeyed he didn't know his own name.

cocksure very sure, overconfident:—He was cocksure that it wasn't going to rain, but it is pouring outside.

cocky conceited, arrogant:—He was a very cocky young man previously, but the army took a lot of that out of him.

C.O.D. cash on delivery:—I told the saleslady to send the package C.O.D.

coffee-break a short time allowed employees in the morning and afternoon to leave their work and have refreshments:—I'll meet you in the cafeteria across the street during my coffee-break.

coin a word or phrase invent, originate:—Many new words have been coined in Harlem.

coin money earn money rapidly and in great quantity:—Ever since Hughes went into that business he has been coining money.

coin See also **pay** one back in one's own coin; **toss** a coin.

Coke a soft drink, a short, popular name for Coca-Cola:—Give me a Coke with lemon, please.

cold war strained diplomatic relations with a foreign power just short of hostilities:—During the 1940's and 1950's the U.S. and Russia were engaged in a cold war.

cold, have cold feet be timid, afraid, cowardly:—His accomplice got cold feet at the last moment and deserted him.

cold, in cold blood coolly, without passion, mercilessly:—He murdered her in cold blood.

cold See also **blow** hot and cold; **catch** cold; **leave** out in the cold; **take** cold.

come about happen:—How did the accident come about?

come across (1) meet or find unexpectedly:—I came across this book in an old bookstore on Fourth Avenue. (2) pay or do what is desired:—I wanted to borrow $50 from Harry, but he failed to come across.

come along (1) accompany:—John wants to come along with us to the movie. (2) succeed, get along:—How are you coming along with the plans for your new house?

come around (1) agree:—If we talk to him I am sure that he will come around to our way of thinking. (2) revive:—After this much-needed rain my flowers will come around again. (3) visit:—He comes around to see us once or twice a week.

come back return:—His words on that subject often come back to me.

comeback (n.) return from obscurity to prominence or popularity:—After several years of absence from the stage, the actress made a very successful comeback.

come by (1) get, acquire:—How did they come by such an expensive car? (2) pass by, approach:—Our dog barks every time a stranger comes by the house.

come clean confess, reveal everything:—The officer warned the suspect that it would be much better if he came clean and told the whole story.

come down off one's high horse become more modest, less arrogant:—After the election when he loses that good job he will quickly come down off his high horse.

comedown (n.) letdown, disappointment, embarrassment:—To have to live in such a small apartment after having lived for years in that mansion was quite a comedown for the Evans family.

come down with become sick with:—I am afraid that I am coming down with a cold.

come easy (or natural) to one be simple for one to do or learn:—Since he has always been interested in automobiles and in driving cars, learning to fly an airplane comes easy to Frank.

come from originate in, be born and reared in:—John comes from Florida and his wife from California.

come in (1) begin, enter—often said of styles, fashions, etc.:—Long skirts came in about ten years ago. (2) share, participate, enter:—When he gave everyone a share of the money except me, I asked him where I came in.

come in contact with meet or mingle with, be exposed to:—In his work Allen comes in contact with all types of businessmen.

come in for receive, be the recipient of:—Woodrow Wilson came in for a good deal of criticism as a result of the failure of his peace plan.

come in handy prove to be useful or handy:—Take this hunting knife with you on your trip. It may come in handy.

come into inherit:—He will come into a large fortune when he becomes twenty-one.

come into existence begin, start, be born:—No one knows when such a custom first came into existence.

come into style become the fashion:—More informal evening dress came into style shortly after the last war.

come into the world be born:—The records show that he came into the world in June of 1942.

come near doing almost do, nearly do:—We came near visiting you last night but decided that perhaps you wouldn't be at home.

come of result from:—After all the time and energy we spent on that advertising campaign, absolutely nothing came of it.

come off (1) take place, happen:—When does Janet's wedding come off? (2) succeed, make the point:—The jokes Bill told in an effort to cheer us up didn't quite come off.

come off it stop being so haughty or superior:—When Henry said that he was the only man in the firm doing his job, I told him to come off it.

come off with flying colors succeed, triumph:—He came off with flying colors in his final exams.

come-on (1) prize, inducement, attraction:—As a come-on the grocer offered his customers a free soap dish with each dozen bars of soap purchased. (2) an inducement to secure the attention of the potential buyer or contributor:—As a come-on the fund-raisers threw a large cocktail party for prospective donors to the hospital.

come on (1) to progress, get along:—How is John coming on with his study of French? (2) appear, make an entrance—said of those on the stage:—Does Hamlet's father come on again in the scene? (3) hurry, come along:—Come on! We'll never catch them if we continue at this slow pace.

come out (1) appear, be published:—Time magazine comes out once a week. (2) be introduced formally to society:—She comes out in June. They are planning to give her coming-out party at the Hotel Pierre. (3) succeed, fare:—How did you come out in that lawsuit you had against the telephone company? (4) result, turn out, develop—said of photographs particularly:—A few of the pictures came out very well, but others came out poorly. (5) finish, end:—How did that movie finally come out? I couldn't wait to see the ending.

come out for declare oneself for, support—especially in an election:—The Governor of New York State came out for the Republican candidate for mayor.

come out in the open declare one's position openly, reveal one's intentions:—He finally came out in the open and admitted that he was a Socialist at heart.

come out with (1) reveal rather suddenly and unexpectedly:—After sitting there quietly all evening Matilda came out with the announcement that she was to be married the next day. (2) put on the market, offer to the public:—Last year, the Ford Company came out with several new models.

come over (1) be affected by rather sudden illness or emotion, happen to:—I don't know what came over me, but suddenly I felt very faint. (2) be received clearly, result, turn out—said of radio or television programs:—My set is working much better now; the President's speech last night came over very well.

come round Same as **come around.**

come to a head reach a climax, come to a point where a final decision is inevitable: —The dispute must come to a head soon; neither the union nor the owners will tolerate these interminable delays much longer.

come to blows begin to fight:—They were both so angry that I thought they would surely come to blows.

come to grips with meet with, be confronted with, engage with:—It was the first case of cholera with which the young doctor had come to grips.

come to light appear, be found, be discovered:—After being lost for years the document finally came to light in an old attic trunk.

come to one's senses become reasonable, logical, sensible:—It's about time he came to his senses and stopped losing all his money at cards.

come to pass happen. occur:—No one knows for sure how the accident came to pass.

come to terms agree, reach an accord:— After considerable argument buyer and seller finally came to terms.

come to think of it an expression meaning "Now that I have begun to think about it," or "Now that I remember":—Come to think of it, John promised to telephone me about this time.

come through perform, deliver:—After some delay they came through with their promise to deliver the necessary merchandise to us.

come true prove to be correct or realized: —One's dreams do not always come true.

come undone, unwrapped, untied, etc. become undone, unwrapped, untied, etc.: —Your shoelace is coming untied; that package you are carrying is also about to come unwrapped.

come up arise:—The question of Jones's sanity came up several times during the trial.

come up to to equal:—The meals served in most restaurants do not come up to those cooked at home.

come up with present, announce, offer:— You can always depend on Holmes to come up with some practical suggestions for increasing sales.

come upon discover, meet or find unexpectedly:—Where did you ever come upon such an odd piece of furniture?

come what may an expression meaning: despite whatever may happen:—Come what may, I shall always consider Ben my best friend.

come, to come—as in the expressions **years to come, life to come, months to come, days to come** The meaning is: future years; future life; future months, etc.:—In the years to come I shall think of his words very often.

come See also **natural,** come natural; **point,** come to the point; **strong,** come in strong.

coming, not to know whether one is coming or going be very confused, be in an excited state:—Ever since he got that good news John has been so happy that he doesn't know whether he is coming or going.

coming-out party a debutante party in which a young girl is formally introduced to society:—They will probably have her coming-out party in the Hotel Waldorf.

command, have a good command of have skill in, have fluency and accuracy in:— Does he have a good command of English?

command, in command of in charge of, in control of:—He is in command of the First Division.

commission, out of commission not working, out of order:—My vacuum cleaner is out of commission and I am trying to get it repaired.

common, in common sharing the same interests:—They should get along well together because they have much in common.

company, good company a friendly and congenial companion:—I always enjoy being with Frank. He is very good company.

company, keep company with to court, go out frequently in the company of:—He has been keeping company with her for more than two years but still hasn't mentioned a word about marriage.

company See also **keep** someone company; **part** company.

compare notes make a comparison of impressions or ideas:—After comparing notes we found that we both had the same opinion of Jones's work.

con one deceive, mislead, cheat, persuade one against his better judgment:—Although Katie hated the shore, she let her husband con her into spending their vacation there.

concerned, be concerned about be worried about:—He is very much concerned about his wife's health.

concerned, be concerned with have connection with, be associated with:—His work is concerned with the preparation of documents for export.

condition, out of condition See **out** of shape.

conscientious objector one whose principles are against war and against conscription into the army:—During the last war most conscientious objectors were assigned non-military tasks.

contrary, on the contrary to mention the exact opposite:—He is not stupid; on the contrary, he is very intelligent.

cook one's goose cause one serious trouble and complications, terminate with serious consequences:—Since it was the third time that the teacher had caught him smoking in the hall, John knew that his goose was cooked.

cook-out a meal cooked outdoors in the backyard:—We have a cook-out in our yard every Thursday night.

cook up invent, fabricate:—The absentee cooked up some excuse about having had to visit a sick friend.

cool it stay calm, don't get excited:—When two men at the bar began to argue violently, someone else cried out: "Cool it."

cool off become cooler, less excited:— I told him to sit down and cool off before he talked to the boss about his grievance.

cool one's heels wait—especially be left waiting intentionally:—We arrived on time, but he let us cool our heels in his outer office for almost two hours.

cool, lose one's cool get excited, incensed. (Compare **keep** one's cool.):—What if we didn't win our point at the student conference. Don't lose your cool and spoil everything.

coop up enclose in a small place, hedge in:—How can he work cooped up in that little office all day long?

cop out back out, evade a duty or what is expected of one:—Although both Ruth and Helen applied for and were accepted for work in the Peace Corps, Helen copped out.

copy cat one who slavishly imitates another:—She is just a copy cat who follows her sister's lead in everything.

corn belt the mid-west, agricultural section of the United States where much corn is grown:—The state of Kansas lies within the corn belt.

corner the market get control of some stock or commodity:—Little by little Frank kept buying up stock until he had finally cornered the market.

corner, just around the corner near at hand, not far off:—They kept telling us every day that prosperity was just around the corner.

corny out-of-date, behind the times, obvious (sl.):—He told several corny jokes that were anything but funny.

correspond to (with) match, be in agreement with:—He explained to me that the signature on the check did not correspond with the signature which they had in their files.

costs, at all costs in any event, regardless of obstacles:—We must arrive there at all costs before midnight.

cough up contribute (sl.):—We all had to cough up a dollar to repair the damage.

count off count in order one after the other, as with a group of soldiers in line:—The sergeant told his squad to count off from right to left.

count on depend upon:—You can always count on Fred in any emergency.

count someone out plan for one's non-participation:—I can't go to that dance; you'll have to count me out.

count up make a sum or total of:—If you count up all the days that he has been absent, you will find that it is hardly worthwhile to keep him on the payroll.

counter, under the counter secretly, said of merchandise sold illegally:—That storekeeper sells pornography under the counter to favored clients.

counter See also **over** the counter.

course, of course naturally:—Of course I'll help you if you need me.

course See also **due,** in due course; **matter** of course.

cover for someone take or assume another's place or duties temporarily:—While our switchboard operator was taking her coffee-break, one of the secretaries covered for her.

cover-story an article in a magazine that is illustrated on the magazine's cover:—Time's cover-story last week was about the President.

cover up cover completely, conceal:—She put a cloth over the chair to cover up the stains.

cover, under cover secret, concealed:—He worked during the war as an undercover agent for the British.

cover, under separate cover separately, apart:—The package will be sent to you under separate cover.

cover See also **ground,** cover a lot of ground; **take** cover.

cows, till (until) the cows come home a long time, forever:—You can wait until the cows come home before Jim pays you what he owes you.

crab, to crab complain (sl.):—Don't pay any attention to him. He's always crabbing about something.

crack a witty or sarcastic remark:—How did you like that crack he made about my not looking a day over sixty years of age?

crack a book read a book:—Thelma hasn't cracked a book in years.

crack a joke tell a humorous story:—He cracked several jokes about the boss which I thought were very funny.

crack down upon censure, punish, descend upon suddenly:—The mayor has threatened to crack down upon every gambler in town.

crack open reveal, split open, expose:—The District Attorney claims to have enough evidence to crack wide open the numbers racket here in the city.

crack up have a mechanical, physical, or mental breakdown:—If he continues to work at that pace he will certainly crack up.

crack, take a crack at try, attempt, take a chance at:—I don't think I can beat him at tennis, but at least I can take a crack at it.

crack See also **nut,** hard nut to crack; **wisecrack.**

cracking, get cracking get down to business, work harder, produce:—When his secretary failed to finish the typed report by three o'clock as her boss had demanded, he told her to get cracking and finish it.

cramp one's style limit one's normal freedom of action (sl.):—Henry likes to entertain the young ladies, but his being without an automobile at present rather cramps his style.

crapehanger a gloomy person, a pessimist:—Instead of saying that he thought our new offices were very nice, he stood around like a crapehanger.

crash the gate (or a party) gain entrance without invitation or without paying:—Tim crashed the Eatons' party and enjoyed himself as much as anybody.

cream of the crop the best, the most select portion:—They advertise their tobacco as being the cream of the crop.

credit, on credit payment on a time or credit basis:—If you don't have enough cash, why don't you make arrangements to buy the car on credit?

creep, make one's flesh creep cause one to feel uncomfortable, to shock, repulse:— The mere sight of a snake makes my flesh creep.

creeps, give one the creeps cause one to shudder:—The sound of the wind in those trees at night gives me the creeps.

cricket acceptable morally or socially:— It's not cricket to wear sport clothes to a wedding.

crocodile tears insincere grief or compassion:—Don't shed crocodile tears over his leaving. I know very well that you detest him and are glad to see him go.

crop out arise, begin, appear sporadically: —Though there were no cases of the disease in our town, several cases cropped out in a nearby village.

crop up happen, occur suddenly:—That kind of problem is bound to crop up in any business.

cross-examine question a witness of an opposing lawyer:—After testifying in his own behalf, the plaintiff was cross-examined by the defendant's attorney.

cross one's mind occur to one:—It never crossed my mind that she might be his sister.

cross one's path meet, encounter, come upon one:—I hope that man never crosses my path again.

cross out cancel, eliminate:—Before approving the contract the lawyer crossed out several clauses to which he objected.

cross up deceive, trick, doublecross, betray (sl.):—The thief fell into the hands of the police after his accomplices crossed him up.

crow over rejoice at someone's else's expense, boast, gloat over:—You needn't crow over beating us at cards last night; just remember how badly we beat you a few weeks ago.

crow, as the crow flies by the shortest and most direct route:—Their house is about ten miles from ours, as the crow flies; but of course the road is much longer since it winds around the mountains.

crow, eat crow apologize, be forced to admit one's mistake:—He is a proud person, and it was a bitter experience for him to eat crow after the election results proved his predictions to be so clearly inaccurate.

crummy poor, tawdry, soiled (sl.):—Our hotel room wasn't bad, but the furniture was certainly crummy.

crush, have a crush on be very fond of, enamored of:—He has had a crush on her ever since they met at that party last summer.

crust effrontery (sl.):—After almost wrecking my car last weekend he had the crust to ask to borrow it again.

cry one's heart (eyes) out cry bitterly:— When her new doll fell and broke, I thought the child would cry her heart out.

cry out protest, speak loudly, shout, scream:—Each time the doctor touched her arm the woman cried out in pain.

cry over spilled milk weep about something which is unalterable or irreparable:—The money was stolen and we had no chance of getting it back, so I explained to her that there was no use crying over spilled milk.

cry wolf give a false alarm:—Politicians often cry wolf in order to obscure the real dangers that exist.

cry See also **far cry.**

cuff, put it on the cuff charge a purchase: —I'll take this tie. Will you kindly put it on the cuff?

cup of tea what one likes to do and is able to do:—Sure I'll go fishing with you. That's just my cup of tea.

curry favor fawn upon, seek to please in order to gain benefit thereby:—He always seems to be currying favor with the boss.

curve, throw one a curve deal unfairly with, to harm, mislead:—You threw me a curve when you recommended me for that distasteful job.

cut (n.) a share:—Each of the robbers got his cut of the stolen money.

cut a class be absent from a class:—In our university each student is permitted to cut five classes each semester; in other words, everyone is allowed five cuts each term.

cut a figure make an impression:—With his handsome face and polished manners Benjamin cuts quite a figure with all the ladies.

cut across proceed transversely, go at an angle:—We can gain some time if we cut across this field.

cut and dried settled, prepared beforehand:—The election will be a cut-and-dried victory for the Democratic candidate.

cut another down to size humiliate or snub a presumptuous person:—Bill assumes so much authority that his employer felt he had to cut Bill down to size.

cut corners go by a shorter route, economize:—If we cut corners on production costs we can probably market the article at about seventy-five cents.

cut down (1) lay an axe to, cut so that something falls to the ground:—Workmen came and cut down the whole row of trees. (2) reduce:—They will simply have to cut down their expenses if they wish to continue in business.

cut down on lessen, economize in:—We'll simply have to cut down on our consumption of meat during the shortage.

cut in (1) interrupt:—The telephone operator cut in and said that I had already spoken three minutes. (2) change partners with a lady who is dancing:—I had only danced with Jane about three minutes when someone cut in. (3) overtake and turn in front of:—The passing motorist cut in so sharply ahead of me that I had to put on my brakes to avoid hitting him.

cut loose become free and independent, lose all restraint:—The speaker suddenly cut loose with a violent attack upon the President.

cut no ice have no effect, achieve no result:—The fact that he is a rich man will cut no ice with that particular judge.

cut off (1) interrupt, terminate:—When he failed to pay his bill, the company cut off his electricity. (2) disconnect—said particularly of telephone conversations:—We were cut off twice during our conversation. (3) cut a part from the whole:—The butcher cut off several pork chops. (4) block:—All the possible escape routes were cut off by the police.

cut off one's nose to spite one's face suffer from an action designed originally to injure another person:—In walking out and leaving his boss in the lurch, he really cut off his nose to spite his face since no other employer cared to hire him thereafter.

cut one dead snub, purposely ignore another person:—He raised his hat to speak to her, but she cut him dead.

cut one in share with another:—That brokerage firm made so much profit that they decided to cut their employees in.

cut out (1) remove by cutting around:—The child sat on the floor cutting out pictures from the magazine. (2) stop, terminate, desist from:—He kept teasing the dog and I finally told him to cut it out. (3) swear off:—I wish I could cut out smoking. (4) outrival, supplant, replace another in the affections of someone:—John used to go with Helen, but Bill cut him out.

cut out for designed for, fitted for:—I doubt whether John is cut out to be a doctor; with his interest in athletics he would make a better physical instructor.

cut short terminate, shorten, stop abruptly:—The meeting was cut short when the chairman fell ill.

cut to the quick hurt one's feelings deeply:—His complete indifference toward her cut her to the quick.

cut up (1) cut into many small pieces:—You should cut up your meat before you eat it; don't try to eat it whole like an animal. (2) disturbed, unhappy:—She was terribly cut up when she heard about his joining the army. (3) misbehave, act in fresh and unconventional manner:—Though he appears very serious, they say that at a party he is quite a cut-up.

cutback a retrenchment:—Ford has announced a cutback in wages and production.

cutrate reduced rate or price:—You can no doubt buy it cheaper in one of the cutrate drugstores.

cutthroat severe, intense, unrelenting:— The cutthroat competition was too much for them and they had to go out of business.

D

damn—to be damned as in "**I'll be damned . . .**" a defiant expression denoting absolute refusal or negation:—I'll be damned if I'll give him one cent more.

damn See also **give** a damn.

dark horse an obscure or unlikely contestant or candidate in a race or election who emerges unexpectedly to replace the previously favored candidate: —If the convention delegates do not choose one of the two chief contenders on the first few ballots, it is possible that Maine's governor may gain the nomination as a dark horse.

dark, in the dark in ignorance:—We were completely in the dark as to his future plans.

dark See also **keep** something dark; **pitch** dark; **shot** in the dark .

darn a polite emphatic expression for **damn**:—I was so darn tired after our walk that I went straight to bed.

darn, not to give a darn (or damn) not to care, not to consider something important:—I don't give a darn whether she ever speaks to me again.

dash something off write or do something else in a hurry:—I must dash off a note to my sister before the postman gets here.

dash, make a dash for run hurriedly towards:—Suddenly I saw a taxi at the corner and made a dash for it.

day by day gradually:—Day by day he seems to grow a little stronger.

day-dream spend time in reverie:—He spends so much time day-dreaming that he never gets anything done.

day in, day out constantly, consistently: —Day in and day out you can hear them arguing about the same silly subjects.

day of grace an extension period after the due date of some contract or bond:—The premium is due on the fifteenth of each month, but they allow you five days of grace.

day, a rainy day a period of misfortune: —One should always put a little money aside for a rainy day.

day, all day long the entire day:—We spent all day long looking for that error in our accounts.

day, have the day off have a holiday, be free from work:—He has Friday and Saturday off each week.

day, not to give one the time of day ignore another person, show little or no interest in him:—He spoke pleasantly to his neighbor's little girl, but she wouldn't give him the time of day.

day, that will be the day said in reply to a prediction that seems very unlikely:— "When that drunk finally gets married he will then settle down and reform." "That will be the day."

day See also **call** it a day; **carry** the day; **many**, for many a day; **one** of these days; **other** day; **red-letter** day; **salad** days; **take** the day off.

days—one's days are numbered meaning that one's death is near, or that the end of something is to be expected soon:— He is becoming less popular all the time, and it is reported that his days are numbered as a member of the Cabinet.

days See also **one** of these days.

daylight, see daylight see that the end of some task is reasonably close:—Although my desk is still piled high with work to do, I am beginning to see daylight.

dead—dead sure, dead certain, dead tired, dead drunk, etc. completely sure, completely certain, etc.:—He said he was dead sure that the thieves would not return.

dead as a doornail completely dead, without any hope of resuscitation:—This battery is dead as a doornail; no wonder your car won't start.

deadbeat one whose unpaid debts appear to be uncollectible:—No one will extend him any credit because he is known everywhere as a deadbeat.

dead-end a street closed at one end:—We drove into a dead-end street and had to back out.

dead-letter office the postal department where undelivered letters are sent:— You might inquire in the dead-letter office to see whether your letter was sent there.

deadline the final date or hour at which something can be filed or accepted:— The deadline for making application for that civil service exam is next Friday.

deadpan with a serious expression on one's face:—That comic always delivers his gags with a perfect deadpan.

dead set against very much opposed to:— I could see that she was dead set against my going abroad.

dead stop a complete and often a sudden stop:—When the traffic light changed to red, I came to a dead stop.

dead to the world deeply asleep:—It was a pity to have to wake him as he was dead to the world.

dead, over one's dead body against one's bitterest opposition:—I told him that if he tried to remove the fence it would be over my dead body.

dead, to be dead to have lost all importance:—The Democrats will never nominate that ex-Senator for the Presidency. He's dead.

deal another in let one participate or share in a business enterprise:—When Rob came of age, his father dealt him in the family business.

deal in sell, do business in:—His firm deals in plumbing supplies.

deal with treat with, have negotiations or business dealings with:—I refuse to deal with that firm any longer.

deal, a good (great) deal of very much, a large quantity of:—He has a good deal of free time, which he usually spends fishing.

deal, a good deal a satisfactory and profitable venture:—He arranged a very good deal for us in the sale of that property.

deal, big deal often said contemptuously, sarcastically, or scornfully, in a belittling fashion:—So the boss is going to give us a twenty-five cents an hour raise. Big deal!

deal See also **fair** deal; **new** deal; **package** deal; **raw** deal; **square** deal.

Dear John letter a letter to a serviceman overseas from his fiancée breaking off their engagement:—After Carl had been in the service for a year, his girl wrote him a Dear John letter and married someone else.

death, be the death of annoy greatly, cause the death of:—My son's constant friction with his school teachers will be the death of me yet.

death See also **do** to death; **meet** one's death.

deck out decorate, adorn or clothe elaborately:—When I met her she was all decked out in a light-blue summer dress.

declare—well, I declare an expression of surprise:—Well, I declare! I never knew William could dance so well.

deep-freeze a large insulated porcelain box used to keep perishable food at sub-zero temperatures:—We keep a month's supply of meat in our deep-freeze.

deep, in deep heavily committed, in debt, etc.:—I hope that oil company will show a good profit this year and pay a higher dividend, because my husband is in pretty deep.

delivery room a hospital room where babies are born:—Mrs. Smith was in the delivery room eight hours before her child was born.

degrees, by degrees gradually:—He is picking up the language by degrees.

depth, beyond one's depth beyond one's normal capacity or ability:—Any mathematical problem more complicated than simple arithmetic is beyond my depth.

depth, in depth thoroughly and profoundly:—Management consultants made an in depth study of that chain of restaurants.

deuce polite form of the word devil:—Where the deuce have you been all afternoon?

devil, give the devil his due acknowledge the merits of a disliked or evil person:—Brown is very unreliable; but to give the devil his due, he is a first-class mechanic.

dial-tone a tone necessary to hear before a telephone can work:—Pick up the receiver, listen until you hear the dial-tone, and then dial your call.

dice, no dice without success or result, ineffective, without acceptance (sl.):—I tried to sell Ellis an insurance policy but it was no dice.

dick a detective (sl.):—The hotel dick kept watching our movements suspiciously.

die away become fainter and fainter in the distance:—The parade passed, and the sound of the calliope gradually died away.

die down subside, become quiet:—The applause died down and the actors were able to continue.

die off cease to exist one after the other:—The older inhabitants of that village are dying off rapidly.

die out disappear, become unfashionable:—That particular style of dress died out years ago.

die, the die is cast an irrevocable decision is made:—Everything was ready for the invasion. The die had been cast and now there was no turning back.

dig in (1) establish oneself firmly, build a trench:—The soldiers dug in and waited tensely for the enemy's attack. (2) apply oneself diligently:—If I expect to finish all this work today I'd better dig in and get started.

dig up unearth, find, bring to the surface:—The reporters dug up some very interesting facts about the candidate's previous connections with left-wing groups.

dim, take a dim view of be skeptical about, have a low opinion of:—Even I myself took a dim view of my chances of winning the tournament, with so many expert players taking part.

dime, stop on a dime. See also **pull** up short, **stop** short.

dine out eat away from home in a restaurant or hotel:—No, we weren't at home last night. We dined out for a change.

dip into scan, sample lightly, briefly:—I haven't had time to read the entire book, but I did dip into it once or twice.

dirt cheap very cheap, literally as cheap as dirt:—I bought this second-hand car dirt cheap.

dirt See also **pay** dirt.

dirty look a look of scorn or displeasure:—Since I hadn't said anything unpleasant, she had no reason to give me such a dirty look.

dirty story an obscene or improper story:—One should be careful about telling dirty stories in mixed company.

dirty, play dirty treat another unfairly or viciously:—It would have been a fair fight except that one of the fighters played dirty by holding a stone in his left hand.

dirty pool See **pool.**

dirty trick an unfair act, a treacherous action:—That was a dirty trick he played on you when he left town owing you so much money.

dish it out scold, abuse another:— She can both dish it out and take it.

disk jockey a radio announcer who plays recorded music:—I prefer live music to disk-jockey programs.

dispose of relinquish, get rid of, sell:—The thieves had difficulty in disposing of the stolen gems.

distance, keep at a distance prevent from being familiar or intimate:—It was difficult to get to know her because she always kept everyone at a distance.

ditch (v.) leave, desert (sl.):—Finding himself saddled with two girls, Carl decided to ditch one of them.

dive (n.) an inferior cafe or restaurant or saloon:—She said she wanted to see some real city night life, so we took her to visit some of the dives along the waterfront.

Dixie the Southern section of the United States, the South:—She is from Dixie, as is shown by her strong Southern accent.

do away with (1) abolish, discontinue:—Recently our state legislature did away with many obsolete laws which had been on the statute books for decades. (2) murder, get rid of, dispose of:—The gangsters did away with the body by throwing it into the river.

do for do household work for another:—An elderly Danish woman does for us twice a week.

do one good benefit one:—This fresh air will do you good after being in the house all day.

do one in kill:—That racketeer was done in by one of his gang.

do over (1) repeat:—Please do that exercise over until it is perfect. (2) renovate, redecorate:—They are going to do over our apartment in the spring.

do one out of cheat:—His cousin, aided by an unscrupulous lawyer, did him out of his entire inheritance.

do, that will do! an expression of impatience meaning: Stop:—That will do, Tommy! I've had enough of your nonsense.

do to death overdo, do so often that it becomes tiresome:—So many movies have had that spy plot that it has been done to death.

do up (1) arrange, prepare:—He did the package up for me very neatly. (2) launder:—In that laundry they do up my shirts just the way I like them.

do up brown do thoroughly, completely, generously:—He did the evening up brown by taking her to dinner, the theater, and a nightclub.

do well by treat exceptionally well, help, benefit:—In his will he did well by all of his old servants and left each of them five thousand dollars.

do with make use of, use with benefit:—I haven't eaten since noon and could do with a little supper.

do without forego, get along without:—Taxes are so high this year that we shall have to do without a new car.

do See also **best,** do one's best; **bit,** do one's bit; **have** something to do with; **have** nothing to do with; **honors,** do the honors; **how** do you do; **justice,** do one justice; **justice,** do justice to; **make** something do; **never** do; **out** do; **proud,** do one proud; **time,** do time; **do** someone a good turn; **well-to-do; worst,** do one's worst.

doctor up artificially alter, adulterate, meddle with:—I don't like my food doctored up with a lot of fancy seasoning.

dog, in the manger one who is unwilling to let another use what he himself has no use for:—Although Rita lives alone in that big house, she is like a dog in the manger when it comes to letting someone share it with her.

dog one's steps follow someone closely:—All the time he was in Moscow the secret police dogged his steps.

dog-tag a metal tag of identification worn around their necks by men in the Service:—They identified the wounded soldier from his dog-tags.

dog, lead a dog's life live or exist unhappily:—With a wife who nags him constantly the poor fellow leads a dog's life.

dog, put on the dog affect an air of elegance, swagger:—He works in the bank, but from the way his wife puts on the dog you would think he owned the bank.

dogs, go to the dogs lose respectability, deteriorate in quality:—Ever since he started drinking he has gone steadily to the dogs.

dogs, let sleeping dogs lie avoid an action which may lead to trouble and complications, let matters stand as they are:—Wait until they notify you that you must appear; why invite trouble? Better let sleeping dogs lie.

doghouse, in the doghouse in disfavor, in disgrace:—Smith has been in the doghouse ever since his wife caught him flirting with another woman.

dole out measure out sparingly:—Since the food supply was running low, the ship's captain doled out the rations.

doll, you're a doll you are wonderful:—Thanks for helping me with my homework. You're a doll.

dollar See also **top** dollar.

dolled up noticeably well dressed, wearing one's finery:—She was all dolled up as though she were going to a formal dinner party.

done for dead, finished:—When I saw him lying there in the street with blood gushing from his mouth, I was sure he was done for.

done, be done with be finished with:—I am done with writing him letters asking him to pay his bill; now I am going to turn the matter over to my attorney.

door, pull the door to close it:—Please pull that door to; I'm in a draft.

dope (1) narcotics:—Peddlers of dope are severely punished when caught. (2) information, details:—I'd like to get all the dope you have on a man named Evans who used to work in your office. (3) a stupid person:—Don't be a dope all your life. Study some trade and then go out and get yourself a good job.

dope out figure out, understand:—Nobody could dope out what he meant.

dot, on the dot on time, punctual, promptly on schedule:—He was there, as he had promised, at ten o'clock on the dot.

doublecross deceive, betray:—The criminals shot one of their gang who they believed had doublecrossed them.

double-date said of a social evening that two couples spend together:—Her roommate and she went on a double-date last night.

double-header two baseball games offered on the same day:—Let's wait until Saturday to see a baseball game, because there is a double-header that day.

double-park park a car parallel to cars parked lengthwise against the curb:—In a large city double-parking occurs a good deal and usually blocks the cars nearer the curb.

double talk slick, assured talk designed to deceive or confuse:—My wife was quite convinced by what the salesman told her, but to me it was just a lot of double talk.

double up (1) double or increase the number of people living within a certain space:—Because of the housing shortage two couples had to double up in one tiny apartment. (2) bend over:—He was obviously suffering greatly; his face was distorted and he was doubled up with pain.

double, on the double hurry!:—Hurry or we'll miss the bus. On the double!

doubt, beyond a shadow of a doubt definite, certain, without any doubt whatsoever:—His guilt was proven beyond a shadow of a doubt.

doubt, in doubt having some question or uncertainty:—Whenever you are in doubt about any of the words, simply consult the vocabulary at the back of the book.

doubt, no doubt doubtlessly, probably:—No doubt he will telephone right after we leave.

doubt, without doubt definitely, unquestionably:—Without doubt he is the best salesman we have ever had.

down and out without money or means of support, financially ruined:—Once a very rich man, he is now down and out and must depend upon his friends for help.

down on one's luck unlucky, to be passing through a period of bad fortune:—First his wife fell ill; then he lost his job; he has certainly been down on his luck recently.

down, be down on someone prejudiced against, opposed to:—Ruth claimed that the poor marks which she always received were due to the fact that the teacher was down on her.

down See also **heels**, down at the heels; **mouth**, down in the mouth; **ups** and downs.

drag on be tedious, monotonous:—The meeting dragged on for more than two hours.

drag out protract, extend so as to become monotonous—use transitively:—The author dragged out the story to such an extent that I lost interest in it.

drag-race a short race between two cars from a standstill to their top acceleration point:—Drag-racing is popular but highly dangerous, especially on a highway.

drag, be a drag on another be in one's way, be dependent on:—When she graduated from college, Susan refused to be a drag on her mother and got herself a job.

draw a check write a bank-check:—He drew a check for fifty dollars payable to me.

draw a conclusion infer:—From his muddy shoes I naturally drew the conclusion that he had been walking through the woods.

draw aside separate, take to one side:—He drew her aside and whispered something into her ear.

draw back withdraw, move away from:—At the sight of the blood she drew back in horror.

draw blood (1) cause blood to flow:—I thought the dog had only scratched her, but his teeth had drawn blood. (2) pique, wound:—The speaker's reference to his opponent's racial stock drew blood.

draw fire become the target of:—The senator's wild insults promptly drew the fire of his opponents.

draw in pull inwards:—It's amusing to watch the cat draw in her claws when playing with the baby.

draw interest earn interest on capital:—My savings account draws 5 per cent interest.

draw lots select at random from a series in order to determine precedence or apportionment:—The scouts drew lots to determine the order in which they would stand watch during the night.

draw near approach, come near:—The time is drawing near when Elliott will have to leave for school.

draw off deflect, drain away:—A light flanking attack was made in order to draw off the enemy's fire.

draw on (1) secure funds from a bank or person:—He kept drawing on his bank account to such an extent that the bank soon notified him that he was overdrawn. (2) arrive, approach:—As midnight drew on, the party became more boisterous. (3) put on—said of clothes:—Hastily John drew on his trousers and rushed out into the street.

draw out (1) cause another to speak freely and without inhibition:—She cleverly drew out from him the whole story of his misadventures. (2) protract, make lengthy, overextend:—His speech was long and drawn out. (3) secure money from one's bank account:—Before leaving town he drew out every cent which they had in their joint bank account.

draw the line stop at a certain point, limit:—I don't mind his taking an occasional cocktail, but I draw the line at heavy drinking.

draw to a close (end, finish) approach an end, terminate:—The meeting drew to a close around midnight.

draw up (1) drive up to a place and stop, approach:—Looking out the window, we saw a police car draw up to our house. (2) stand up very erect:—Before addressing the jury the lawyer drew himself up to his full height. (3) draft a document:—I had my lawyer draw up my will.

draw See also **beat** one to the draw; **blank,** draw a blank; **horns,** draw in one's horns; **quick** on the draw.

drawback a handicap, obstacle:—Her lack of education was a serious drawback to her.

drawing card attraction, special feature:—The main drawing card, which brought thousands to the theater, was the group of Balinese dancers.

dream up invent, originate, design—not always in a complimentary sense:—Who dreamed up that ugly modernistic courthouse?

dress a window prepare and mount a display in a store window:—Albert learned how to dress windows when he worked at Macy's.

dress up put on one's best clothes, dress in formal garments:—When I met her she was all dressed up in her new mink coat.

dressing down, give someone a dressing down scold, reprimand:—His sister gave him a real dressing down for wasting so much time.

dressing See also **window dressing.**

dribs and drabs small bits or portions:—He paid me back what he owed me in dribs and drabs.

drift off (1) fall asleep:—His head kept nodding and he kept drifting off to sleep while we talked. (2) leave gradually, depart:—One by one the couples drifted off into the moonlight.

drink-in a party where there is a lot of drinking:—We had a drink-in in our apartment last night.

drink down drink in one draught swallow:—He was so thirsty that he drank down one glass of water after another.

drink in absorb deeply, take in with great interest:—The tourist stood there drinking in the magnificent mountain scenery.

drink to another to toast, honor:—We all drank to Dan's success in his new undertaking.

drink up finish, drink completely:—The mother told her young son to drink up his milk.

drink See also **drive** another to drink; **take** to drink.

drip-dry said of fabric that can be washed without having to be pressed or ironed:—When Jim travels, he wears drip-dry shirts.

drive a bargain haggle, over, secure the lowest possible price and greatest gain:—Since the victors held all the advantages, they drove a hard bargain at the peace conference.

drive another to drink irritate one excessively:—That rock-and-roll music is enough to drive me to drink.

drive at hint at, aim towards, mean:—None of us understood what the lecturer was driving at.

drive-in a place where customers are served or entertained while remaining seated in their automobiles:—We had lunch along the highway at a drive-in restaurant. In the evening we went to a drive-in movie.

drive someone to the wall ruin, defeat completely:—When his funds were exhausted, Mr. Zell's creditors drove him to the wall.

drive something home prove conclusively, argue strongly:—By citing specific examples, the orator drove home his points.

driveway a private vehicular road leading from the main thoroughfare to a home, garage, or other building:—Yesterday I spent all morning shoveling the snow out of my driveway.

drop by (drop over) visit informally, pay a short visit:—Mr. Evans dropped by my office yesterday to talk with me about the new book he is writing.

drop in visit informally—same as **drop by**:—Mr. and Mrs. Jones dropped in to see us last night on their way home from the movie.

drop in the bucket relatively a very small amount, a small part of the whole:—To meet its budget the city needs ten million dollars, so that the few thousand dollars which it will gain from the new liquor tax is only a drop in the bucket.

drop off (1) fall asleep:—In the middle of our conversation he suddenly dropped off to sleep. (2) lessen in quality or amount:—Sales of that type of article always drop off during the winter months. (3) discharge a passenger:—I picked up my wife at home and dropped her off at the shopping center.

drop one a line write briefly to someone:—Be sure to drop us a line as soon as you get to California.

drop out leave, resign, cease to attend:—The class began with ten students, but several have dropped out within the last month.

drop, at the drop of a hat immediately, at once:—Luke will argue about politics at the drop of a hat.

drop, have the drop on draw one's gun more quickly than the other person does:—Both cowboys started to reach for their guns, but the sheriff got the drop on them both.

drop, let drop (1) hint, disclose:—Quite unexpectedly he let drop that he was thinking of leaving for Europe. (2) cease to talk about, set aside, forget:—It is an unpleasant matter, and I suggest that we let the whole thing drop for a few days.

drop, take a drop (1) partake of alcoholic drinks:—He takes a drop now and then but not to the extent that he used to. (2) fall in price, lose value:—Stocks took a big drop yesterday when the Treasury Department announced it was tightening credit controls.

drown out overwhelm, obscure, eliminate by some overpowering force:—His voice was drowned out by the roar of the waves.

drug on the market an article for which the demand has fallen off thus causing an oversupply:—Men's knickers went out of style and are now a drug on the market.

drum up promote, encourage through energetic methods:—Our department store is offering reductions on many types of merchandise, in an effort to drum up business.

dry behind the ears mature, grown up, experienced:—Don't trust young Ames's judgment in such matters; he is scarcely dry behind the ears.

dry out become dry through loss of moisture:—Don't leave that bread on the table; it will dry out.

dry-run putting some plan into operation temporarily as for testing purposes, a rehearsal:—Let's have a dry-run of that presentation we are to submit to our clients tomorrow.

dry up (1) dry completely:—The sun came out and dried up the streets in a half-hour. (2) cease talking, become quiet (sl.):—When she continued to complain about the food he told her to dry up.

drygoods cloth materials, textile goods:—At the information desk they told us that we must go to the drygoods department to buy that particular material we wanted.

duck (v.) avoid, escape from:—Let's duck those bores by slipping out the back door before they see us.

duck out escape from, avoid by skillful maneuvering:—Somehow or other he always manages to duck out of any hard work which has to be done.

duck soup anything easy to do:—Selling cars is duck soup for that star salesman.

duck See also **water** off a duck's back.

due, in due course eventually, at the proper time:—After they were engaged, the wedding followed in due course.

due See also **devil**, give the devil his due.

dumb luck undeserved good fortune or luck obtained without much effort or intelligence:—When his car collided with another, Henry had the dumb luck to be thrown into a haystack.

dumb stupid, unintelligent:—She is the dumbest student in the class.

dumbwaiter a small elevator arrangement for carrying food, dishes, etc. from one floor to another:—The banquet was delayed because the dumbwaiter broke down and all the food had to be carried upstairs by hand.

dumps, in the dumps sad, depressed:—I have been in the dumps ever since I got that letter early this morning.

dust off clean any flat surface by dusting:—Before we sat down she hurried and dusted off each of the chairs.

Dutch, be in Dutch be in trouble:—He is in Dutch with the police for carrying a loaded revolver.

Dutch, beat the Dutch be extraordinary, unusual:—It beats the Dutch how he always manages to get the highest marks in the class.

Dutch, get in Dutch get into trouble. See **Dutch**, be in Dutch.

Dutch treat a party or "treat" where each person pays his own way:—Nobody had much money, so we decided to make the party a Dutch treat.

Dutch, go Dutch pay, each one, his own way or expenses. See **Dutch** treat:—We decided to go Dutch on the luncheon.

duty, do duty for serve as:—This sheet will do duty for a tablecloth.

duty, off duty not at work, not in service, having time off:—Though the policeman was off duty at the time, he recognized the man as a wanted criminal and arrested him.

duty, on duty at work, in service:—Policemen are not allowed to sleep while on duty.

dyed in the wool complete, inveterate, unchanging:—He is a dyed-in-the-wool Republican.

dying to very eager, having a great desire to:—I am dying to get home and try out my new television set.

E

eager beaver said of an employee, student, etc., who is over-anxious to please: —Jerry is such an eager beaver that he is getting everybody's goat.

ear, bend one's ear: talk endlessly:— Whenever I sit next to that old lady, she bends my ear until I'm ready to scream.

ear, by ear by sound, without ever reading printed music of the pieces played:— He plays the piano by ear.

ear, have an ear for be sensitive to, have a taste for, have a keen aural perception of:—I have no ear whatsoever for music.

ear, have an ear to the ground be attentive to public opinion, watch carefully the movement of current events:—One of the reasons for his success as a politician has been that he has always kept his ear close to the ground.

ear, have one's ear have access to someone:—Our first step is to speak with Jones because, as you know, he has the President's ear.

ear See also **play** it by ear.

earful, get an earful hear more than one expects or wants to hear:—I asked him how he and his new partner were getting along, and I certainly got an earful.

ears, be all ears very attentive:—When I heard them mention my name, I was naturally all ears.

ears, up to one's ears immersed in:—At this season of the year I am always up to my ears in work.

ears See also **box** one's ears; **dry** behind the ears; **prick** up one's ears; **pin** back one's ears; **stop** one's ears.

early bird an early riser from bed:—Helen and Will were the real early birds; they were up at six each morning ready to take a dip in the lake.

earnest, in earnest serious, not joking:— I thought at first he was joking, but he was really in earnest when he said he never planned to see her again.

earshot, within earshot within hearing distance:—The hall was so crowded that we could not even get within earshot of the speaker.

earth, down-to-earth practical, simple:— He is the everyday down-to-earth kind of lawyer that I like to have represent me.

ease out discharge an employee:—The board of directors recently eased out the president of that motor corporation.

ease up lessen, make lighter:—The enemy has begun to ease up on their continuous bombing of our front lines.

ease See also **ill** at ease.

easy does it it can be done if you'll take it easy and gently:—Help me carry this sofa into the next room. Careful. Easy does it.

easy going relaxed, unexcited, amiable in manner:—Tom is an easy-going type of person who gets along well with everyone.

easy mark a foolishly generous person, one from whom it is easy to get money: —All the bums and beggars in the neighborhood know Bill as an easy mark.

easy terms said of an installment contract, a number of small payments seemingly easier than one large payment:—We bought that furniture on easy terms, paying an exorbitant interest.

easy, on easy street well-off financially: —A lucky speculation in the stock market put Tyler on easy street for the rest of his life.

easy See also **free** and easy; **take** it easy.

eat away consume gradually:—Ocean waves are gradually eating away the coastal rocks.

eat one's heart out mourn, grieve bitterly: He is eating his heart out because she hasn't written to him for two months.

eat one's words retract, apologize humbly: —When confronted by such clear evidence, the Senator was forced to eat his words in public.

eat out eat in a restaurant rather than at home:—We prefer to eat at home, but once in a while we eat out.

eat out of house and home eat voraciously, eat to a ruinous extent:—We have two young sons with appetites like wild animals, and I wouldn't be surprised if one day they ate us out of house and home.

eat up eat completely:—I told him that he had better eat up his meat if he wanted to get any dessert.

eating, be eating someone causing someone to be angry or ill-humored:—I don't know what's eating Mabel, but she hasn't spoken a pleasant word all day.

eat See also **crow,** eat crow.

economy class second class on an airline: —Economy class is cheaper and more crowded than first class.

edge away retreat or withdraw gradually: —Becoming more and more frightened of the snarling dog, Marion began to edge away.

edge out win over someone by a slight margin:—At the last moment Bob edged out Henry for first place in the election.

edge up to reach by twisting through a crowd:—After the lecture Ruth edged up to the speaker and asked him for his autograph.

edge, be on edge be nervous, irritable:— I have been on edge all day ever since that argument with my wife at the breakfast table.

edge, have an edge on (1) have a slight advantage over:—According to the reports, the Yankees have a slight edge on the Dodgers in their pitching and batting. (2) be slightly drunk:—He came to the office yesterday with quite an edge on.

edge, take the edge off soften, lessen the intensity of:—Those two pieces of candy I ate took the edge off my appetite so that I didn't want dinner.

edge See also **get** a word in edgewise; **gilt** edge; **set** one's teeth on edge.

effect, in effect actually, for all practical purposes:—They have no formal contract, but he is, in effect, her manager.

effect See also **go** into effect; **take** effect.

egg on incite, encourage:—It was Helen who egged him on to write the letter.

egg, lay an egg be unsuccessful, fail:— That new show laid an egg and closed after one performance.

egg See also **goose** egg; **nest** egg; put one's eggs in one basket.

eke out extend by adding to gradually, supply the deficiencies of:—He ekes out his small salary by doing odd jobs in the neighborhood.

elbow grease effort, exertion, energy:— You have to use plenty of elbow grease, when you polish brass candlesticks.

elbow one's way into (out of) force one's way by using the elbows:—Since they all stood there like a pack of sheep, we had to elbow our way out of the crowd.

elbow room sufficient room in which to work without difficulty or crowding:— I don't require a lot of space, but I must at least have elbow room.

elbows, be out at the elbows shabbily dressed, poor:—Though I knew they were in reduced circumstances, I was surprised to see Smith so out at the elbows.

elbows, rub elbows with associate with:— During the intermission at the opera we rubbed elbows with the great and the near-great.

element, in one's element in one's natural environment, in one's own field:—Whenever the discussion touches on music, Jane is right in her element.

eleventh hour near the time set, at the last moment:—The editors made several eleventh-hour changes in the magazine.

else sometimes used with the meaning of "otherwise":—Hurry, or else we'll be late.

else, or else an expression added to a command or order and used as a threat, implying a penalty for non-compliance:—Wash those dishes before you go to bed —or else.

end up slightly emphatic form of **end:**—Though friends for many years, they finally ended up enemies.

end, at one's wit's end at the point of having exhausted one's last idea or mental resource:—I had searched unsuccessfully all summer and was at my wit's end to find the right school for my daughter.

end, no end very much, a great deal:—On our trip we had no end of trouble with our car.

end, on end (1) upright:—If you stand the box on end, it will fit into that corner. (2) consecutively:—For three weeks on end the firing continued.

end See also **finger,** have at one's fingertips; **keep** one's end up; **loose,** at loose ends; **odds** and ends; **put** an end to.

ends, at loose ends without direction, aimless, unintegrated:—Ever since she left town, Frank seems to have been at loose ends.

ends, make both ends meet stay within one's financial means, make one's income cover one's living expenses:—With high taxes and his small income Henry had great difficulty in making both ends meet.

equal to the occasion capable of handling the situation:—Although he had never before practiced artificial respiration, Fred proved equal to the occasion and saved the swimmer's life.

error, in error mistaken, wrong:—You were in error in assuming that he would wait for us.

even so nevertheless, regardless:—He appears to be honest but, even so, I don't think we should trust him with all our money.

even, be even (1) be fully repaid, be both on an equal basis, be quits:—After I pay you the five dollars which I owe you, we will be even again. (2) be revenged upon, paid back in kind:—Now that I have caused him just as much trouble as he once caused me, we are even.

even, get even with pay back, retaliate:—I'll get even with him for his insulting remarks if it takes me ten years.

even See also **break** even.

event, in any event in any case, anyway, regardless:—In any event I'll telephone you before I make a final decision.

event, in the event of if such happens, in the case of:—In the event of fire, break the glass and push the small red button.

events, at all events nevertheless:—She may not be very pretty, but at all events she makes a good appearance.

ever so much very much:—We are ever so much obliged to you for your help.

every now and then occasionally, now and then:—I meet him every now and then on Fifth Avenue.

every other alternate, every second one:—The buses stop at every other corner.

every so often frequently:—I no longer see him regularly, but he drops in at my office every so often.

every which way in all directions:—A sudden gust of wind blew our papers every which way.

explain away remove suspicion through force of argument:—Despite his best efforts he was still unable to explain away the fact that the money had not been returned to the safe.

expose oneself reveal one's nakedness in a public place:—Terence was arrested for exposing himself in a theater.

eye, have an eye for have an appreciation of, be ever alert for:—Rogers always has an eye for a good bargain.

eye, in one's mind's eye in one's imagination, visualized:—After looking at the architect's plans, it was easy for him to see the completed house in his mind's eye.

eye, in the eyes of in the opinion of, regarded by:—Though you may consider him innocent, in the eyes of the law he is guilty of murder.

eye, keep an eye on watch, guard:—Please keep an eye on my suitcase while I go to buy my ticket.

eye, keep an eye out for be on the alert for, look for:—The police have been instructed to keep an eye out for pickpockets at the fair.

eye, keep one's eyes open be watchful, alert:—The agent said that he would keep his eyes open and notify me as soon as he found the right piece of property.

eye, see eye to eye be in agreement:—I must say that I don't see eye to eye with you on that matter.

eye, with an eye to with the purpose of:—He bought the property with an eye to building a home for himself there.

eye See also **apple** of one's eye; **black** eye; **catch** one's eye; **set** eyes on.

eye-opener a surprise:—The sudden financial success of that dull fellow was certainly an eye-opener to me.

eyes, make eyes at flirt with:—She makes eyes at all the handsome men.

eyes See also **keep** one's eyes peeled.

F

face down (up) with the head or face turned downwards (upwards):—The cards were placed on the table face down.

face the music incur the penalty:—Cooley spent all his money, then got into debt, and now must face the music.

face to face confronting one another, two people facing each other:—I hadn't seen him in ten years when suddenly there we stood, face to face.

face up to confront or meet hardship calmly and gracefully:—It was hard for Charles to face up to long months of illness.

face value apparent value:—Without inquiring into Walter's record, the employer hired him at his face value.

face, about face in a reverse position:—They suddenly turned about face and marched off in the opposite direction.

face, in the face of threatened by, confronted by:—He remained calm even in the face of such obvious danger.

face, keep a straight face refrain from smiling, remain serious:—John looked so comical up there on the stage that no one could keep a straight face.

face, make a face show an expression of disgust or repugnance:—Every time I mentioned taking a swim in the lake Jack made a face.

faces, make faces at scowl, grimace:—Instead of eating, the two children sat at the table making faces at each other.

face, on the face of on the surface, superficially, apparently:—On the face of it the document seemed genuine.

face, put a new face on change, alter the aspect of:—Smith's announcement of his candidacy puts an entirely new face on the political campaign.

face, show one's face put in an appearance:—He says that if Hilton ever shows his face around here again he'll throw him out bodily.

face, to one's face directly to a person:—I dare you to say those same things to his face.

face, with a long face with a sad or displeased expression:—What's the matter with Grace? She's been walking around here with a long face for two days.

face See also **lose** face.

faced with confronted with:—We are all faced with the same problem of rising costs.

faced, two-faced deceitful, disloyal:—Don't confide too much in Holmes. He has the reputation of being two-faced.

fact, as a matter of fact in reality, to speak the truth, truthfully:—He appears to be strong and healthy but, as a matter of fact, he suffers from a very weak heart.

fact, matter of fact (adj.) literal, factual: —She is a very matter-of-fact person who never seems to get excited or enthusiastic over anything.

fail to do something not to do something which is expected of one, neglect to do: —We waited for him until nearly seven o'clock but he failed to appear.

fail, without fail positively, without exception: —The summons directed the motorists to appear in court the next day without fail.

fair and square absolutely honest and straightforward: —Since everything had been covered in a fair-and-square manner, I had no hesitation in signing the agreement.

fair deal See **square** deal.

fair play justice: —The contestants agreed to observe the spirit of fair play in all of the games.

fair sex the feminine sex, women: —That shop caters exclusively to the fair sex.

fair, in a fair way to tending toward, likely to: —He is in a fair way to becoming the best player we have ever developed.

fair See also **play** fair.

faith, in good faith trustingly: —I signed the agreement in good faith, and I expect you to live up to it.

faith See also **pin** one's faith on.

fall all over someone shower with attention, be excessively attentive: —The hostess fell all over her distinguished guest in an attempt to make him completely comfortable.

fall asleep go to sleep, pass suddenly from a waking to a sleeping state: —He began to nod and fell asleep right in the middle of our conversation.

fall asleep at the switch fail to perform an expected task, be remiss in one's duty: —He was supposed to signal us at the proper time by flashing a light in the window, but apparently he fell asleep at the switch.

fall away diminish, decline: —I was shocked to see how thin she is. She is falling away to a shadow.

fall back retire, retreat: —Our troops fell back before the withering fire of the enemy.

fall back on rely on, turn to as a final recourse: —In an emergency we can always fall back on our savings.

fall behind lag: —Our receipts are falling behind those of last year.

fall down (1) fall striking the floor or ground: —Each time the child fell down, her mother ran out and picked her up. (2) fail to fulfill: —They have fallen down so often on their promises to pay that I no longer believe a word they say.

fall down on the job fail to produce, prove to be a disappointment: —Though he promised to do everything possible to clean up the city, the mayor has certainly fallen down on the job.

fall due become due or payable: —The next payment falls due in thirty days.

fall flat misfire, fail to interest or entertain: —He told some funny jokes, but they fell completely flat before that humorless crowd.

fall for (1) become enamored of, succumb to the attractions of: —It looks as though Bill is falling for your sister. (2) accept, be deceived by: —His story was so convincing that everyone fell for it.

fall-guy a dupe, sucker: —The rich playboy was a natural fall-guy for the shrewd gamblers.

fall in (1) collapse: —The explosion caused the walls of the house to fall in. (2) to form ranks: —"Fall in!" the sergeant shouted to his men.

fall in love begin to love, become enamored of: —All the boys seem to fall in love with Laura.

fall in with associate with: —He fell in with a group of tough kids and in that way started his career as a thief and criminal.

fall into line conform, take a position of agreement: —After the big operators had agreed to accept our terms, the smaller ones immediately fell into line.

fall into the habit of develop the custom or habit of: —He has fallen into the bad habit of stopping off at the corner bar each night on his way home from work.

fall off decline, lessen in intensity:—The demand for this article always falls off when the weather gets warm

fall on (1) attack:—The robbers hid in the bushes and fell on him from three sides. (2) take place on—said of dates: —This year Decoration Day falls on a Friday.

fall-out (n.) radioactive dust in the atmosphere after an atomic bomb has been exploded:—Traces of the fall-out are often found thousands of miles from the site of the exploded bomb.

fall out (1) quarrel, cease to be friends:— Mary and John fell out over the question of who was to be best man at the wedding. (2) break ranks—a military term:—After a long drill the sergeant told his squad to fall out.

fall short be insufficient, stop short of a goal, fail to measure up to:—The performance fell far short of our expectations.

fall sick become ill:—She fell sick last week and has been in bed ever since.

fall through fail to materialize:—Our plans for a picnic fell through.

fall to (1) devolve upon, be one's duty:— When Joel died without leaving anything, it fell to his brother to support Joel's family. (2) start eating:—After grace was said the guest fell to and ate heartily.

fall to pieces disintegrate:—After the death of Napoleon his empire began to fall to pieces.

fall upon (1) devolve upon, become one's responsibility:—It fell upon John as an only child to support his mother after his father died. (2) strike, attack unexpectedly:—The police fell upon the rioters and routed them in a matter of minutes.

fall, let fall reveal, hint, let escape:—From something he let fall during our conversation I believe he is planning to give up his share in the business.

fall See also **ride** for a fall; **windfall.**

false, play one false betray one, be disloyal:—Bert's wife played him false by having an affair with another man.

family tree ancestry:—There are at least two kings in his family tree.

family, in the family way pregnant:—She appears to be in the family way.

fan mail letters and packages received by a celebrity from his admirers:—That top movie actress receives hundreds of pounds of fan mail every week.

fan out spread in several directions:—The main road fans out at that point in at least three directions.

fancy doing something an expression of surprise meaning "Imagine . . .":— Fancy meeting you here at such an unexpected place!

far afield far from the starting point, remote:—When he began to discuss philosophy he was obviously getting far afield from his subject.

far and away clearly, obviously, by far:— He is far and away the best-prepared candidate for the Presidency.

far and wide over a great distance:—You will search far and wide before meeting another friend like him.

far cry something a long distance from, completely different from:—His poor performance today was a far cry from that of last year when he easily beat every player in the tournament.

far-fetched exaggerated, fantastic:—He told some far-fetched story about having been in Tibet at the time.

far gone in an extreme and critical state: —He was so far gone when the ambulance arrived that little help was possible.

far out avant garde, very modern and unconventional, extreme:—That new Swedish movie is very far out.

far, as far as to the extent that:—As far as I am concerned, we can leave either this week or next.

far, be far from one be distant from, have no intention of:—Far be it from me to interfere in such matters, but I would never attempt to talk to him in such an autocratic way.

far, by far obviously, clearly, by a great difference:—He is by far the best player on our team.

far, insofar as to the extent that:—Insofar as money alone is concerned, I am ready to contribute my share.

far, so far up to now, up to the present:— So far this month we have covered ten lessons in the grammar book.

far, so far so good satisfactory up to this point:—"How is the new employee working out?" "So far so good."

farm out delegate a job or part of a job to another person or concern:—They may farm out production of some of the machine parts to other factories.

fashion, after a fashion a little, in an unprofessional, mediocre, or amateurish way:—She cannot prepare elaborate meals, but she cooks after a fashion.

fast See also **pull** a fast one.

fasten on attach:—What can I use to fasten on this corsage?

fat chance ironic for "slim" chance or little chance:—With tickets for that show sold out for two months in advance, we have a fat chance of getting anything for tonight.

fat of the land the best, the richest part:— Ever since he inherited that fortune he and his family have been living off the fat of the land.

fat's in the fire a critical situation has been provoked, trouble has started:— The newspapers report that the fat is in the fire now that the Senate has rejected the President's recommendations and has openly challenged his whole foreign policy.

fault, at fault in error, mistaken:—You were at fault for speaking to him so sharply.

fault, to a fault excessively, to an exaggerated and mistaken degree:—He is generous to a fault in his treatment of his employees.

fault-finding critical, nagging:—He is so fault-finding that it is difficult to work with him.

fault See also **find** fault with.

favor one resemble another person in appearance and manner:—Mary favors her mother, but John seems to favor his father.

favor, do one a favor (1) Give, lend, or buy something for someone, get introductions for, etc.:—You did me a big favor when you introduced me to my future wife. (2) oblige one:—Do me a favor and get out of my light. Also used ironically in "Don't do me any favors," meaning "What you propose to do as a favor is really unwelcome and harmful."

favor, in one's favor to his credit:—Good looks and a good mind are in his favor.

favor See also **curry** favor.

favorite son a political candidate favored by his own state:—Indiana is seeking the presidential nomination for its favorite son.

favorites See **play** favorites.

fear, in fear of afraid of, fearful of:— Situated so close to the border, they live in constant fear of attack by the enemy.

feather in one's cap a triumph:—Winning the scholarship was a feather in his cap.

feather See also **birds** of a feather; **nest,** feather one's nest.

fed up with out of patience with, bored with:—I am fed up with his laziness and carelessness.

feel for sympathize with:—We all feel for the plight of the displaced persons of Europe.

feel in one's bones feel intuitively, have a feeling of certainty:—I feel it in my bones that they will never get along well together.

feel like a new man feel refreshed, recreated:—After a vigorous massage he felt like a new man.

feel like doing be inclined to, have a desire to:—I don't feel like going to the movie. Let's take a walk instead.

feel one's way probe, proceed cautiously by trial and error:—I won't ask him directly to lend me his car. I'll feel my way first.

feel one out get a person's reaction:— Let's feel Gross out and see if he would be interested in the promotion.

feel out test, try experimentally:—Let's feel out the situation first before we take any definite steps.

feel small be embarrassed, humiliated:— He felt very small when it was discovered that he had slipped in without buying a ticket.

feel up to feel equal to, be capable of:— I am so tired I don't think I feel up to going shopping today.

feel See also **get** the feel of; **home,** make one feel at home; **pinch,** feel the pinch.

feet, carry (sweep) one off one's feet overpower emotionally, overwhelm:—His ardent courtship carried Janet off her feet.

feet See also **cold,** have cold feet; **grass,** let the grass grow under one's feet; **stand** on one's own feet; **take** a load off one's feet; and see entries under **foot.**

fellow traveler a communist sympathizer: —The government is trying to weed out the fellow travelers from the civil service.

fence in enclose, limit:—My room was small and looked out on a narrow courtyard, so that I always felt fenced in.

fence, on the fence neutral or undecided: —When asked whether he was going to support the Democrats or the Republicans, Evans replied that he was on the fence.

fence See also **mend** one's fences.

ferret out find out, discover through careful and painstaking investigation:—The district attorney has said that he will ferret out the truth even if it means calling fifty witnesses to the stand.

few and far between widely separated, very few in number:—Really good cooks are few and far between.

few See also **not** a few; **quite** a few.

fiddle around with Same as **fiddle with.**

fiddle with play with, toy with:—If he keeps fiddling with the dials on that radio, he is sure to put it out of order.

fiddle See also **play** second fiddle to.

field, have a field day enjoy great success, have unlimited opportunity:—Their opponents were so weak that our team had a field day and raced up and down the gridiron at will.

field, play the field not limit oneself to one girl friend:—John isn't ready to settle down yet and still plays the field.

fifth column the traitorous element within a country:—Norway was taken over by its Fifth Column even before the German army appeared.

fifty-fifty equally, each paying or contributing half:—Let's go fifty-fifty on the dinner check.

fight it out fight to a conclusion:—The crowd refused to interfere and let the two men fight it out.

fight off struggle against, push back:— After our long walk in the fresh air I had to fight off my desire to sleep.

fight shy of avoid, escape from:—He always fights shy of anything that resembles hard work.

fighting chance a slim chance, a chance necessitating courage and a struggle:— His illness is serious, but the doctor says he has a fighting chance to recover.

fight See also **put** up a fight; **show** fight.

figure of speech a simile, metaphor, etc.:— When we say that "War is Hell" we are speaking metaphorically and using a figure of speech.

figure on count on, expect:—Bill's failure to pay his share was something we had not figured on.

figure out (1) reason out, discover, determine:—I can't figure out what he was hinting at. (2) calculate:—Please help me to figure out my income tax.

figure up add up, calculate:—If you'll figure up exactly how much I owe you, I'll pay you right away.

figures, it figures that's what one would expect:—"That incompetent employee is always late to work." "It figures."

file away put away or store in a place for keeping records:—All those documents were filed away more than a year ago.

file out leave by marching in a single file or column:—The children filed out of the schoolroom at the end of the period.

file, on file on record, placed in a file:—Do you have an application on file with us?

fill in complete, usually said of something left blank or missing:—There are one or two lines more on this application which you must fill in.

fill one in give one background information:—I've been away for a month. Please fill me in on that change in administrative personnel.

fill out complete—said of forms, applications, etc.:—Every place he went he had to fill out an application blank before they would interview him.

fill the bill satisfy the needs or requirements:—I am sure that the new secretary will fill the bill perfectly.

fill up fill to the top, complete:—When the attendant asked Bill how much gas he wanted in the tank Bill told him to fill it up.

fill, have one's fill be satisfied, surfeited, over-indulged:—He says he has had his fill of travel in foreign countries.

filling station a gasoline station:—We'd better stop for gas at the next filling station.

find fault with criticize, complain about:—He is constantly finding fault with my work.

find oneself discover what one is really suited for:—After trying various jobs, he finally found himself and became a very successful newspaper reporter.

find out discover, learn:—How did you find out that Burns was going to be promoted?

finger, at one's fingertips readily available, at one's command, memorized:—He has all kinds of production statistics at his fingertips.

finger, have a finger in the pie participate in, share in:—He can't plan a thing without his wife's having a finger in the pie.

finger, keep one's fingers crossed hope, through crossing the fingers superstitiously, that things will turn out well; be emotionally prepared for the worst that can happen, ward off by crossing one's fingers:—I am sure that nothing will happen to him, but we had better keep our fingers crossed.

finger, lay a finger on harm, beat, maltreat physically:—"Never lay a finger on your child again!" was the judge's warning to the prisoner.

finger, put (lay) a finger on find, locate:—That timetable is somewhere in the room, but it may take me a few minutes to put my finger on it.

finger, slip through one's fingers escape:—Just when the police thought that they had him surrounded, he slipped through their fingers.

finger, twist (turn) another around one's little finger influence easily, dominate completely:—When she wants anything, she can twist her husband around her little finger.

finger See also **lift,** not to lift a finger.

finish up finish completely—slightly emphatic form of **finish:**—If I don't finish this work tonight, I'll surely finish it up tomorrow.

firebug an arsonist, one who willfully sets fire to property:—The police nabbed the firebug just as he was about to set another fire in the basement.

fire, catch on fire begin to burn:—First the curtains caught on fire and then the bedclothes.

fire, hang fire be postponed or delayed, in a state of suspension:—Plans for alteration of the city's water-supply system have been hanging fire for months.

fire, miss fire fail to appeal:—All the comedian's jokes seemed to miss fire with the audience.

fire, on the fire in preparation:—They say that he has several new plays on the fire.

fire, open fire begin to shoot or attack:—The enemy opened fire on our lines at early dawn.

fire, play with fire court danger, risk grave consequences:—Joan is playing with fire when she lets strange men pick her up.

fire, set fire to cause to burn:—Fletcher set fire to his house in order to collect the insurance.

fire, set on fire cause to burn. Same as **set fire to:**—Fletcher set his house on fire in order to collect the insurance.

fire, under fire being attacked or criticized:—Leslie is constantly under fire for giving out confidential information to the press.

fire See also **draw** fire; **fat's** in the fire; **irons** in the fire; **sure-fire**.

first-hand from the original source:—He says he got the information first-hand from the Senator himself.

first-rate of the best quality:— The virtuoso's playing was first-rate.

first thing off the bat immediately, at once:—He fired him first thing off the bat when he got to the office in the morning.

first, at first at the beginning:—At first he was a little shy in class, but now he acts more natural.

first, not to get to first base have no success whatsoever, fail to make initial progress:—I tried various ways to make him lend us the money, but I couldn't get to first base.

first, not to know the first thing about not to know anything whatsoever about:—He assured us that he didn't know the first thing about John's leaving.

first See also **name**, on a first-name basis.

fish out of water one out of his element or natural surroundings:—Not knowing anything about music, I felt like a fish out of water among so many musical experts.

fish story an unlikely or improbable tale:—Though some of his listeners were impressed, John's tale sounded to me exactly like a fish story.

fish, queer fish an odd or eccentric person:—Our high school science teacher was certainly a queer fish.

fish See also **pretty** kettle of fish; **soup** and fish.

fishy improbable, suspicious, illegal, unethical. See **fish story:**—The fact that the mayor's son-in-law received the contract, although he was not the lowest bidder, looks very fishy to me.

fit in with accord with, fall into agreement with:—His plans to take his vacation early in August fit in very nicely with mine.

fit, be fit for be suited for, prepared for:—What kind of work is he fit for?

fit, throw a fit become very angry:—When he told his mother he was going to get married, she almost threw a fit.

fits, by fits and starts (jerks) erratically, by a series of starts and stops:—He never accomplishes much because he always works in fits and starts.

five and ten Woolworth's or any similar inexpensive variety store:—I bought these paper plates at the five and ten.

fix a flat repair a flat or punctured tire:—Some garagemen don't like to fix flats.

fix one up arrange a date with a young woman:—Can you fix me up with that blonde?

fix over alter, make like new:—She will fix over her old party dress and give it to Mary.

fix up (1) repair:—We are having our old house fixed up. (2) arrange:—I think I can fix it up with Bill so that we can use his car this weekend.

fix, get a fix get an injection of a narcotic:—That dope addict would kill in order to get a fix.

fix, in a fix in trouble:—Last night he wrecked his dad's car, and now he is in a pretty fix.

flame, old flame a former love:—Didn't you know that Mary was an old flame of Henry's?

flare up (1) arise suddenly:—Minor outbreaks have flared up in several sections of the country. (2) become suddenly very angry:—I meant no harm by my remark, but she flared up at me as though I had insulted her.

flash in the pan a brief success:—That play of his was a flash in the pan; he hasn't written a thing of value since.

flash, in a flash quickly, suddenly:—I told him that I would be with him in a flash.

flashback in a story, novel, or play, the revealing of a scene earlier in time than the time at the beginning of the literary work:—That novel about a business man started with his early years in business, with subsequent flashbacks to his boyhood and college years.

flat tire See **tire.**

flesh, in the flesh alive, in person:—It was quite a thrill to see a real movie star in the flesh.

flight of stairs a section or series of stairs between floors:—To get to his apartment you have to walk up four flights of stairs.

flight See also **put** to flight.

fling, have one's fling dissipate, have a riotously good time:—He has had his fling and now seems ready to get married and settle down.

flip, flip one's lid to react strongly:—When I told Harry that I was getting a divorce, he flipped his lid.

floating island a custard dessert with beaten whites of eggs floating on top:—We had floating island for dessert.

floor show a show in a nightclub where the entertainers act on the same floor-level that the diners are on:—They had an outstanding floor show in that café.

floor someone overwhelm, astound, nonplus:—His announcement that he was leaving the company for good floored all of us.

floorwalker a section manager in a department store:—To exchange this merchandise you must first get the floorwalker's approval.

floor, have the floor have one's turn to speak:—Please don't interrupt. I believe I have the floor.

floor See also **ground,** get in on the ground floor; **take** the floor.

flop a complete failure:—The show was a flop and closed after only three performances.

flop down on fall or lie down heavily upon:—He flopped down on the couch as though he never wished to get up.

flop, take a flop fall heavily:—I took a nasty flop on that slippery sidewalk.

flunk out fail in one's studies and have to withdraw from school:—If you flunk out of one university, it is sometimes difficult to get into another.

fly at attack—figuratively, become angry at:—She is so irritable these days that she flies at me for nothing at all.

fly-by-night unsubstantial, tending to disappear without notice:—If you're going to insure your car, do it with one of the established companies and not with some little fiy-by-night concern.

fly in the face of defy or resist authority:—It was a mistake for those students to fly in the face of the administration and carry guns.

fly in the ointment a drawback, a defect spoiling the whole:—Although his mother-in-law paid for his trip to Paris, there was a fly in the ointment—she went along.

fly into a rage (temper) become very angry:—Each time we mentioned Carl's name she flew into a rage.

fly off the handle lose one's temper or control, become suddenly very angry:—There was no reason for him to fly off the handle just breause she arrived a little late.

fly, go fly a kite an expression meaning: Leave! Go to the devil! Beat it! (sl.):—He kept bothering me so much with his silly questions that I finally told him to go fly a kite.

fly, on the fly hastily, enroute:—We had so little time to catch the train that we had to eat our lunch on the fly.

fly See also **come** off with flying colors; **get** off to a flying start.

fob off lie down on the job, fail to complete a task:—Although I expressly told Mary to finish those leters, she fobbed off and I had to type them myself.

fold up (1) double over or fold completely:—He folded up the letter and put it in his pocket. (2) fail, go bankrupt:—Several large investment houses folded up during those difficult years.

follow out proceed in accordance with:—It is important that you follow out his instructions carefully.

follow suit copy or imitate the lead of another:—Burke resigned from the club, and Jones immediately followed suit.

follow through carry to completion:—He is good at initiating projects but rarely follows through with anything.

follow up pursue steadily, act on a lead that may bring in business:—Every inquiry which the company receives is turned over to a salesman who immediately follows it up. If no action results, the company also writes a follow-up letter later.

food See **soul** food.

fool around waste time, pass time foolishly and without result:—He spends so much time fooling around that he never accomplishes anything.

fool around with play with, toy with, waste time. Same as **fool around**:—He spends almost his whole lunch-hour fooling around with the girls.

fool away waste, lose foolishly, dissipate:—He fools away so much time on his stamp collection that he never gets anything done.

fool-proof so constructed that even a fool can use it without error:—A new signal system recently developed for railroads is said to be fool-proof.

foot the bill pay for, stand the expense of:—It was the bride's father who footed all the bills.

foot, on foot walking:—Our car is being repaired, so we came on foot.

foot, one foot in the grave close to death:—I doubt whether Bates will ever get well. He looks as though he had one foot in the grave.

foot, put one's best foot forward make the best impression possible:—Instead of putting his best foot forward and mentioning his excellent qualifications for the job, Clark sat there without opening his mouth.

foot, put one's foot down assert oneself, be firm in one's attitude:—Mary is running around too much, and it is high time that her father put his foot down.

foot, put one's foot into it make a social blunder, faux pas:—When you told Pearson, whose father is a politician, that all politicians are dishonest, you certainly put your foot into it.

for all I know to the extent of my knowledge:—For all I know, he may already have left for Europe.

for all that despite what has been said:—For all that, I still feel that he is the most capable man in our organization.

for, be for something to be in favor of, support:—I am for peace at any price.

for See also **good**, for good; **have** it in for; **part**, for my part.

force, in force in effect, active:—That traffic regulation hasn't been in force very long.

forget oneself make a scene or an unpleasant remark, take the wrong attitude:—In the heat of the discussion, John forgot himself and called his boss a liar.

fork out pay, surrender:—Each of us had to fork out five dollars to defray the costs of the trip.

fork over hand over, deliver:—They stuck a gun in his ribs and made him fork over all his money.

form, a matter of form a question of appearance, etiquette, or formality:—We will have to attend the ball just as a matter of form.

fortune, tell someone's fortune predict someone's future:—Let's go to an astrologer and have our fortune told.

fortune See also **read** one's fortune.

foul play treachery, unfair action—especially criminal action:—After examining the body, the police began to suspect foul play.

four-in-hand a necktie:—Which do you prefer: a bow tie or a four-in-hand?

four-letter word one of a few English words, referring to bodily functions, which are seldom used in polite society or mixed company:—Until recently publishers had to be careful about printing four-letter words.

four-poster a bed with four upright posts: —The bedroom had two Colonial-type, four-poster beds.

fours, on all fours (1) walking on both hands and feet:—Most animals except man move on all fours. (2) in agreement with:—Your argument is on all fours with the judge's.

fourth estate the newspaper or journalistic profession:—He is proud of his years of service in the fourth estate.

frame (v.) to victimize, to arrange so that the responsibility for some crime falls on an innocent rather than guilty person:—The prisoner claimed that he had been framed by his enemies.

frame of mind state or condition of mind: —There is no use talking to him while he is in that low frame of mind.

frame-up the result of wrongly attributing a crime or misdeed to a person:—At the trial it was discovered that the accused's supposed theft was all a frame-up by his enemies.

free and easy liberal, wasteful:—The guests were rather free and easy with their host's liquor.

free-for-all a fist-fight in which everyone present participates:—It started as an argument between one player and the referee but ended up as a free-for-all.

free, give a free hand allow one complete freedom of choice, carte blanche:—Mrs. Brown gave the interior decorator a free hand in furnishing her living room.

freeze out force out, render inactive:— The competition became so keen that many of the smaller companies were frozen out.

French, take French leave slip away secretly:—While the family was in Europe, two of the servants packed up all the silver and took French leave.

fresh from recently returned from or experienced in:—He was fresh from two years spent abroad and very condescending in manner regarding everything American.

fresh out of be without, to have run out of a commodity recently:—Sorry, we are fresh out of milk.

freshen a drink get a fresh or new drink for a guest:—Your highball is almost gone. May I freshen your drink?

fringe benefit something given to employees over and above their wages:— Fringe benefits in that company include free hospital insurance and retirement pensions.

front for take one's place, act for, insulate one from the press, etc.:—During the divorce proceedings the husband got his assistant to front for him at the office.

front, put up a front aim to impress, make an impressive appearance:—Although the Smiths put up quite a front, they really are not very well off.

frosting on the cake an extra dividend or bonus:—Besides a high salary there is a frosting on the cake—a free trip to Europe every summer.

frown upon look with disfavor upon:— Everyone in her family frowns upon the match.

fry, small fry small children; also, people or things of little importance:—We spent several hours watching the small fry playing in the park.

full-bodied mature, of maximum quality: —The wine of that particular year has a rich, full-bodied flavor.

full, in full swing at the maximum point of activity:—By midnight the party was in full swing.

full See also **blast**, full blast; **hands**, have one's hands full.

fun city a humorous term for New York City where it is supposed to be lots of fun to live:—Fun City needs a lot more policemen and street cleaners than it has.

fun, in (for) fun in a spirit of amusement:—He didn't mean to frighten her; he just did it in (for) fun.

fun, make fun of ridicule, kid:—When Albert took to using perfume, all the boys in the office began to make fun of him.

funny bone the sensitive elbow nerve:— Ouch! I just hit my funny bone.

fur, make the fur fly cause a commotion: —When the boss finds out that they failed to secure that contract, he will certainly make the fur fly.

G

G-string a scanty garment designed to cover a woman's sexual organ:—The burlesque queen wore nothing but a G-string.

gaff, stand the gaff endure the strain:— Our mayor had to resign because he couldn't stand the gaff.

gain on come closer to in a race:— Although Driver No. 32 was in the lead, Driver 18 was gaining on him.

game, be game be sporting, cooperative, willing:—When I asked him whether he would join us in presenting our grievances, he said that he was game if we were.

gangway! move out of the way!:—Gangway! Here come the piano movers.

gang up on conspire against, unite against:—That small nation is afraid that if she makes one false move the other countries may gang up on her.

garbage (sl.) used loosely for all sorts of trash or useless or disliked material:—I asked my secretary to get rid of all the garbage on my desk.

gas up fill up a car tank with gasoline:— We'd better stop at a station soon and gas up.

gasser a term of approval (also **it's a gas**): —That lecture on Rubens was a gasser.

general, in general generally, on the whole:—In general he is quite a satisfactory student.

get (1) Used in the sense of "become":— Henry got sick after eating the pie. I get hungry every day at this hour. Compare: get tired, get sleepy, get busy, get drunk, get well, get better, get worse, get rich, get poor, get dressed, get shaved, etc. (2) Used in the sense of "arrive":—I got home at about six o'clock. What times does this train get to Washington? He finally got to be president of the company. (3) Used in the sense of "catch" or "understand":—I don't

get what you mean. Did you get what he said? (4) Used emphatically in conjunction with verb "have":—I've got a bad cold. What have you got against him? It has got to be done today.

get a move on leave, show some activity, hurry:—If we want to finish this today, we'd better get a move on.

get a word in edgeways (edgewise) enter with difficulty into a conversation:— They both talked incessantly, and it was impossible for anyone else to get a word in edgeways.

get about (1) travel, move from one place or position to another:—It is hard for Jones to get about. (2) circulate, spread: —How did the story of her marriage get about?

get across cause to understand, communicate, instill:—He was unable to get across to the group what he meant.

get ahead prosper, succeed:—He is the type of young man who will get ahead in any business he goes into.

get along (1) progress, succeed:—How is your son getting along in school? (2) leave, depart:—It's rather late, and I think I'd better be getting along.

get along in years grow old:—Smith is getting along in years and can't work so hard as he used to.

get along with live or work in harmony with:—He doesn't get along with anybody in the office.

get around (1) circulate, travel. Same as get about:—It is difficult for him to get around without a cane. (2) circumvent: —How can we get around that tax regulation?

get around one manage, influence, circumvent:—Whenever she wants something from her father, she knows very well how to get around him.

get at (1) reach:—The baby tried his best to get at the brightly colored candles. (2) intimate, hint:—I don't know what you are trying to get at. If you have something unpleasant to say, tell it to me directly. See **drive** at.

get away (1) escape:—The prisoner had little difficulty in getting away from the police. (2) leave, depart on a trip or vacation:—I hope to get away next Tuesday for at least a week.

get away with escape without punishment or reprimand:—Joan never arrives at the office on time. I'd like to know how she manages to get away with it.

get away with murder See above **get away with**:—Some of the people in our office get away with murder, but if I arrive late just one morning the boss calls me down.

get back (1) return:—He left for Washington on Tuesday and won't get back until Saturday. (2) receive back:—Stop worrying about the money you lent him. You'll get it back.

get back at gain revenge:—If it takes me ten years I'll get back at him for spreading those lies about me. See **even, get even** with.

get behind (1) fall behind in one's normal schedule of work or studies:—During my illness I got behind in my school work, and now it is difficult to catch up. (2) support, assist:—If we all get behind Campbell we can easily elect him to that office.

get by (1) circumvent, pass alongside of, gain admittance:—How can I get by that guard at the door? (2) succeed by a very narrow margin, be barely acceptable:—I didn't do too well on the exam, but I think I got by.

get down (1) bring down, descend:—Will you help me get down those dishes off that shelf? John, get down off that table. (2) swallow, digest:—The medicine was so bitter I couldn't get it down. (3) depress, break the spirit of a person:—Having to work for a person like him will sooner or later get you down.

get going start, go into action, make haste:—If we expect to reach there before they leave, we'd better get going.

get his, hers, etc. receive one's proper reward or punishment:—Johnny will get his when his father learns that he did not attend school today.

get hold of grasp, obtain:—If the cat gets hold of that bird, he will surely kill it. I'd like to get hold of two tickets for a Broadway musical.

get in (1) enter:—He invited us to get in the car and go for a ride with him. (2) join, become a member of:—He has been trying for years to get into that club. (3) arrive:—What time does the train from Washington get in? (4) receive, put in stock:—Macy's has just gotten in a new shipment of furs.

get in Dutch See **Dutch**, be in Dutch.

get in on be included, be allowed to participate:—This is your chance to get in on a good thing and perhaps make a fortune on a small investment.

get in with join up with, begin to associate with:—He got in with the wrong crowd of boys and ended up a petty criminal.

get into one's head become possessed of an idea:—He has gotten it in his head to become a pilot, and nothing we say can change him.

get it (1) be scolded, punished:—He'll get it when his mother finds out that he has broken her new set of dishes. (2) solve a problem, understand:—Now I get it. You really want to leave me, don't you.

get left be stranded or miss or be deprived of something:—When we got to the party the food was all gone, so we got left with nothing to eat.

get next to succeed in knowing well, become familiar with:—He is a very hard man to get next to.

get off (1) leave or alight from a vehicle or public means of transportation:—We got on the subway at 79th Street and got off at 42nd Street. (2) remove:—He can't get the ring off his finger. (3) mail, send:—I want you to get both these letters off right away. (4) deliver, produce:—The speaker got off one or two very amusing jokes.

get off easy escape with a light penalty or punishment:—If all you had to do was pay a two-dollar fine, you got off very easy.

get off on the wrong foot make a blunder or poor start:—He got off on the wrong foot when, after working there only a week, he asked the boss for a day off.

get off to a flying start begin successfully: —The bond drive got off to a flying start when two wealthy citizens subscribed for ten thousands dollars worth each.

get off with escape with:—The prisoner got off with a very light sentence.

get on (1) board or enter a vehicle:—I get on the subway every morning at 79th Street and get off at 42nd Street. (2) progress, succeed:—How is he getting on with that novel he is writing? (3) grow older:—His white hair and his wrinkles are enough to show that he is getting on. (4) live or work harmoniously with:—For two people with such different personalities they get on quite well with each other.

get on in years Same as **get along in years.**

get on one's nerves make one nervous or irritable:—Turn off that radio. It's getting on my nerves.

get on the ball become attentive, efficient, more alert:—He'd better get on the ball if he expects to advance in this type of work.

get on to succeed in understanding, grasp: —Although at first shorthand seemed difficult to me, I soon got on to it.

get on toward approach, draw near:—It was getting on toward eleven o'clock when he finally arrived.

get one's hand in accustom oneself, gain one's usual proficiency:—This is a different type of business from what he is accustomed to, and it may take him a few months to get his hand in.

get one's second wind get renewed strength:—I felt I couldn't move another step, but after lunch I got my second wind and pushed ahead with the rest.

get out (1) leave, depart from a vehicle: —I told the bus driver that I wanted to get out at 72nd Street. (2) publish, produce:—They are getting out two new books on atomic energy this season. (3) escape:—We must not let news about this secret invention get out.

get out of (1) avoid, be excused from:—He got out of serving on the jury by claiming that he was engaged in essential government work. (2) extract from, gain from:—How much did Dayton get out of the deal?

get over (1) recover from:—It took me a long time to get over my cold. (2) visit, call upon:—I'll try to get over to see you sometime next week. (3) move over:— You'd better get over on your own side of the road.

get round Same as **get around.**

get someone's goat annoy, or exasperate someone:—That constant hammering got his goat.

get something down cold learn or memorize a thing perfectly:—I thought that I had gotten all those formulas down cold, but when I took the examination I couldn't remember one of them.

get something off one's chest unburden oneself of, communicate an annoying matter:—It was something I had wanted to tell him for a long time, so I finally got it off my chest.

get something over with terminate, finish in order to be free from:—It's an unpleasant task, so let's get it over with as soon as we can.

get the feel of understand, learn:—It will take at least two weeks before that new employee gets the feel of that computer.

get the gate be fired, told to leave. See also **give** someone the gate:—He was very careless in his work and disloyal in his attitude, so that he really deserved to get the gate.

get the goods on obtain conclusive evidence against:—The police had two good clues to follow and they soon got the goods on the murderer.

get through (1) finish:—We got through work at five o'clock. (2) pass a course or examination:—I got through everything except biology.

get through one's head understand:—He couldn't seem to get it through his head that his wife was really leaving him.

get through to penetrate to, succeed in reaching:—Several telephones lines were down because of the storm, so that we could not get through to Montreal.

get to another person (1) manage to get an interview:—I think I could sell that executive some life insurance if I could ever get to him. (2) obtain one's confidence or trust:—The teacher says if she could only get to Tommy she could help him improve his poor school work.

get together unite, meet as a group:—We all try to get together at least once a year at Christmas time.

get under way leave, get started:—It was almost four o'clock before we got under way.

get up (1) arise from a bed, chair, etc.:—I usually get up at about eight o'clock every morning. (2) organize, plan:—Our social club is getting up a picnic for the first of the month.

get-up costume, odd mode of dress:—What an old-fashioned get-up Mrs. Green was wearing last night.

get up on the wrong side of the bed arise in a bad or unpleasant mood:—He hasn't spoken to any of us all day long; he must have gotten up on the wrong side of the bed this morning.

get with it adjust to, become more efficient or skillful:—Jim's father was displeased with Jim's poor grades in high school and told Jim to get with it.

get See also **axe**, get the axe; **bottom**, get to the bottom of; **brass**, get down to brass tacks; **breaks**, get the breaks; **better**, get the better of; **cheap**, get off cheap; **even**, get even with; **grip**, get a grip on; **hard** to get; **line**, get a line on; **line**, get into line; **hair**, get into someone's hair; **hand**, get the upper hand of; **hand**, get out of hand; **kick**, get a kick out of; **lowdown**, get the lowdown on; **neck**, get it in the neck; **raise**, get a raise; **raspberry**, get the raspberry; **rattled**, get rattled; **rise**, get a rise out of; **rid**, get rid of; **runaround**, get the runaround; **run**, get the run of things; **sack**, get the sack; **side**, get on someone's good side; **stuck**, get stuck; **tell**, tell someone where to get off; **wrong**, get one wrong; **wrong**, get in wrong; **warmed**, get warmed up;

touch, get in touch with; **wind**, get wind of.

ghost of a chance the very slightest chance:—John doesn't have the ghost of a chance of winning that game.

ghost writer a writer whose identity remains unknown and who writes for another who gets all the credit:—They say that book of Senator Smith's on international finance was done by a ghost writer.

ghost See also **give up the ghost.**

G.I. short for "Government Issue," used to designate any American soldier of World War II:—Many G.I.'s after the war failed to take advantage of the educational benefits contained in the G.I. Bill of Rights.

gift of gab ability to talk freely and persuasively:—With his gift of gab, he should make an excellent politician.

gilt-edged of the highest quality:—U.S. government savings bonds are considered a gilt-edged investment.

gin mill a bar where liquor is sold:—New York City's Third Avenue is full of gin mills.

girl Friday an indispensable secretary:—My girl Friday is leaving me, and I'm frantically trying to replace her.

girl See also **go-go girl.**

give a damn (not to give a damn) be concerned (indifferent) about, to consider of the greatest (slightest) importance:—I don't give a damn whether he goes with us or not.

give a good account of oneself perform well, leave a good impression of one's abilities:—Despite the stiff opposition, Henry gave a good account of himself throughout the tennis tournament.

give and take compromise, mutual exchange:—Married life is said to be a matter of give and take.

give away (1) give to another:—The rich man gave away most of his fortune to the poor. (2) reveal something hidden:—Although he pretended to be French, his German accent gave him away. (3) give the bride to the groom in marriage:—According to custom, the bride's father gave her away.

give back return:—He got angry when I asked him to give me back my pencil.

give birth to bear a child:—Mrs. Reese gave birth to her second child this morning.

give forth emit, produce:—The bell, when struck, gave forth a hollow sound.

give in (1) surrender, assent:—Although her father was at first reluctant to let her go abroad alone, he finally gave in. (2) collapse, cave in:—The floor gave in under the weight of the heavy safe.

give it to scold, censure:—When Irma stole money out of her mother's pocketbook, her mother gave it to her.

give notice announce, inform:—The tenant gave notice that he was going to move on the first of the month.

give off produce, release:—The flowers gave off a heavy, sickly odor.

give on (give out on) look out upon, adjoin:—Our bedroom window gives on a lovely park.

give one pause cause one to stop and think, astonish:—His subsequent failure as an artist after such a brilliant beginning gives one pause.

give one to understand assure implicitly, cause one to believe:—He gave me to understand that he might have a job for me within a few weeks.

give out (1) wear out, terminate, be used up:—After two days our food gave out, and we had to return to camp. (2) hand out, distribute:—An usher stood at the door giving out programs. (3) release, publish:—The State Department has refused to give out any further information on the matter.

give place to yield a position to:—At eleven o'clock the entertainment provided for the guests gave place to dancing.

give rise to cause, precipitate:—The President's death gave rise to much speculation as to the fate of many of his personal appointees.

give someone a hand (1) help, assist:—Give me a hand with this table; it's too heavy for me to move alone. (2) applaud:—Mr. Holmes is responsible for this wonderful banquet. Let's give him a big hand.

give someone the gate discharge, dismiss, send away unceremoniously:—Though they went together for two years, she finally met someone she liked better and gave George the gate.

give someone the go-by disregard, snub, ignore completely:—He raised his hat and was about to speak, but she gave him the go-by as though she had never seen him before.

give up (1) renounce, abandon:—I am going to give up smoking. (2) surrender: —When they saw that they were surrounded by the enemy, they gave up.

give (oneself) up surrender to the authorities:—After hiding from the police for several weeks, the criminal finally gave himself up.

give up as a bad job discontinue, cease to do something which appears hopeless or impossible:—Several times I tried to help him to stop drinking, but I finally gave it up as a bad job.

give (someone) up for dead consider dead or abandon hope for:—His pulse was so weak that the doctor gave him up for dead.

give up the ghost die:—After ten weeks in the hospital he finally gave up the ghost.

give way (1) retreat, move back or away: —The crowd slowly gave way before the troop of mounted policemen. (2) collapse, crash to the ground:—Several hundred people were hurt when the railing against which they were leaning suddenly gave way.

give, something's got to give there must be a concession, change, or adjustment somewhere along the line:—She won't sell her house nor will she pay her back taxes. Something's got to give, otherwise she'll lose her home.

give See also **airs**, give oneself airs; **berth**, give a wide berth; **devil**, give the devil his due; **dressing**, give one a dressing down; **going-over**, give someone a going-over; **lift**, give one a lift; **mind**, give one a piece of one's mind; **rap**, not to give a rap for; **rein**, give rein to; **ring**, give someone a ring; **show**, give one a fair show; **right**, give one's right arm; **show**, give the show away; **sign,** give signs of; **slip,** give one the slip; **straight,** give it to one straight; **talking,** give a talking to; **thought,** give thought to; **word,** give one's word; **works,** give one the works.

giveaway (1) something given away free: —We get many giveaways in the mail which are nothing more than samples of toothpaste, razor blades, etc. (2) revelation, exposure:—Roger claimed to speak French fluently, but when he met a real Frenchman, his imperfect use of French was a dead giveaway.

given name one's first name:—His given name is Frank; his surname, Smith.

given to addicted to, in the habit of:— He is given to telling fantastic stories about his travels in Europe.

glance off strike a glancing blow, be deflected:—The bullet glanced off the wall and struck an innocent bystander.

globetrotter a world traveler, one who has traveled widely:—He is famous both as a journalist and as a globetrotter.

glory, be in one's glory be in a happy or triumphant state:—Whenever he is behind the wheel of any high-powered motor car, Frank is in his glory.

gloves, handle with kid gloves treat with great diplomacy and tact:—My aunt is so touchy and irritable that we all have to handle her with kid gloves.

go—sometimes used in the sense of "become" as in the expressions go mad, go blind, go crazy, go insane, go dry, go bad, etc.:—The doctors are afraid that he is going blind. The well went dry after a few months of use. This can of preserves has gone bad.

go ahead (1) proceed, continue:—After the rain stopped, the men went ahead with their work of digging up the street. (2) go first, precede, go in front:—You go ahead and tell them that we will be there shortly.

go along (1) succeed, progress. See also **get along:**—How is your work on that novel going along? (2) agree with, proceed in accordance with, cooperate:— We can count on England to go along with us in any efforts we make toward securing peace.

go around satisfy the need, supply everyone:—Only a few guests came, so there were more than enough sandwiches to go around.

go astray become lost:—The letter has obviously gone astray; otherwise it would have been delivered several days ago.

go away leave, depart:—When are you going away on your vacation?

go back on betray, desert:—After George lost his money, even his wife went back on him.

go by employ, make use of:—The police are looking for a tall man who goes by the name of Smith.

go down (1) become lower in price:—The newspaper states that prices of all farm products are expected to go down soon. (2) deteriorate in quality:—This hotel, which was once one of the best in New England, has gone down steadily in the past few years. (3) sink:—The ship went down with all on board.

go for (1) call for, go to seek:—I'll go for the ice cream while you go to the bakery for the cakes. (2) attack, charge at:— Our dog goes for any stranger who appears at the door. (3) sell for:—How much did the Rembrandt painting go for at the auction? (4) be attracted toward, pursue:—She is simply not the type of girl that Bill goes for.

go from bad to worse deteriorate, become even worse than before:—His marks at school are going from bad to worse.

go halves Same as **go fifty-fifty.** See **fifty.**

go hard with be difficult for, involve severe penalty:—It will go hard with him if his father learns that he has been absent so frequently from school.

go in for study or follow seriously as a hobby or profession, favor, use customarily:—He goes in for tennis, but his brother goes in more for football and baseball.

go into (1) discuss, consider:—Why go into that matter now? (2) be divisible into:—Three goes into twelve four times.

go into effect become effective, active:— The new regulation does not go into effect until the first of March.

go off (1) explode:—The firecracker went off with a bang. (2) turn out, result:—How did the party go off? (3) terminate, leave:—At what time does the feature picture go off?

go on (1) continue:—He went on talking as though nothing had happened. (2) proceed, continue walking or riding, go along:—Let's go on a little further along this same road. (3) approach:—The child says that she is six, going on seven. (4) a scornful expression suggesting disbelief:—Go on! You never had a hundred dollars in your whole life. (5) proceed upon, use as a basis:—The police feel that he is guilty, but they have little evidence to go on.

go one better surpass another:—John told a very funny story but Henry went him one better.

go out (1) stop burning or giving off light:—Put more wood on the fire; otherwise it will go out. (2) pass out of date or style:—Long skirts went out years ago. (3) accompany, go out in the company of:—Henry goes out with any girl with whom he can get a date. (4) leave:—When I telephoned, his mother told me that Edward had just gone out.

go out for strive for, seek to gain or enter into:—He plans to go out for the tennis team next spring.

go out of one's way make a special effort, exceed what is one's normal duty or obligation:—He is the type of restaurant owner who goes out of his way to see that all his guests are well-satisfied.

go over (1) repeat, restudy:—Actors have to go over their lines many times in order to learn them perfectly. (2) be successful:—That new musical went over in a big way. (3) examine, check over:—I want to go over the contract carefully with my lawyer before I sign it.

go round Same as **go around.**

go straight live an honest life, be upright and respectable:—The prisoner said that he would promise to go straight if the judge gave him a suspended sentence.

go the rounds circulate:—There is a rumor going the rounds that Jackson will become the sales manager.

go whole hog do something thoroughly:—We first drove to Washington and then decided to go whole hog and continue on to Florida in order to make it a real vacation trip.

go through (1) suffer, pass through with great difficulty:—I never want to go through again what I have gone through in the past year with my wife's various illnesses. (2) succeed, be completed:—After months of negotiation the merger finally went through. (3) spend, waste, dissipate:—In less than six months he went through his entire inheritance.

go through with complete, carry to completion:—They are planning to open a branch office in Chicago, but I doubt whether they will go through with it.

go to bat for help or assist in an emergency:—It was Mr. Reese who went to bat for Jack when he got into trouble with his teacher.

go to it go ahead, proceed, an expression of encouragement:—I had to get the professor's permission before starting my thesis, but he finally told me to go to it.

go to one's head (1) cause one to become dizzy or light-headed:—I drank only two glasses of beer, but they went right to my head. (2) cause one to become conceited:—George's promotion to the position of vice-president has gone to his head with the result that he scarcely recognizes his old friends now.

go to pieces become very nervous or hysterical, lose control:—At the news of her son's death she went completely to pieces.

go to pot deteriorate completely:—He gave the farm less and less attention each year until it finally went to pot.

go to show serve to demonstrate or make clear:—His success goes to show how much an ambitious young man can accomplish.

go to the trouble suffer the inconvenience, extend oneself unduly:—I asked him not to go to the trouble of fixing up the room for me.

go to the wall See also **drive to the wall.**

go up rise:—Prices are going up every day.

go under fail, become bankrupt:—During the depression many a solid business went under.

go up in smoke burn, be destroyed:—The war caused all his plans for a trip abroad to go up in smoke.

go up in the air become angry, lose one's temper:—He is so irritable these days that he goes up in the air for no reason at all.

go upon proceed upon, use as a basis. See also **go on**:—The police feel sure that he is the guilty party, but they have no evidence to go upon.

go with (1) to match:—I want to buy a new tie to go with this brown suit. (2) court, go out in the company of:—He went with Helen Smith for about two years, but now they say he is going with someone else.

go without lack, be without:—Cut off by the storm, they were forced to go without food for several days.

go without saying be unnecessary to mention, implicitly understood:—It goes without saying that an experienced person will do that work better than someone without experience.

go wrong (1) fail, become out of order:—Something went wrong with our car and we got stalled on the bridge. (2) Sink into an immoral or criminal existence:—In a large city many girls go wrong every year.

go, from the word go from start to finish, completely:—He may look like an American, but he is French from the word go.

go, have a go at try, attempt:—I don't think I can finish in one day, but I am willing to have a go at it.

go, on the go busy, active:—She is one of those energetic persons who are on the go every minute.

go-between an intermediary:—They expect Mr. Hartford to act as a go-between in the dispute between the union and the owners.

go See also **after**, go after; **against**, go against the grain; **bail**, go bail; **bat**, go to bat for; **business**, go about one's business; **dogs**, go to the dogs; **go-by**, give

someone the go-by; **hammer**, go under the hammer; **huff**, go off in a huff; **fly**, go fly a kit; **let go**, let oneself go; **mill**, go through the mill; **make** a go of it; **name**, go by the name of; **no go**; **outgo**; **spin**, go for a spin; **business**, go about one's business; **rocks**, go on the rocks; **stag**, go stag; **story**, as the story goes; **touch** and go; **under**, go under; **wagon**, go on the wagon.

go-by, give one the go-by shun one, avoid a person:—When he tried to speak to Elsa, she gave him the go-by.

go-go girl a solo dancer in a night club:—John is taking out a go-go girl.

going-over, give someone a (good) going-over examine thoroughly, sometimes maltreat physically:—The police gave the suspect a thorough going-over but were unable to get a confession out of him.

going places succeeding impressively:—That new movie star is going places and will soon be in the front ranks in Hollywood.

going strong showing no signs of abatement or lessening ability:—Although he is pretty old to be a major-league pitcher, he is still going strong.

going, have something going for one have success:—Jones has something going for himself with that popular folk-song record he cut.

going See also **about**, going about; **hard** going.

goings-on events, happenings:—The neighbors report some strange goings-on in the building every night at midnight.

goner someone for whom there is little hope:—If he has another heart attack like this one, he is a goner.

good and . . . very, extremely:—I'd like a glass of water and, if possible, make it good and cold.

good copy newsworthy:—The President's wife is always good copy.

good Joe a nice fellow:—He is a good Joe.

good time an enjoyable occasion:—We all had a good time at Jane's party.

good, for good permanently, forever:—
After the war he decided to leave the
service for good.

good, never have it so good be better off
at present (economically) than ever before:—At the political rally, we were
told that we had never had it so good
until now, under a Democratic Administration.

good, to the good profit gained (sometimes expressed as all to the good):—
Counting our money after the dance, we
found that we were fifty dollars to the
good.

good See also **hold** good; **make** good;
mind, have a good mind to; **nothing,**
good for nothing; **pretty** good; **terms,** on
good terms; **turn,** do a good turn; **word,**
put in a good word for.

goodness, for goodness' sake an exclamation suggesting impatience:—For goodness sake! I've already waited a half
hour for you.

goods, have the goods on have clear evidence against:—If they have the goods
on him, why don't they arrest him?

goods See also **get** the goods on; **sell** one
a bill of goods

goof (v.) make a mistake or an error:—
Sorry that your bank balance is $300
less than I told you. The bank certainly
goofed.

goof off (sl.) lie down on the job, pretend
to work, be absent from work without a
good reason:—When the boss leaves
early, Price goofs off for the rest of the
day.

goose egg a zero, nothing:—Bill's mark
on his mathematics exam was a great
big goose egg.

goose See also **cook** one's goose.

got to go have to go to the toilet:—Where
is your bathroom? Johnny's got to go.

grabs, up for grabs available to the highest
bidder or to the person who gets there
first:—The last tenant left a lot of furniture in the apartment which is now up
for grabs.

grace, say grace ask God's blessing before a meal:—Before eating, we bowed
our heads while our host said grace.

grace See also **day** of grace; **saving** grace.

grade, make the grade succeed in a particular objective:—After many years of
study Oliver finally made the grade and
got his engineering degree.

grain, go against the grain displease,
offend, irritate:—To say anything uncomplimentary about the Republican
Party goes against Smith's grain.

grammar school elementary school covering grades one through eight:—Although he had never even completed
grammar school, he became a very successful man.

grandstand play an action designed to
attract much attention, a form of ex-
hibitionism:—According to his opponents, the senator's advocacy of guaran-
teed annual income was just a grandstand play designed to gain more votes.

granny glasses spectacles with square lens
of the type worn by old ladies years ago:
—Ella wore a pair of colored granny
glasses to the beach.

grapevine a roundabout, unofficial source:
—It has been learned via the grapevine
that a cabinet shakeup is imminent.

grass widow a divorced woman:—Helen
is a grass widow.

grass, let the grass grow under one's feet
delay, loiter, procrastinate:—In that
type of business, which is very competitive, you simply cannot let the grass
grow under your feet.

grass See also **snake** in the grass.

grave, turn over in one's grave said of the
reaction of a dead person if he were
alive:—If her deceased husband knew
how she was spending his money, he
would turn over in his grave.

grave See also **foot,** one foot in the grave.

gravy train something soft and easy such
as money received for little or no work,
graft, etc.:—When Alex married a rich
wife, he hit the gravy train.

grease paint facial makeup used by artists
on the stage:—It took him at least a
half hour to remove the grease paint
after each performance.

grease See also **elbow** grease; **palm,** grease
the palm.

Great White Way Broadway, near Times Square, in New York City:—We walked along the Great White Way and admired the sights.

great, be great on be in the habit of, have a strong tendency towards:—He is great on telling jokes which, for me, have little point.

Greek, be Greek to be incomprehensible to one:—His whole lecture was Greek to me.

green, give someone the green light give someone the signal to go ahead:—As soon as the President gives them the green light, the Party Leaders will begin their campaign for a greater congressional appropriation.

green, have a green thumb have a marked ability to cause plants and other green things to grow:—Helen seems to have a green thumb, with the result that all her house plants grow beautifully.

greenhorn a green and inexperienced person—originally an immigrant:—The manager was warned not to hire any more greenhorns as clerks.

grill (v.) to question closely and intensively:—The police grilled the suspect for eight hours.

grip, get a grip on grasp, control, take a firm hold of:—If he wants to hold that job, he'd better get a grip on himself and settle down to work.

grip, lose one's grip find one's habitual ability diminishing; show signs of weakening:—He was formerly one of our best salesmen, but recently he has begun to lose his grip.

gripe complain (sl.):—Stop griping about the food; it's the best we can afford.

groomed, well-groomed well cared for, particularly with respect to the hair, face, hands, etc.:—They chose Bailey for the job because he always looks so well-groomed.

ground, cover a lot of ground deal with a wide area by traveling over it or by writing or discussion:—We had a business-management conference all day yesterday and covered a lot of ground.

ground, gain (or **lose**) **ground** make (or lose) headway:—Though his condition was very critical, the patient now seems to be gaining ground.

ground, get in on the ground floor become one of the first to enter or participate:—Evans, who got in on the ground floor, made a fortune in the promotion of that stock.

ground See also **break** ground; **stamping** ground; **stand** one's ground.

grow on one increase in one's favor, gradually impress with one's charm or manner:—At first I didn't care much for Della, but she is the kind of girl who grows on one.

grow out of (1) outgrow, become too mature for:—As a child he had a habit of blinking his eyes, but gradually he grew out of it. (2) arise or result from:—His illness grew out of his tendency to overwork and neglect his health.

grow up reach maturity:—He says he wants to be a lawyer when he grows up.

guard, on (**off**) **guard** alert, watchful:—The citizens were warned to be on guard against a sudden night attack.

guess, have another guess coming be mistaken:—If you think I'll apologize to Tom for hitting him after he insulted me, you have another guess coming.

gum up the works obstruct, limit progress by one's clumsiness or stupidity:—It was John who gummed up the works by failing to arrive in time with the money.

gun-shy afraid of something unpleasant happening again:—Since Blake's elder daughter had run away with a worthless loafer, Blake was rather gun-shy when his younger daughter told him she was engaged.

guts courage, fortitude:—It takes a lot of guts to speak up that way to one's superior.

gyp (v.) deceive, cheat:—If you paid more than two dollars for that pen, you were gypped.

H

habit, be in the habit of have the habit of, be accustomed to:—He is in the habit of drinking coffee with all his meals.

habit, get into the habit of become accustomed to:—While living in South America, he got into the habit of drinking strong black coffee.

hail-fellow well met a particularly friendly person—one who is immediately on good terms with everyone he meets:—Frank is the hail-fellow well met type who calls everyone in town by his first name.

hail from come from as a place of origin:—What town in Texas does he hail from?

hair-do style or manner of combing the hair, coiffure:—How do you like Helen's new hair-do?

hairpiece a wig:—That bald man wears a hairpiece.

hair, get in someone's hair annoy, irritate:—Grace, with her baby talk and affected gestures, is one person who simply gets in my hair.

hair, let down one's hair become confidential:—After a few drinks we both let down our hair, and it was then I got the real story on why she was leaving her husband.

hair, to a hair exactly, perfectly:—My friend's dress and mine matched to a hair.

hair, without turning a hair calm, unintimidated, skillful:—When the thug demanded money from the bank teller, she pressed the alarm button without turning a hair.

hairs, split hairs argue over minor points:—Instead of deciding the important issues before us, the committee spent the whole two hours splitting hairs over matters of procedure.

half-baked immature, mentally deficient, foolish, impractical:—He has a lot of half-baked notions about how to run the department.

half-hearted lacking interest or enthusiasm:—He made several half-hearted attempts to learn golf, but I could see that he had little interest in the game.

half the battle half the work, half the struggle:—In teaching, when you have aroused the student's interest, you have already gained half the battle.

half See also **better** half; **shot**, half shot.

halt, come to a halt stop, terminate:—For the second time this week the peace negotiations have come to a halt.

halt See also **call a halt**.

hammer and tongs with much noise and energy:—In his usual energetic manner Jones went after every new prospect hammer and tongs.

hammer, go under the hammer be auctioned off, sold at auction:—James sat there watching all his precious works of art, which he had collected at such expense, go under the hammer.

hand down (1) bequeath:—Their home contains many rare antiques which have been handed down to them from one generation to another. (2) give a decision from the bench:—The Supreme Court handed down a decision enforcing desegregation.

hand in deliver something due, submit:—Each student has to hand in a composition once a week.

hand in glove in close alliance with:—It is rumored that several police officers have been working hand in glove with the gamblers. (Also expressed as **hand in hand**.)

hand it to one give praise or proper credit:—I have to hand it to you; you certainly predicted the elections results very accurately.

hand over surrender, give over:—The robber forced the bank messenger to hand over all the money he was carrying.

hand over fist rapidly, in great quantity:—They say that he is making money hand over fist in that business.

hand to hand in close, personal contact:—Our troops advanced and engaged the enemy in hand-to-hand fighting.

hand to mouth day to day, lacking provision or preparation for the future:—The land has been so overworked that most of the peasants are forced to live a bare, hand-to-mouth existence.

hand, a big hand enthusiastic applause:—When Smith appeared on the stage, he received a big hand from the audience.

hand, an old hand an experienced person: —He claimed it was his first offense, but the police soon learned that he was an old hand at safecracking.

hand, ask for one's hand ask to marry someone, propose:—Somehow he could never summon up the courage to ask for her hand.

hand, at first hand from the original source:—He got the information at first hand from the senator himself.

hand, at hand close by, near, soon to occur:—Christmas was at hand, and I still had no money to buy Marge a present.

hand, be a poor (good) hand at be inept in, have little ability in:—Being a dreamer, Cyril proved to be a poor hand at running a store.

hand, by hand done or delivered by a person rather than by a machine:—The rug was obviously made by hand.

hand, get out of hand become excessive, out of control:—Government spending is getting a little out of hand.

hand, get the upper hand gain control over, dominate:—Fighting went on for hours, but the authorities finally got the upper hand and put down the riot.

hand, give one a big hand applaud enthusiastically and at length:—After the famous torch singer finished her number, the audience gave her a big hand.

hand, give one's hand accept a proposal of matrimony, marry:—She finally agreed to give him her hand in marriage.

hand, have a hand in participate, take part in:—Since it is the kind of job in which he has always specialized, the police feel sure that Sutton had a hand in the Boston bank robbery.

hands, have one's hands full be very busy or occupied:—With a sick husband at home and three children to care for, Mrs. Jones has her hands full.

hands, in good hands aided by an expert or other reliable persons:—If you go to Dr. Brown, you are in good hands.

hand, in hand under control:—The police now have the situation well in hand, and no further outbreaks are expected.

hand, keep one's hand in retain one's ability or proficiency, not to lose one's ability or proficiency through lack of practice:—He no longer plays tennis regularly, but he enters a tournament now and then just to keep his hand in.

hands, lay hands on (1) seize, capture:—I would like to lay hands on the person who threw that stone through our front window. (2) obtain, secure:—Where can I lay my hands on a tall ladder?

hand, on hand (1) present, in attendance: —All his old friends will be on hand to see Jack receive the Medal of Honor. (2) in stock, available:—I asked the grocer what kinds of canned meat he had on hand.

hands, on one's hands responsible for, faced with the necessity of getting rid of, saddled with:—At the end of the year the dealer found himself with twenty-five new cars on his hands which he naturally had to sell at a big discount.

hand, on the other hand conversely, to mention the opposite:—He is clever, but, on the other hand, he makes many mistakes.

hand, try one's hand experiment with, test one's ability:—Have you ever tried your hand at writing a novel?

hand, with a heavy hand inexpertly, imperfectly:—She salts her cooking with a rather heavy hand.

hand, with a high hand imperiously:— That absolute monarch reigned with a high hand, and none of his subjects ever dared to criticize him.

hand See also **bird** in hand; **change** hands; **first**-hand; **four**-in-hand; **free,** give one a free hand; **give** someone a hand; **high** handed; **hold** a good hand; **hold** up one's hands; **keep** one's hand in; **lend** a hand; **near** at hand; **offhand; play** into the hands of; **red**-handed; **second** hand; **shake** hands; **shorthanded; show** of hands; **show** one's hand; **take** a hand in; **take** something off one's hands; **throw** up one's hands; **time** hanging on one's hands; **turn** one's hand to; **wash** one's hands of; **whiphand; win** hands down.

handwriting on the wall a warning of future disaster:—Six months before the stock-market crash he saw the handwriting on the wall and shrewdly sold all his securities.

hang around loiter, frequent:—He is crazy about horses and spends all his free time hanging around the racing stables.

hang back show signs of timidity, be disinclined to:—We tried to get her to go in swimming with us, but she hung back.

hang on (1) grasp, take a firm hold upon:—The child hung on to her mother's hand as they crossed the street. (2) persevere, hold fast:—All throughout his illness, despite his intense suffering, he hung on desperately to life.

hang one's head feel shame or embarrassment:—As the prosecutor enumerated the prisoner's various offenses, the latter hung his head.

hang out loiter, frequent. Similar to **hang around**:—If he continues to hang out with that group of tough boys, he will eventually end up in jail.

hang something on another transfer the blame or guilt to:—Since Tom was ashamed of banging up the family car, he tried to hang it on his younger brother.

hang together unite, join, associate closely:—Benjamin Franklin declared that if the colonists failed to hang together, they might eventually hang separately.

hangover the unpleasant physical effects that follow in the morning after a night of excessive drinking:—Henry, who was grouchy and ill-humored at breakfast, was obviously suffering from a hangover.

hang up (1) put on a hook or hanger:—There are hangers in the closet on which to hang up your clothes. (2) replace a telephone receiver on a hook or cradle:—After she finished her conversation, she hung up.

hang-up (n) frustration, obstacle:—Despite some hang-ups, that actress has gotten work on Broadway every year since she started acting.

hang, get the hang of understand how to proceed or operate:—It took me weeks to get the hang of that computer.

happening an unconventional party where the guests all take part in some far-out creative or artistic activity:—We went to a happening at a friend's house and found ourselves cutting each others' hair.

hard frequently used in everyday speech with the meaning of "difficult":—Physics was always a hard subject for me in high school.

hard and fast inflexible, rigid:—Our factory has a hard-and-fast rule against smoking.

hard-boiled tough, merciless, unrefined:—Her pretty face and engaging smile can be counted upon to soften up the heart of the most hard-boiled traffic cop.

hard-core adamant, immoveable, unchangeable:—Bliss is a hard-core Communist.

hard going difficult of progress:—He found the study of law to be hard going.

hard headed stubborn, also shrewd, practical:—Sloan is a hard-headed, intelligent business man who made money even during the worst years of the depression.

hard-hearted without pity, merciless:—Her hard-hearted father disowned her when she married outside the Church.

hard luck bad luck, ill fortune:—Henry has had a lot of hard luck lately; he lost his job, then got sick.

hard of hearing partially deaf:—Some theaters have special hearing devices in the first few rows for those who are hard of hearing.

hard put under great difficulty:—When his secretary resigned, Smith was hard put to find another as efficient.

hard sell (soft sell) a forceful insistent selling message:—Many listeners turned off the radio when that hard-sell car ad came on.

hard to get, play hard to get act or pretend to be uninterested:—Cecile played hard to get until she learned that Roy was wealthy.

hard up (1) in need of money, in very reduced circumstances:—Ever since Smith lost his job, the Smiths have been hard up. (2) desperate, unresourceful:— He must be very hard up for a date if he has to invite someone like her to go out with him.

hard, be hard on be severe, strict, or critical with another:—He is very hard on his children and permits them few privileges.

hard See also **go** hard with; **ride** something hard; **pressed**, hard pressed.

hare-brained foolish, thoughtless:—Most of the hare-brained things Claude does can be attributed simply to his youth and lack of experience.

harness, in harness serving in one's accustomed work or duties:—He has always sworn that when he died he would die in harness.

harp on dwell upon continuously to the extent of causing boredom:—He is always harping on the fact that people are so much less religious today than they were previously.

has-been a person or former celebrity whose popularity has waned:—He continues to write novels but is generally considered to be a has-been.

hat, high hat conceited, given to putting on airs:—Jones has been very high hat ever since he became a member of the country club.

hat, pass the hat make a collection, solicit money:—At the club's annual dinner they always pass the hat to raise money for the various scholarships which the club sponsors.

hat, take one's hat off to express deference or admiration for the ability of another:—I certainly must take my hat off to you for the clever way in which you got that document back from Bill.

hat, toss one's hat into the ring enter a political contest:—Three candidates have already tossed their hats in the ring for the mayoralty.

hat See also **keep** something under one's hat.

haul, make a good haul be successful in obtaining something:—The robbers made a good haul when they broke into that bank last night.

have (sometimes used colloquially with the meaning of "permit"):—I won't have their dog running all over my flower beds.

have a time experience some difficulty:— What a time we had trying to find your apartment in this big building.

have got to Same as **have to:**—I've got to go to the hospital tonight to see an old friend.

have it in for hold a grudge against, wait for a chance to harm or injure another: —Ever since John insulted her, the teacher has had it in for him.

have it out with someone discuss some grievance with the culprit:—She has been saying unpleasant things about me for some time, so today I am going to have it out with her.

have nothing on another have no superiority over another:—Though they have two cars, they have nothing on us because we also have two cars and in addition a home in the country.

have nothing to do with have no connection with:—We have nothing to do with the work of the shipping department.

have on (1) be wearing—said of clothes: —That's a pretty dress you have on. (2) have an appointment or engagement:— What do you have on for tomorrow night?

have one up (over, out, down) invite someone up (over, out, down) depending upon the direction and location of one's home with respect to the residence of the one invited:—Let's have Mary and Bill up to dinner some night. (The suggestion here is that those who are to be invited live either downtown or in an apartment at a lower geographical level.)

have something on someone have some damning evidence or information against another:—They say that he is afraid to fire her because she has something on him.

have something to do with concerned with:—The rising birthrate has something to do with religion.

have to must, be obliged to:—I have to go to the hospital tonight to see an old friend.

have, I've been had an expression meaning: I have been taken advantage of, I've been cheated or fooled:—The butcher charged you ten dollars for that roast? You've been had!

have See also **affair,** have an affair; **best,** have the best of; **better,** had better; **cake,** have one's cake and eat it too; **day,** have the day off; **edge,** have an edge on; **fill,** have one's fill; **fling,** have one's fling; **heart,** have a heart; **laugh,** have a laugh on; **mind,** have a mind to; **mind,** have in mind; **run,** have a long or short run; **run,** have the run of; **say,** have one's say; **say,** have a say in; **sleeve,** have something up one's sleeve; **shot,** have a shot at; **string,** have on the string; **way,** have a way with; **way,** have one's own way; **wits,** have one's wits about one; **word,** have a word with.

hay, make hay while the sun shines take advantage of a timely opportunity:—Business conditions are now very good, so we should make hay while the sun shines and try to build up our sales to the highest point possible.

hay, That ain't hay an expression meaning: That's important:—That oil stock of mine had a split and then rose, and that ain't hay.

hay See also **hit** the hay.

haywire, go haywire go crazy, act upset, do the wrong thing, get out of control:—Whenever Rob starts drinking, he goes haywire and breaks lots of windows.

head and shoulders above considerably higher than, superior to:—As a salesman he is head and shoulders above any other man in our organization.

head for go in the direction of:—We set sail at dawn and headed straight for Southampton.

head off intercept, get ahead of in order to block or turn back:—The party campaign managers went into action at once in order to head off the movement toward nomination of an entirely new candidate.

head on facing frontward, frontally:—The two cars crashed head on.

head over heels completely, enthusiastically:—He fell head over heels in love with Helen.

head start a time advantage gained through leaving or beginning earlier:—They had a good head start on us, but after a few hours we caught up with them.

head, be out of one's head insane, irrational:—He must be out of his head to make such a foolish statement.

head, bring to a head precipitate a crisis:—It was Smith's direct challenge of the report that brought the whole matter to a head.

head, (eat, cry, scream, run) one's head off to an excessive degree:—When one little mouse ran across the floor, I thought Esther was going to scream her head off.

head, have a head on one's shoulders be intelligent, capable, practical:—Young Bacon has a good head on his shoulders and can be trusted to do any job well.

head, keep one's head maintain one's self-control, presence of mind:—Henry, who was driving, kept his head when our car skidded; otherwise we might have been involved in a serious accident.

head, keep one's head above water manage to stay out of debt, remain solvent:—Jones' business fell off seriously, and he had difficulty keeping his head above water.

head, neither head nor tail nothing:—I could make neither head nor tail out of that modern poem.

head, over one's head beyond one's ability to grasp or understand:—Calculus is over the heads of most students.

head, turn one's head cause one to become conceited or to feel superior:—The fact that she was selected as the prettiest girl in the class turned her head completely.

heads or tails the two sides of a coin—especially when a coin is tossed into the air to decide which of two alternatives shall be followed:—Bill tossed the coin into the air and said: "Heads I win and tails you win."

heads, put heads together discuss together, consult:—We finally put our heads together and arrived at a very satisfactory plan.

heads, two heads are better than one a second person's opinion or assistance is often helpful:—The changes which Henry suggested in my plan proved very valuable, and it goes to show that two heads are often better than one.

head See also **come** to a head; **double-header; get** through one's head; **go** to one's head; **hard-headed; hit** the nail on the head; **lose** one's head; **make** neither head nor tail of; **put** out of one's head; **rear** its head; **take** into one's head.

headway, make headway to progress, advance:—He says that he has made little headway in writing his thesis because he has had so many interruptions.

hear from receive a message from:—Have you heard from your son in the service recently?

heartbreaker one with whom others fall in love readily, a person with many admirers of the opposite sex:—Jack, who has three girls at school in love with him, is fast developing a reputation as a heartbreaker.

heart-to-heart confidential, intimate, frank:—I think if we could once have a good heart-to-heart talk we could clear matters up and arrive at an understanding.

heart, at heart basically, fundamentally:—At heart he is a simple, generous fellow.

heart, broken-hearted inconsolable, grieved:—She was broken-hearted at the loss of such a good friend.

heart, do one's heart good cause one to be happy, contented:—It would have done your heart good to see how pleased he was to receive your gift.

heart, hard-hearted merciless, stern, unsympathetic:—He is so hard-hearted that even his own children ask and expect little from him.

heart, have a heart be understanding and sympathetic, considerate:—I asked him to have a heart and give the old lady a little more time in which to pay her bill.

heart, have one's heart in the right place be basically good and generous despite appearances to the contrary:—He may appear like a very miserly landlord, but you'll soon discover that his heart is in the right place.

heart, have the heart to have the courage, have the necessary degree of hard-heartedness:—I wanted to tell him that after this week we might not have any more work for him, but in view of all the troubles he has had recently, I didn't have the heart to.

heart, learn (know) by heart memorize:—Everyone in the class has to learn Lincoln's Gettysburg Address by heart.

heart, lose heart become discouraged, dispirited:—Though he spent weeks and weeks at the task Holmes never once lost heart.

heart, set one's heart on desire greatly, plan for with much interest:—William has set his heart on going to college.

heart, take heart become encouraged, gain inspiration:—The general took heart from his first minor victory and succeeded in routing the enemy completely.

heart, take to heart take seriously, be deeply affected and depressed by:—Although our joking was all in fun, Joseph took it to heart.

heart, to one's heart's content to one's complete satisfaction, to the extent that one wishes:—It's a perfect vacation spot, and there is a small stream nearby where you can fish to your heart's content.

heart, wear one's heart on one's sleeve show one's feelings for all to see:—Since Alice was not the type who wears her heart upon her sleeve, William was not quite sure whether she loved him or not.

heart See also **after** one's own heart; **break** one's heart; **chicken-hearted**; **soft-hearted.**

hearty, hale and hearty strong and healthy:—John's father is sixty-five years old but still hale and hearty.

heat up become hot, overheat:—Climbing the steep mountain caused our car to heat up.

heave-ho, give something the heave-ho throw out, discard:—We gave the heave-ho to all the furniture found in the apartment we had just rented.

heel a disloyal or traitorous fellow (sl.): —When his father died, William, like a heel, refused to support his mother.

heels, be at one's heels follow closely:— My dog is always at my heels.

heels, down at the heels be shabbily dressed and showing signs of poverty:— Ever since he lost his job, he has been looking rather down at the heels.

heels, on the heels of following closely upon, immediately thereafter:—The numerous bank failures coming on the heels of the stock-market crash were more than the nation's economy could stand.

heels, take to one's heels run away, escape:—When the robber heard the dog bark, he took to his heels.

heels See also **cool** one's heels; **head** over heels; **heeled**, well-heeled; **turn** on one's heel.

heeled, well-heeled well supplied with money (sl.):—He was well-heeled at the time and was living at one of the more expensive hotels.

hell, a hell of a . . . a term used to give strong emphasis, usually indicating disfavor:—Those boys are making a hell of a lot of noise.

help, so help me (sometimes expressed as **so help me God**) an expression of asseveration, a pledge, a solemn declaration: —It was, so help me, one of the most embarrassing situations I had ever been in.

hem in enclose, surround, limit:—Our troops were hemmed in on three sides by enemy detachments.

herd See **ride** herd on.

here goes an expression meaning: Watch! Here I go! I am doing what I am expected to do!:—Do you really want to see me dive from this high spot? Well, here goes.

here, neither here nor there irrelevant, having no connection with the subject under consideration:—I know you like him personally, but that is neither here nor there. We are discussing the question of his honesty.

hide and seek a popular children's game in which several children hide and one goes to find them:—The children gave us little trouble because they spent the whole evening together playing hide and seek.

hide out (1) go into hiding as in the case of a criminal hiding from the police:— He tried to hide out, but the police tracked him down. (2) the place where one hides:—Apparently the criminal had used several hideouts, but the police trailed him from one to the other.

high and dry deserted, abandoned:—She excused herself saying that she would be back in a moment, but she left him there high and dry for the rest of the evening.

high and low everywhere:—The detectives looked high and low for the missing jewels.

high-handed arbitrary, arrogant, overbearing:—The seizure of the smaller nation's territory was a high-handed act which should be punished.

high pressure forceful, persuasive, dominating:—Only high-pressure salesmanship can sell luxury goods in this community.

high sign a signal:—We waited for Henry to give us the high sign, and then we slipped silently out the back door.

high-strung tense, sensitive:—The leading lady was a great artist but extremely nervous and high-strung.

high time said of an unaccomplished action that is desirable now and may even have been desirable long before now:— It is high time he stopped running around and found himself a good wife.

high, on one's high horse arrogant, superior. Also sometimes expressed as **get on** or **get down off one's high horse** become humble or less arrogant:—When she discovered that her dinner companion was also a man of great wealth, she immediately got down off her high horse.

higher education education on the college or university level:—Each year many high-school graduates go on to study in schools of higher education.

higher-ups those in authority:—I always find it easier to do business with the higher-ups than with those who have little authority.

hip, be hip to be in the know, be informed, experienced, sophisticated (sl.):—Oscar is hip to progressive jazz.

hit-and-run driver one who leaves the scene of an accident without stopping to identify himself or assist the injured:—She was struck by a hit-and-run driver who drove off at once and left no trace of his identity.

hit below the belt strike or treat unfairly, be unsportsmanlike:—When he began to refer to his opponent's unsavory family background, he was really hitting below the belt.

hit home go directly to the mark, strike a vulnerable spot:—His remarks hit home when he referred to those who did not take sufficient interest in our schools.

hit it off get along well with each other, agree:—Fortunately Jones and his new son-in-law hit it off from the very beginning.

hit-or-miss aimless, without definite direction or plan:—He is a hit-or-miss type of workman who is not sufficiently expert for this particular job.

hit the ceiling become very angry:—When Lester reported the accident he had in the family car, his father hit the ceiling.

hit the hay go to bed (sl.):—It's been a long hard day, and right after supper I am going to hit the hay.

hit the nail on the head reach the mark through careful aim, be very accurate:—When you said that what he chiefly lacks is self-discipline, you hit the nail right on the head.

hit the spot satisfy, please by suiting the need perfectly:—I was dying of thirst, and that Coca-Cola just hit the spot.

hit town arrive in town:—There will be plenty of activity here tonight because the American Legion delegates have just hit town.

hit upon discover, come upon by accident, invent:—After many experiments Edison finally hit upon a suitable filament for the electric light bulb.

hit, make a hit become very popular:—The new Fords are making a great hit with the public.

hit See also **jackpot,** hit the jackpot; **sack,** hit the sack; **smash hit; stride,** hit one's stride.

hitched, get hitched (sl.) get married:—Joan and Rob got hitched last June.

hold a good hand have good cards:—Doris usually wins at cards because she always seems to hold a good hand.

hold back (1) restrain oneself:—I was so angry that it was with great difficulty that I held back from telling him exactly what I thought. (2) limit, control, resist:—The narrow sea wall was unable to hold back the surging flood waters. (3) conceal, be reluctant to reveal:—I could tell from his nervousness that he was holding something back.

hold forth preach, talk, discourse at length:—The main speaker held forth on the same theme for at least two hours.

hold good remain valid, effective:—For how long will your offer hold good?

hold off (1) resist, push back, restrain:— The best that we could do was to hold off the enemy's attack for a few hours. (2) delay:—I only hope that the rain holds off for a few hours more.

hold on (1) wait:—He asked me to hold on while he left the telephone to find a pencil. (2) grasp, take a firm hold:— Hold on to my hand tightly while we cross this street. (3) resist, survive, stay safe:—If he can just hold on a little longer, we can get help to him. (4) Stop: —Hold on! You can't talk to me like that!

hold one to something insist on the fulfillment of a contract, promise, etc.:—At the time they reorganized the business, they promised him a partnership, and I am sure he will hold them to it.

hold one up to another mention someone as a model to be followed:—Father is always holding up my older brother to me.

hold one's horses be patient, not to act impulsively:—The bell had rung and we were all eager to leave, but the professor asked us to hold our horses until he had finished.

hold one's own be a match for, be equal to, not to surrender or retreat:—When it comes to a discussion on music or the arts, Henry can hold his own in any group.

hold one's tongue restrain oneself from speaking, remain silent:—Since Marie knew all the facts of the case, it was difficult for her to hold her tongue while the police officer questioned the other servants.

hold out (1) to tender, make:—The oil company is holding out a very attractive offer to him. (2) delay, resist, refuse to agree:—Most of the members of the ball team have signed their contracts for next year, but their star pitcher is still holding out. (3) survive, last:—The rescuers must hurry, because the trapped miner cannot hold out much longer.

hold out on keep information or facts from another:—Why he held out on me I do not know, but for several months he had known that the house was going to be sold.

hold over (1) postpone:—The regular Wednesday meeting will be held over until next week. (2) retain beyond the regular or normal period of time:—The picture now being shown at Radio City is being held over another week.

hold still remain motionless:—It is hard for a child to hold still while being photographed.

hold the bag be victimized, made liable for:—We all agreed to share in the rent of the cottage, but when it came time to pay, the others left me holding the bag.

hold true be true or be valid:—What I told you about Henry's lack of tact also holds true for his brother.

hold up (1) rob, extort money from:— Thieves held him up in the park and took his watch and wallet. (2) overcharge:—That dealer certainly held you up for that new car. Tom got the same model for $200 less. (3) delay:—The steel strike may hold up production of all new cars for several months. (4) survive, endure, last:—The last paint which we put on our house seems to be holding up particularly well.

hold up one's hands a gesture of dismay or surprise:—When her husband came into the house all covered with blood, Mrs. Bloom held up her hands in horror.

hold water serve, be valid:—None of his arguments seemed to me to hold water.

hold with accept, approve:—I don't hold with these new women's styles.

hold See also **brief,** hold a brief for; **candle,** hold a candle to; **lay** hold of; **peace,** hold one's peace; **take** hold of; **tight,** hold tight.

hole, in the hole owing, said of a debt:— Lenny has no funds and owes for his TV set. So far, he is fifty dollars in the hole.

hole up hide, withdraw:—Since the reporters were looking for him, the notorious movie star holed up in an Adirondack camp.

home, at home with familiar with, comfortable with:—That scholar is at home with other intellectuals.

home, make one feel at home be hospitable, make one feel comfortable and at ease:—She is a popular hostess because she has the happy faculty of always making her guests feel at home.

home, nothing to write home about too insignificant to tell about:—Her playing was nothing to write home about.

home See also **bring** home to; **bring** home the bacon; **cows,** until the cows come home; **drive** something home; **hit** home; **make** oneself at home; **see** one home; **steal** home; **strike** home.

honors, do the honors preside as host, serve at a dinner:—The host being absent, the hostess asked me to do the honors and carve the roast.

hooey (sl.) nonsense:—The President's promise to end the war is a lot of hooey.

hook, get one off the hook relieve one of a burden or distasteful obligation, help one out of a difficulty:—Ralph doesn't want to marry that girl he just proposed to, and he wants his sister to try to get him off the hook. Tired of an unwanted visitor, the executive signaled to his secretary to get him off the hook.

hook, line, and sinker completely, totally —as when a fish swallows the entire hook, line, and sinker:—He is naturally a gullible person anyway, and he accepted our fantastic story hook, line, and sinker.

hook-up a series of radio or TV stations linked together for occasional special broadcasts:—The President will go on the air tonight over a nationwide hook-up.

hook, by hook or by crook by one means or another, by fair means or foul:—She assured us that she would get the money by hook or by crook.

hook, on one's own hook independently, upon one's own initiative:—The lieutenant said he had planned and executed the entire maneuver on his own hook.

hooky, play hooky be a truant from school:—Yesterday several of the younger boys from our class played hooky and went to the ball game.

horn in intrude:—Although he was not invited, Henry as usual managed to horn in on the party.

horns, draw in one's horns cease to be hostile or threatening:—When George finally arrived with our official pass, the guard, who had been so belligerent up to then, drew in his horns.

horns, take the bull by the horns grapple directly with a problem:—There's no use waiting any longer; let's take the bull by the horns, go directly to his office, and state our demands.

horse around fool around, talk boisterously:—He spends most of his lunch hour every day horsing around with some of the girls from the office.

horse-laugh a loud, derisive laugh:—When the speaker remarked that politics was one of the noblest of all the professions, his listeners gave him a loud horse-laugh.

horse of another color something completely different. Sometimes expressed as a **horse of a different color:**—We're not discussing the salary I make; we are discussing your extravagance. That's a horse of an entirely different color.

horseplay rough, practical joking:—After the wedding there was a good deal of horseplay on the part of some of the groom's young friends.

horse sense common sense:—Though his wife is very impractical, Jones fortunately has a lot of good horse sense.

horse trade said of clever bargaining:—In a horse trade Mexico agreed to police narcotic pushers if the United States would give up intensive border searches.

horse See also **cart,** put the cart before the horse; **dark** horse; **high,** on one's high horse; **look** a gift horse in the mouth; **straight** from the horse's mouth; **wheelhorse; wooden** horse.

horses See **hold** one's horses.

hot-rod a souped-up racing car that can exceed the speed of most conventional stock cars:—That hot-rod has two carburetors.

hot seat the electric chair (sl.):—If convicted, he will certainly get the hot seat.

hot, be in hot water be in trouble, have difficulties:—He is in hot water with the law again for accepting bets on the horses.

hot, not so hot ineffective, not so good:—His plan to raise the money in a hurry obviously wasn't so hot.

hot See also **blow** hot and cold; **air,** hot air.

hours, after hours after the regular or legally scheduled time:—Bars found serving drinks after hours are subject to a fine.

hours, at all hours at various times, at almost any time:—The baby was so sick that we were up at all hours last night.

hours, keep good hours arise and go to bed early—at a reasonable hour:—The doctor told him that he should rest for a few months and try to keep good hours.

hours, keep late hours habitually stay up late, go to bed late:—He cannot keep such late hours without feeling the ill effects in time.

hours, wee hours the early hours of the morning between one and three o'clock:—We waited until the wee hours of the morning, but he did not call.

hour See also **eleventh** hour; **strike** the hour.

house of ill fame a brothel. Also sometimes expressed as a **disorderly house:**—Most large cities have laws prohibiting houses of ill fame.

house, like a house afire with great speed or energy:—Patton's troops, encouraged by their previous advances, swept like a house afire across the enemy territory.

house, on the house free to the customer:—We each bought a round of drinks, and then the bartender announced that the next drink was on the house.

house See also **bring** down the house; **clean** house; **doghouse,** in the doghouse; **keep** house; **keep** open house.

housebroken trained—said of animals trained to go outside to relieve themselves:—All young puppies have to be housebroken.

how, and how! an expression emphasizing a fact or opinion just given previously:—"Grace certainly can dance well." "And how!"

how about it? what's your decision?:—I've offered you $500 for your old car. How about it?

how about that! how remarkable that is:—"Your old girl friend Janice is married and has three children. How about that!"

how come an expression meaning: why, how does it happen that:—How come Mary is not going on the picnic with us?

how goes it? an expression meaning: how are you and your affairs in general progressing:—How goes it in your office since your new boss arrived?

huddle, go into a huddle confer, group closely together in order to talk confidentially:—Before resuming the game, the coach and the team went into a huddle.

hue and cry a proclamation for the capture of a criminal, a great clamor, widespread alarm:—There was a great hue and cry on the part of the crowd but the thief escaped.

huff, go off in a huff in anger:—She went off in a huff just because we failed to nominate her as club president.

hum, make things hum make things proceed briskly, efficiently:—As soon as our new manager came in he began to make things hum.

hump See **over** the hump.

hunky dory satisfactory, O.K. (sl.):—He asked me whether we liked our new apartment, and I told him that so far everything was hunky dory.

hunt down track down with intent to capture:—They hunted down the escaped convict and found him hiding in a cabin in the woods.

hunt up look for, search for:—If you ever visit Scranton, be sure to hunt me up.

hurry on with make haste with:—He promised to hurry on with the report and send it to us today.

hurry up make haste, hasten—an emphatic form of hurry:—Hurry up or we will miss the train.

hush-hush said of an important matter kept very secret by an exclusive few:—That agreement our President made with an unfriendly foreign power is strictly hush-hush.

hush money money paid to a person to be silent:—That blackmailer extorted hush money from a husband who had been unfaithful to his wife.

I

ice, on thin ice in a dangerous or embarrassing position:—When the art lecturer got into the realm of science, he was on thin ice.

icing on the cake See **frosting** on the cake.

ill at ease uncomfortable:—He naturally felt ill at ease since he was the only one present who was not in evening clothes.

ill-favored unprepossessing, ugly:— Strangely enough he had less trouble in marrying off his ill-favored daughter than her two prettier sisters.

imagination, stretch of the imagination imaginative attempt or effort:—By no stretch of the imagination can I see William as a research scientist.

impression, be under the impression have the idea, believe:—I was under the impression all the time that he was well pleased with my work.

in keeping with consistent with:—Russia's attitude in this matter is certainly not in keeping with the spirit of the United Nations Charter.

in line with in agreement with:—His ideas on politics are exactly in line with mine.

in step with closely joined to, in unison with:—If he expects to be able to continue in office, a politician must keep in step with his backers.

in the know having information not available to the general public:—Those in the know maintain that the President will not run for office again.

in the pink in the best possible condition: —After two weeks of training, the heavyweight champion claims to be in the pink.

in, be in for it be liable for punishment or censure:—When the editor called me to his office, I knew from the expression on his face that I was in for it.

in, be (let) in on be informed, participate in, be a party to:—We decided to let Frank in on our plan because he would be very helpful to us.

in, be in with be familiar with, be on good terms with:—My lawyer can help you in that matter, because he is in with many influential people.

in, have an in with have influence with, be liked and accepted by:—Perhaps I can get Harry to lend you his car. I have an in with him.

in, have it in one be capable of:—I did not know that he had it in him to speak so forcefully.

in, the in-thing the style, action, etc. that is fashionable:—Miniskirts were the in-thing in 1969.

inch along proceed slowly and with difficulty:—The best our troops could do was to inch their way along the mine-filled road.

inclined to have the tendency to:—I am inclined to fall asleep after a heavy meal.

increase, on the increase increasing, growing:—Crime is certainly on the increase in many of our big cities.

Indian-giver one who gives something and later asks for it back:—One does not give an engagement ring to a young woman and then, like an Indian-giver, ask for it back.

Indian Summer a dry, warm period in late autumn, usually in October:—We had a brief cold spell, followed by Indian Summer, when the weather turned warm and pleasant again.

ins and outs all the details:—George, who knew all the ins and outs of the case, was the only one of us who was able to follow the course of the trial intelligently.

inside of within—used with reference to time:—He said that he would be back inside of an hour.

inside out with the inner side turned toward the outside:—John had one of his socks on inside out.

inside, have an inside track have a preferred or favored position:—Martin, whose father is well acquainted with the president of the company, naturally has an inside track towards getting that contract.

instance, for instance for example:—He will earn, for instance, about twice as much as I earn.

I.O.U. a promissory note (I Owe You): —I had no money so I gave him my I.O.U. for a hundred dollars.

iron out smooth out, untangle:—All the difficulties were finally ironed out and the contract signed.

iron, strike while the iron is hot do something at the opportune moment:—He was in a very good mood so I decided to strike while the iron was hot and to ask him to lend me his car for the week-end.

irons, have many irons in the fire have various enterprises or resources all at the same time:—He says that he is not very worried about his drop in sales because he has several other irons in the fire.

itch, have an itch to have a strong desire to. Also expressed as **be itching to**:— He has an itch to tour Mexico this winter.

Ivy League a group of eight colleges in the northeastern United States:—Harvard and Yale belong to the Ivy League.

J

jack of all trades a handyman capable of doing many small repairs adequately: —There is an old saying that a jack of all trades is very often master of none.

jack up (1) to raise by using a jack:— To remove the wheel we had to jack up the whole rear end of the car. (2) raise, increase:—It is the wholesaler rather than the retailer who has jacked up the prices.

Jack, before you can say Jack Robinson very quickly:—I'll be back before you can say Jack Robinson.

jackpot, hit the jackpot be the lucky winner, come suddenly into a large sum of money:—When oil was discovered on his land, he hit the jackpot.

jailbird a convict, either one in prison, or one recently released:—He was a jailbird, and naturally it was difficult for him to find work after leaving prison.

jam, in a jam in difficulties, in a predicament:—If you continue to disregard those "No Parking" signs, you'll certainly get into a jam with the police.

jar on irritate:—The noise of that radio going all day is beginning to jar on my nerves.

jaywalk walk across a city street against the lights:—There is a fine for jaywalking.

jerry-built badly and hastily constructed: —Those new jerry-built homes will be needing expensive repairs very soon.

jet-set said of the rich who travel frequently overseas to parties, etc.:—Many members of the jet-set spend part of the year in Monte Carlo.

jiffy, in a jiffy immediately, in a moment: —I'll be with you in a jiffy.

jig is up the end is near; no hope remains: —When the man on the roof saw that the police had surrounded the building, he knew that the jig was up.

Jim Crow bus a bus on which blacks were once segregated:—In Alabama Negroes used to have to ride in the back of Jim Crow buses.

job, be on the job alert, attentive:—We gave him a raise because he is a good worker and always on the job.

job, inside job a crime committed by an employee:—That robbery of the cash register looked like an inside job.

job See also **give** something up as a bad job; **lie** down on the job; **odd** jobs; **neat** job; **put-up** job.

john a toilet, water-closet:—There are three johns in that house.

joint a low place of entertainment, a bar, cabaret, etc. (sl.):—In their drive against narcotics the police raided several joints on the East Side.

joke, play a joke on victimize, make the butt of a joke:—Let's play a joke on the teacher and lock the door so that she can't get in.

joke See also **crack** a joke; **practical** joke; **take** a joke.

joker a drawback:—Our store bought that merchandise at a very low figure, but the joker is that we cannot expect delivery for over six months.

jot down make a note of, write down quickly:—Let me jot down your telephone number so that I can call you later.

jug, in the jug (sl.) in prison or jail:—They put Tom in the jug for driving while intoxicated.

jump at accept with alacrity, eagerly:—Arthur naturally jumped at the chance to invest in such a promising business.

jump to conclusions arrive too hastily and possibly mistakenly at a decision or conclusion:—I see no reason to jump to conclusions and say it was John who made the mistake unless I have further evidence.

jump on scold, criticize:—Ross left his job because his supervisor was continually jumping on him for no reason.

jump the gun start something before the scheduled time or before the signal is given:—The strike was called for Wednesday, but many steel workers jumped the gun and did not report for work on Tuesday.

jump, get the jump on start in advance of another, gain the initiative:—While all our plans were still in the blueprint stage, our competitors got the jump on us by announcing their new model.

junkie a heavy user of narcotics, a dope addict:—The police arrest junkies and then they are set free the next day.

just now at this very moment—also, a moment ago:—I met him just now in the hall as I came in.

just so perfect, in excellent order or condition:—His trousers were neatly pressed and his new jacket fitted just so.

justice, do justice to treat in a just manner, appreciate properly, demonstrate a keen appetite:—There was no doubt that they all did justice to his wife's Spanish cooking.

justice, do one justice be fair to one:—Although I am repelled by Frank's coarse manners, to do him justice he has a kind heart.

K

keel over fall or faint suddenly:—After drilling in the hot sun for several hours, several recruits keeled over.

keen, be keen about be enthusiastic about:—I'm very keen about the new Ford sports model.

keep a close check on follow or watch carefully:—The police are keeping a close check on the movements of both suspects in the case.

keep a stiff upper lip be firm and courageous, literally not to let one's upper lip quiver from fear or emotion:—The trip at night through the dark woods was enough to frighten even the bravest adult, but both youngsters kept a stiff upper lip.

keep at continue doing, persist in:—I'm sure that if he keeps at it long enough he will learn to play quite well.

keep away remain away from, avoid:—The doctor told her to keep away from all sweets and other fattening foods.

keep back refrain from or be restrained from entering, remain back:—As the President's car approached, the police had great difficulty in keeping back the crowd.

keep cool (1) remain cool:—How do you manage to keep so cool in this hot weather? (2) remain calm, unexcited:—The main thing to remember, if the man starts any trouble, is to keep cool.

keep doing something continue to do something:—He kept working at the problem until he found the solution.

keep good time run accurately—said of watches and clocks:—My watch keeps good time.

keep house manage or take care of a home:—It was quite a new experience for Sylvia to keep house.

keep in mind remember:—You must keep in mind that he is somewhat younger than you.

keep in touch with remain in communication with:—Be sure to keep in touch with me while you are away.

keep off stay off, away from: —There were signs everywhere in the park reading: "Keep off the Grass!"

keep on continue:—He kept on telling me the same story over and over.

keep one company accompany or stay with someone:—Why don't you come over and keep me company tonight while I sit with the children? See **company,** keep company with.

keep one waiting cause one to wait:—He kept us waiting in his outer office for more than an hour.

keep (lose) one's balance retain one's balance:—To cross the stream we had to jump from stone to stone, and it was difficult to keep one's balance; Bill lost his balance and fell into the water.

keep one's cool stay calm:—Despite the disorder that five kids can create in a household, their mother always managed to keep her cool.

keep one's end up do one's part, fulfill that which is expected of one, hold one's own:—With all the difficulties that faced them, they nevertheless kept their end up.

keep one's hand in still be occasionally working at what one is skilled in or trained to do:—Although that carpenter is retired, he still keeps his hand in by helping a few of his neighbors.

keep one's nose to the grindstone to slave continuously:—In order to meet his heavy expenses, Lyman has to keep his nose to the grindstone.

keep one's shirt on remain calm, not to become excited or angry:—I told him to keep his shirt on, no matter what the provocation

keep one's temper remain calm, retain one's self control:—Only a saint could keep his temper under such irritating circumstances.

keep one's word fulfill one's promise:— Bill kept his word and arrived exactly at the time he had promised.

keep open house entertain all those who come at any time:—They have a cottage at a nearby lake where they keep open house all summer long.

keep out stay or remain outside of **or** away from:—The sign on the door said, "Danger! Keep out!"

keep out of stay or remain out of:—It's his own fault if he got hit by the ball; I told him several times to keep out of the way.

keep pace with maintain, match, the same rate of speed as:—Our limited budget makes it difficult for us to keep pace with their extravagant way of living.

keep peace between maintain peaceful relations between:—My mother always had all she could do to keep peace between my brother and me.

keep the peace (See under **peace.**)

keep plugging along continue working steadily and industriously — often against difficulties:—He did not have great ability, but he kept plugging along year after year, and eventually attained the rank of captain.

keep (one) posted inform oneself or receive current information:—My secretary telephoned me daily and kept me posted on everything that went on at the office.

keep something dark maintain as a secret:—I'll tell you something quite interesting about that family if you promise to keep it dark.

keep something under one's hat keep secret:—I'm going to get married next week but please keep it under your hat. I don't want my former wife to know.

keep tabs on check on, watch, keep a record of:—She keeps tabs on every movement her husband makes.

keep time play or perform music in time, giving notes and rests their proper values:—An orchestra conductor keeps time with his hands and his baton.

keep to bear toward, said of directions, as in the expressions **keep to the right, keep to the left,** etc.:—Instead of keeping to the right, most drivers, when they are learning, tend to stay in the middle of the road.

keep track of maintain a record of:—We have to keep track of every cent we spend.

keep up (1) maintain, support:—It costs a lot of money to keep up a car; it is said that it is not the original cost which is so important but rather the upkeep. (2) continue, endure doing:—I have been working at this ten hours a day for the last month, but I don't know how much longer I can keep it up.

keep up with remain abreast of, maintain pace with:—Don't walk so fast. I can't keep up with you. The newspaper is so large that it is hard to keep up with the news.

keep up with the Joneses duplicate or imitate the manner of living of one's friends or neighbors, aspire to a social level slightly above one:—The poor fellow went broke because his wife was always trying to keep up with the Joneses.

keep watch to guard, be vigilant:—The police have asked everyone to keep watch against an escaped convict who is armed and masquerading in women's clothes.

keep See also **appearances,** keep up appearances; **arms,** keep at arm's length; **ball,** keep the ball rolling; **body,** keep body and soul together; **books,** keep books; **company,** keep company with; **distance,** keep one at a distance; **eye,** keep an eye on; **eye,** keep an eye open; **eye,** keep an eye out for; **face,** keep a straight face; **hand,** keep one's hand in; **head,** keep one's head; **head,** keep one's head above water; **moving,** keep moving; **peace,** keep the peace; **sight,** keep sight of; **step,** keep step with; **straight,** keep a straight face; **wolf,** keep the wolf from the door; **in** keeping with.

keeps, for keeps permanently, never to be returned, given outright:—I only lent her the ring, but she was under the impression that it was for keeps.

keyed up nervous, excited:—I was so keyed up over the prospect of our long trip that I did not sleep a wink all night.

kick (v.) complain:—To me the meals were very poor, but nobody seemed to kick about them.

kick a habit stop, cease doing:—It took a year in the hospital before that dope addict could kick the habit.

kick back return or pay part of one's wages to one's boss:—That municipal street supervisor went to jail for making his subordinate workers kick back ten percent of their wages.

kick in pay, contribute:—Each of us had to kick in a certain amount toward the general campaign expenses.

kick one upstairs get rid of an employee in one department by transferring him to a less-important but better-paying job elsewhere:—Since the sales-manager's assistant was better than the sales-manager, the company kicked the latter upstairs into a vice-presidency.

kick out expel, throw out:—When we found out that he had lied, we immediately kicked him out of the club.

kick something around discuss or debate an idea or suggestion:—Your plan to improve our mail-order department seems good. Let's kick it around.

kick the bucket die (sl.):—They tell me that old man Jenkins has finally kicked the bucket.

kick, get a kick out of obtain a thrill or intense pleasure from:—He gets a kick out of just walking along Broadway and looking in the store windows.

kicks, do something for kicks do it for pleasure and excitement (also **just for kicks**):—After the party was over, the guests broke all the windows for kicks.

kid (1) (v.) joke, make fun of:—We often kid him about the loud ties he wears. (2) (n.) a child:—We want to send our two kids to the country for the summer.

kid See also **gloves,** handle with kid gloves.

kill off eliminate by killing:—Hitler's original plan was to kill off all the German Jews.

kill time waste time, cause the time to pass more rapidly:—The train trip was long and tiring, but we killed time playing cards.

kill two birds with one stone accomplish two objectives in one action:—We can visit Aunt Jennie and also see New York City on the same trip, thus killing two birds with one stone.

kind of rather, somewhat:—He looks kind of pale after his illness.

king-size larger than customary:—The Browns paid a lot of money for a king-sized bed.

kiss of death firing or letting an employee go:—When you reach 55 in that company it's the kiss of death, for that is the retirement age.

knife, go under the knife have a surgical operation in the hospital:—My wife went under the knife at Mercy Hospital.

knock around (about) wander without purpose but often gaining in experience:—He had knocked around Europe a good deal and consequently spoke several languages.

knock cold render unconscious:—The blow on the chin knocked him cold.

knock down ′(1) knock to the floor or ground:—He knocked the challenger down in the third round and again in the seventh round. (2) reduce, make lower:—He said that if I agreed to buy the car right away they would knock down the price another hundred dollars.

knock it off cease doing something objectionable to others:—When the two antagonists started to fight, the other men in the bar told them to knock it off.

knock off (1) stop, leave work:—Let's knock off early today and go to see a ball game. (2) reduce:—The dealer knocked $5.00 off the list price. (3) accomplish, do:—Last night he knocked off five hours of work before he went to bed.

knock one's block off hit or punish severely, literally—knock someone's head off his shoulders:—He was bigger than I, but I told him that if he ever used such foul language again I would knock his block off.

knock out render unconscious by a strong blow:—The champion knocked his opponent out in the third round.

knockout something or someone exceptionally attractive:—Bill's new girl friend is certainly a knockout.

knock over upset, overturn:—I inadvertently knocked over the vase, which fell to the floor and broke.

know a thing or two about have a fairly considerable knowledge of, be experienced in:—He had traveled widely and knew a thing or two about the Far East.

know-how experience with, ability to devise and construct:—It soon became clear that the United States had the technological know-how necessary to win the war.

know one's own mind be definite in one's plans or ideas, not to vacillate:—It is difficult to plan anything with him because he doesn't know his own mind.

know one's place be polite and deferential to one's elders or superiors:—He's an attractive child, but someone ought to teach him to know his place.

know one's way around be experienced and familiar with places, customs, etc.:—Bill can serve as our guide, because he has lived in New York for many years and really knows his way around.

know the ropes experienced in the routine of:—Until I got to know the ropes a little better, I figured that the best thing to do would be to follow instructions.

know what's what have considerable knowledge of, understand thoroughly:—For this particular case, we need a lawyer who really knows what's what about corporation law.

know, in the know be informed, have information:— Before the merger was announced, only two of us in the firm were in the know.

know See also **heart,** know by heart; **in** the know; **let** someone know; **not** to know what to make of something.

kosher (sl.) all right, acceptable, honorable, honest:—Flirting with your boss's wife isn't kosher.

L

labor under suffer from, be the victim of:—He is obviously laboring under the delusion that I am going to help him.

labor, be in labor suffer the pains of childbirth:—She was in labor for ten hours before her baby was finally born.

ladies' man one who likes women, a man who tries to be attractive to women:—He's a handsome chap but too much interested in his work to be a ladies' man.

ladies room a public toilet and restroom for women:—Can you please tell me where the ladies room is?

lady-killer a man attractive to women, a male flirt:—Bill fancies himself to be quite a lady-killer.

lady of the house the owner or wife of the owner of the house:—Would you like to speak to the lady of the house?

laid out arranged:—Their apartment is very conveniently laid out.

laid up confined to one's bed, sick:—He has been laid up for several months with a sprained back.

lame duck specifically a member of Congress who has failed to be reelected but whose term of office has not yet ended, an ineffectual person:—The present Congress contains only three lame-duck members.

land-office business a sudden flourishing business:—By underselling their competitors the store did a land-office business in radio and television sets.

land on (1) fall upon, strike:—The child fell from the fence and landed on his head. (2) criticize, abuse:—As soon as I got home Father landed on me for using the car without his permission.

land, make land arrive at land after a voyage:—On our seventh day out, we made land in the Caribbean.

land See also **fat** of the land; **lay** of the land; **see** how the land lies.

landslide an overwhelming victory:—The 1964 election was a landslide for the Democratic candidate.

large order a difficult job, a task difficult to fulfill:—Having to educate three sons at college is a large order for any father.

large See also **at** large; **by** and large; **scale,** on a large scale.

lash out at strike at suddenly, burst out in angry words:—In his speech he lashed out at the labor leaders, who he said were the real enemies of labor.

last lap the final stage:—The trip had all been very interesting, but it was a relief to know that we were on the last lap of our long journey.

last, at last finally:—We waited until midnight, and at last he telephoned.

last, on one's last legs ready to fall exhausted, about to fail completely:—Anyone could see that the business was on its last legs.

last See also **stick** to one's last; **straw,** last straw.

late, of late recently, lately:—He has been working very hard of late.

late bloomer said of a young person, often a student, who doesn't achieve very much until he is older than most of his peers were when they achieved success:—With poor grades in college, Jones finally proved to be a late bloomer in graduate school.

laugh off dismiss, treat with little concern:—When they told him that his life had been threatened, Smith just laughed it off.

laugh on the other side of one's mouth be disappointed, be the opposite of amused:—He will laugh on the other side of his mouth when he finds out that that seemingly valuable land he boasted of having bought has turned out to be almost worthless.

laugh one down mock, ridicule:—When the legislator proposed that all voters be given a bonus, he was laughed down by his colleagues.

laugh one out of cause another to forget his sorrow or worries by joking:—He was very much worried about getting seasick, but his fellow-travelers laughed him out of it.

laughs, for laughs for fun, for pleasure (sl.):—They throw things out of the window late at night just for laughs, but sometime they are going to hurt someone.

laugh, have (get) the laugh on turn the tables on, prove to be the victor rather than the victim:—Henry had the laugh on all of us when his blind date turned out to be the prettiest girl at the party.

laugh See also **horse** laugh; **sleeve**, laugh up one's sleeve.

laughing matter something to be treated lightly:—Anyone could see that the blow Henry had received was no laughing matter.

law-abiding following or obeying the law: —He had been a law-abiding citizen all his life.

law, take the law into one's own hands act precipitately, anticipate the normal course of legal action:—The tenants threatened to take the law into their own hands, if the landlord persisted in ignoring their reasonable demands.

law See also **lay** down the law; **letter** of the law; **pass** a law.

lay aside (1) put to one side:—Why don't you lay that problem aside for a while and work at it later when your mind is fresher? (2) put aside, save:—I plan to lay aside five dollars each week toward my next summer's vacation fund.

lay-away plan custom of holding a piece of wanted merchandise for a customer until he has entirely paid for it:—We paid fifty dollars down on a $200 bedroom suite on the lay-away plan.

lay bare reveal, expose:—In his confession, the man laid bare the whole story of his life.

lay by save:—Every week I would like to lay by five dollars toward buying a new carpet.

lay down one's arms cease fighting—also, surrender:—After four long years of war, our troops were finally able to lay down their arms and return home.

lay down one's life sacrifice one's life for some cause or person:—Smith volunteered for the dangerous mission, saying that, if necessary, he was ready to lay down his life for his country.

lay down the law scold, reprimand severely:—When she arrived home at about two o'clock in the morning, her dad was waiting up for her, and he certainly laid down the law in no uncertain terms.

lay eyes on see:—She was one of the most beautiful girls he had ever laid eyes on.

lay for wait for someone with the intention of attacking, scolding, or playing a joke on (sl.) (cf. **lie** in wait for):— They were laying for him in the dark, and when he stepped out of his car, they all fell upon him.

lay hold of grasp, obtain:—Where could I lay hold of a good used car? (cf. **hands,** lay hands on.)

lay in to store, put away and keep:—With the new home freezers now on the market, any housewife can lay in a complete store of fresh vegetables sufficient to last the whole winter.

lay it on thick give exaggerated or excessive praise, fulsome flattery:—Of course Ross deserved praise for getting that contract, but I couldn't see the reason for everybody laying it on so thick.

lay it on with a trowel Same as **lay it on thick.**

lay of the land the general situation, topographical arrangement:—Before ordering the attack, the general sent out several scouts to get the lay of the land.

lay off (1) dismiss workers during a slack period:—A sudden slump in business caused many of the plants to lay off workers. (2) cease, stop (sl.):—I didn't like some of the things he was saying about her so I told him to lay off.

lay oneself open to expose oneself, make oneself vulnerable to:—They warned the candidate to be careful in his comment on racial questions; otherwise he might lay himself open to criticism from certain groups.

lay out (1) spend, provide:—He laid out a tremendous sum of money just for a special playroom for his children. (2) prepare for burial:—The deceased man was laid out in the neighborhood funeral parlor. (3) bring and place or arrange properly:—The valet laid out his master's evening clothes.

layout (n.) plan, general situation:—The layout of their apartment was rather unusual with several bedrooms opening out from a circular living room in the center.

lay over stop overnight, a scheduled stopover on a passenger route:—He had to lay over in Pittsburgh while they made repairs on the bus.

lay stress on emphasize:—In his speech he laid stress on the need for better understanding among the nations of the world.

lay to rest bury:—After a special ceremony the dead soldier was laid to rest in Arlington National Cemetary.

lay up See **laid up.**

lay waste destroy completely:—The retreating army laid waste the fields and farm buildings along their path.

lay See also **egg,** lay an egg; **finger,** lay a finger on; **hands,** lay hands on.

lead by the nose manage, control completely:—His wife, being more aggressive, is able to lead him by the nose.

lead off begin, start:—In the fourth inning Crocker, the Yankee outfielder, led off with a double to right field.

lead one a merry dance tire someone by causing him to overdo, cause him unusual discomfort or expense:—With her personal extravagances and constant social activities she led her husband a merry dance.

lead one on mislead, deceive:—She assumed at first that he was serious in his courtship but soon learned that he was simply leading her on.

lead the way go first, indicate the correct course or direction:—It is so dark here in the garden I think you'd better lead the way.

lead to result in, go towards:—Such an armament race can only lead to one thing—war.

lead up to approach indirectly:—Anyone could see what he was leading up to; he wanted to borrow some money from us.

lead, have the lead star, take the most prominent part in:—Grace has the lead in the school play.

lead, take the lead go into the first or head position, command:—As soon as the race started the gray horse took the

lead and maintained it throughout the entire race.

lead See also **dog,** lead a dog's life; **ringleader.**

leaf through turn the pages of, scan through a book or other reading matter:—We had only enough time to leaf through our programs before the play started.

leaf See also **take** a leaf from the book of; **turn** over a new leaf.

leak out escape, become known:—The movie star tried to keep her marriage a secret, but news of it soon leaked out.

leak to said of confidential information given to a newspaper reporter, etc.:—The secret illness of the President was leaked to the radio commentator.

leak See also **spring** a leak.

leap year every fourth year, during which the month of February contains twenty-nine instead of twenty-eight days:—During leap year any unmarried woman is supposed to have the privilege of proposing matrimony to the man of her choice.

leaps and bounds rapidly:—Their business has grown by leaps and bounds.

lease, a new lease on life a new chance to live, an improved manner of living:—Living in Florida each winter will give him a new lease on life.

least, at least at the minimum:—If you can't go to the party, you should at least send your regrets.

least, not in the least not at all:—Of course I'd be glad to help you with the dishes. I'm not in the least tired after my trip.

least, to say the least understate, express as mildly as is possible:—After all his family had done for him, his complete neglect of them was, to say the least, a poor way of showing his appreciation.

leave alone not to interfere with or interrupt, permit to be alone:—No one dared to disturb him, because when Father said that he wished to be left alone, he meant precisely that.

leave behind (1) go away without, forget:—We were well on our way when we discovered that we had left behind our box of fishing tackle. (2) abandon:—Sometimes those who are left behind at home suffer more during a war than those who actually participate.

leave in the lurch desert, abandon one who is in a dangerous or difficult situation:—To remove the wheel was a job requiring two men, so that when John walked blithely off he left me in the lurch.

leave it at that not to discuss or argue further, avoid further and more bitter disagreement:—Your opinion of Oscar and mine are apparently quite opposed, but let's leave it at that instead of getting ourselves excited and quarreling.

leave no stone unturned spare no effort, use every possible means:—The police promised to leave no stone unturned in their search for the missing girl.

leave off desist, refrain from:—I ordered Sam to leave off playing jokes on our guests.

leave one's mark influence, leave an impression upon:—Nothing that he wrote was very popular in his day, but that does not mean that he did not leave his mark upon the course of 19th century fiction writing.

leave out omit, skip:—The printer has left out two lines from this paragraph.

leave out in the cold forsake, abandon:—We felt left out in the cold when we learned later that we had not been invited to the wedding.

leave up to (See **put** up to)

leave word leave a message:—He left word with his secretary that he would be back at five o'clock.

leave, take leave of say goodbye to another, say one's farewells to:—Before he went abroad, he took leave of all his associates.

leave, take one's leave depart:—After a short visit, he suddenly got up and took his leave.

leave See **French**, take French leave; **open**, leave open; **take it or leave it.**

left, be left remaining:—How much money is there left?

left-handed compliment doubtful praise, a well-intentioned compliment which turns out to be rather uncomplimentary:—When he said that he enjoyed playing tennis with me because I was one of the few persons he could beat, he was paying me a left-handed compliment.

left See also **get** left, **right** and left.

leg, not a leg to stand on have no facts or evidence to support an argument:—When the chief witness' testimony was thoroughly discredited by the prosecutor, the defendant didn't have a leg to stand on.

leg, shake a leg hurry (sl.):—Come on! Shake a leg or we shall never get there in time.

legs, stretch one's legs take a walk, go walking:—I'm getting tired sitting around so much. Let's stretch our legs before dinner.

leg See also **last**, on one's last leg; **pull** one's leg.

lend a hand help, assist:—I had to get a porter to lend a hand with the luggage.

lend an ear listen:—If the public would only lend an ear to what the Senator has to say on foreign policy, some of our problems would be made easier.

length, at length (1) finally:—After a long journey they arrived at length in Naples. (2) completely, in considerable detail: —He told us about the trip at some length.

lengths, to any lengths to any extremes:—He said he would go to any lengths to protect his good name.

let alone (1) avoid, allow to remain undisturbed:—After it had scratched him several times, the boy let the cat alone. (2) not to mention:—He can't speak his own native language well, let alone French.

let be cease to bother, let alone:—I told him to let the cat be.

let blood cause blood to flow, bleed, perform phlebotomy:—In olden times in the case of fevers, the physician always let blood from the patient.

let bygones be bygones forget past differences:—We finally decided to let bygones be bygones and resume our former partnership.

let down disappoint, fail, desert:—He promised to help me, but at the last minute he let me down.

let down easy refuse or reject gently, treat sympathetically:—He started to apologize and Bob, who has had much practice in these matters, let him down easy.

let George do it let someone else perform a task which one should do himself:—The reason that we often have such poor government is that too many people say, "I don't have time to interest myself in politics. Let George do it."

let go (1) release:—The judge let the prisoner go with only a few words of warning. (2) start, deliver, speak vociferously or intemperately:—In the course of his speech, the lawyer let go with a vicious attack on the tactics of his opponent. (3) dismiss:—Since we are going away for the summer, we will have to let our housekeeper go.

let go of release one's grasp:—As soon as I let go of the leash, the dog ran away.

let oneself go throw off restraint, cast aside one's inhibitions:—At a party, when Smith lets himself go, he can be quite amusing.

let in-out permit to enter-leave:—You can let the cat out and at the same time let the dog in.

let know inform:—He will let us know as soon as he arrives in Washington.

let off (1) permit to go free, excuse:—The judge let the traffic violator off with just a warning. (2) release, discharge:—He likes to let off steam once in a while by scolding his secretary.

let on reveal, tell:—Don't let on to Helen that we are planning to go to the movie tonight.

let one have it scold, strike, punish:—A stranger insulted Mrs. Bloom, and her husband let him have it.

let one in on permit someone to share in, reveal a secret to:—If I let you in on something big that we are planning will you promise not to mention a word of it to anyone?

let out (1) dismiss, release:—After forty years of service in the same company, Collins was suddenly let out. (2) alter, enlarge:—If she gets much fatter she will have to let out all her dresses. (3) award:—The contract was finally let out to the lowest bidder.

let pass overlook, disregard:—I heard what he said about me but decided to let it pass.

let slide be negligent or careless in the execution of one's duty or work:—At first he got good marks, but then he began to let his studies slide, and finally flunked out of school.

let slip reveal unintentionally:—The girl let slip that she had been a witness to the accident.

let up cease, moderate:—It doesn't look as though this rain is ever going to let up.

let See also **cat,** let the cat out of the bag; **dogs,** let sleeping dogs lie; **fall,** let fall; **grass,** let the grass grow under one's feet; **hair,** let down one's hair; **in,** be (let) in on; **ride,** let something ride.

letdown a lowering of one's interest, a strong reaction of depression:—After the excitement of a year's travel, it was a letdown to find herself living in that small town.

letter of the law a strict, literal interpretation and application of a law:—The judge held the offending motorist to the letter of the law and gave him five days in jail.

letter, hold (keep) to the letter adhere strictly to the literal interpretation:—Holding to the letter of the law, the judge sentenced the prisoner to the maximum penalty.

letter perfect perfect to the last letter, memorized perfectly:—The actor was letter perfect in his role.

letter See bread-and-butter letter; **dead**-letter office; **man** of letters; **open** letter; **red**-letter day.

level best one's very best, one's utmost:—Tim refused to stay in school although his mother tried her level best to make him do so.

level-headed practical, reasonable, having good common sense:—What that home needs is a good, level-headed manager.

level off tend to become stable, normalized:—The economists report that the inflation curve seems to be leveling off.

level with another tell the truth, reveal something:—Level with me. Is Jane Gary's wife or his mistress?

level, on the level honest, trustworthy, sincere:—Though he was a complete stranger to her, she trusted him because she felt that he was on the level.

liberty, at liberty free to accept work:—That actress has just finished a road tour and is at liberty to work for others.

lick defeat, beat:—He says that even with one hand tied behind his back, he can lick Tom.

lick into shape train, drill, make perfect:—It was a difficult job to take raw army recruits and lick them into shape in just three months of basic training.

lick and a promise, a said of a job done very superficially:—It's hard to get a good cleaning woman today. Most of them clean with a lick and a promise.

licks, get in one's licks get an opportunity to do something:—After the first guest musician had played, the other musician who had also been invited got in his licks.

lie around be unused, inert:—This old gun has been lying around the house ever since grandfather's time.

lie down on the job be remiss, fail to fulfill one's duty or obligations:—This particular task requires close teamwork, and if any one of us lies down on the job, we shall never be able to finish it in time.

lie in wait for ambush, hide and wait for:—The man lay in wait behind a tree, ready to attack whoever might pass by.

lie, white lie a harmless untruth told with some justifiable motive:—When I said that her boy friend was very attractive, I was really telling her a white lie, because I couldn't possibly tell her that I really thought he was the ugliest man I had seen in a long time.

life-preserver a floating block or ring designed to support the victim of a shipwreck while in the water:—During the boat drill each of the passengers had to put on a life-preserver.

lifesaver something or someone that helps another out of a predicament:—You can lend me $10.00? You're a lifesaver.

life, for the life of me an expression meaning: even if it meant losing or giving up my life:—For the life of me I couldn't remember where I had put my keys.

life, not on your life never, an expression of unwillingness:—You expect me to date that unattractive girl? Not on your life.

life See also **change** of life; **dog,** lead a dog's life; **lease,** a new lease on life; **not** on your life; **walk** of life.

lift steal, take. See **shoplifter:**—The author had lifted an entire passage from an old historical novel and used it verbatim in his book.

lift, give someone a lift (1) give someone a ride:—I waited on the corner a long time hoping that someone might give me a lift home. (2) stimulate, cause one to feel better:—Take a drink with us. It may give you a lift.

lift, have one's face lifted have one's face altered and beautified by surgery, be changed completely for the better:—The town needs more than a row of trees along the main street; it needs its whole face lifted.

lift, not to lift a finger not to help in the slightest degree:—He said he wouldn't lift a finger to help him.

light-fingered having a tendency to be dishonest, thieving:—I had often suspected that Owens was light-fingered; my suspicions were confirmed when the stolen money was found on him.

light into attack, scold:—When Jennie came home at 4 a.m., her mother lit into her.

light-struck said of a photograph that was exposed to too much light:—Because Wally faced his camera right into the sun, his snapshot was light-struck.

light up (1) to ignite:—Jones, apparently feeling rather prosperous and opulent that day, lit up a second cigar as soon as he had finished the first. (2) illuminate completely:—The house was all lit up as though a big celebration was going on.

light, make light of treat as inconsequential, minimize:—Larry was pretty badly hurt, but he tried to make light of it in front of his wife.

light, see the light be won over from one point of view to another:—The inspector was obviously averse to approving the building plans, but when the builder slipped twenty-five hundred dollars into his hand he immediately saw the light.

light, throw light on clear up, illuminate:—The contents of the desk failed to throw any light on the man's mysterious disappearance.

light See also **bring** to light; **come** to light; **tail** light.

like anything to an extreme degree:—He swore like anything when he found out she wasn't going to give him the watch.

likelihood, in all likelihood probably:—In all likelihood the leading candidates will not begin their campaigns for another month.

likes, the likes of anyone like:—I told him I wouldn't want the likes of him working for me.

limb, out on a limb openly exposed, in a compromising position from which it is difficult to withdraw or escape:—The party obviously favors Smith for the office, but as yet no one is prepared to go out on a limb by saying so publicly.

limit, be the limit an extreme case, dreadful—a colloquial expression indicating exasperation:—That child is the limit. If he is not in trouble at school, he is in trouble at home or with the neighbors.

line up (1) form into a line:—All the recruits were ordered to line up in front of the barracks. (2) (n.) the row of suspects or criminals that are lined up each morning by the police for examination:—They asked us to visit the line-up in the police station the next day to see whether we might identify the thief. (3) the regular team participants in a game or enterprise:—They say that Gomez may not appear in the line-up tomorrow in the game against Brooklyn.

line, get a line on obtain information about:—Two detectives were sent out to get a line on the past business dealings of the company.

line, get out of line be uncooperative, intractable, disobedient or insubordinate:—At the cocktail party one guest got rather out of line and had to be taken home.

line, get into line cooperate, conform:—The radical members were told that if they didn't get into line at once they might be expelled from the union.

line, on the dotted line on the line reserved for signature on a document:—All the terms have been agreed to; the only thing lacking is Smith's signature on the dotted line.

line, to be in one's line said of something that a person is skilled in:—Let Smith try to sell our house. Real estate is in his line.

line See **draw** the line; **drop** one a line; **fall** into line; **in** line with; **toe** the line; **underline.**

lines, read between the lines interpret or understand what is said indirectly rather than directly in a letter or document:—He wrote that he liked camp life very much, but I could read between the lines that he was homesick.

lion's share the largest part, a disproportionate share:—Since Holmes had done no more than the rest of us, there was no reason for him to claim the lion's share of the profits.

lips, hang on the lips of listen to eagerly:—Those students hang on the lips of their adored professor.

listen in overhear, tap telephone or other communications lines:—The police had tapped his telephone wire and listened in on his conversations with his confederates. See also **bug** (v.)

listen to reason heed or accept advice, be reasonable:—Hall refused to listen to reason, went swimming right after lunch, and almost drowned with stomach cramps.

little by little by degrees, gradually:—At first he made poor progress in English, but little by little Albert became the best student in the class.

little does one think one hardly expects:— Little did he think, when his wife went to the hospital, that he was to become the father of twin boys.

little ones children:—We went in the canoe, but we thought it would be safer for the little ones to go in the flat-bottomed row boat.

little, make little of modestly minimize:— To all of us it seemed a great honor, but Dad himself made little of the fact that he had just been nominated for the United States Senate.

live down live in such a way as to cause others to forget a personal tragedy or disgrace, gradually overcome some disgrace:—Mary often felt that she could never live down the fact that her father had been convicted of embezzling.

live high live luxuriously or extravagantly:—Ever since he got his promotion, John and his wife have lived rather high.

live (rhymes with give) **in** sleep in the place one works:—Although Mary gets a good salary as a cook, she has to live in.

live it up have a good time regardless of expense:—When we traveled in Europe, we lived it up for six weeks.

live on, exist on, support oneself on:— Since Smith fell ill, the family has had to live on what Mrs. Smith earns.

live up to match or equal the mark set by another:—Harry was a capable lawyer, but it was difficult for him to live up to the reputation established by his more brilliant father.

live wire (1) an electrically charged wire, usually uninsulated:—The lineman was severely burned by the live wire. (2) an alert, energetic person:—To sell that type of merchandise, they need several live-wire salesmen.

live See also **hand,** live from hand to mouth.

living in sin said of an unmarried man and woman living together:—Jack and Melba aren't married; they are living in sin.

load, get a load of listen, notice, learn about, be informed of:—When your father gets a load of your drinking, he'll raise hell.

loaded (adj.) very rich, well-supplied with money:—Why don't you try to borrow from Martin? He's loaded.

loaded, get loaded get drunk:—Every Saturday night Burns gets loaded and staggers home.

loan shark a moneylender who charges excessive interest:—Why go to a loan shark when you can borrow from the bank at the legal rate of interest?

lock, stock and barrel completely, everything—literally the three parts which comprise a gun:—I intend to buy the business—lock, stock, and barrel.

lock in (out) keep in (out) by locking:— They told me that if I didn't get home by twelve o'clock, I might find myself locked out.

lock up (1) lock completely—intensive form of "to lock":—I can't imagine how the rain got in, because we had locked up all the windows tightly. (2) imprison:—When he became violent, the drunk was taken to the police station and locked up for the night.

lock, under lock and key well protected, secured, locked up:—I keep all my valuables under lock and key.

lock See also **pick** a lock.

lodge a complaint complain, make a complaint:—If they don't stop their noise, I am going to lodge a complaint with the police.

long and short of it the substance of it, that which may be stated briefly:—The long and short of it is that John is lazy and doesn't want to find work.

long (and) drawn out See **draw** out (2).

long for want very much:—Elsa longs for a trip to Europe.

long-hair said of an intellectual artist, musician, writer, etc.:—Bobby's mother took her unwilling young son to a long-hair concert.

long shot a remote possibility or chance, a rather reckless gamble:—He took a long shot and invested money in a copper mine in Arizona; fortunately it proved to be a very profitable investment.

long standing established for considerable time:—Their friendship is of long standing.

long suit what a person does well:—Keeping house was never Mollie's long suit. She preferred to have a business career.

long-winded overlong, tedious:—We were bored by his long-winded stories.

long, in the long run eventually, with time, when things run their natural course:—I am sure that in the long run John will prove to be the better friend.

look a gift horse in the mouth examine a gift very critically for defects:—Even though the watch she gave you is not an expensive one, you should be quite contented with it and not look a gift horse in the mouth.

look about search around, examine:—As soon as we get there we will begin to look about for a good piece of land on which to build.

look after take care of:—Our neighbors have promised to look after our dog while we are away.

look back on view in retrospect:—I like to look back on my high school days, which were among the happiest of my life.

look down one's nose despise, show contempt:—Whenever I mention jazz to that classical musician, he looks down his nose at me.

look down upon despise, scorn, consider inferior:—Just because they owned their own home and were slightly better off, they always looked down upon us as poor relations.

look for search for, seek:—John looked everywhere for the ball which he had lost.

look for a needle in a haystack look for something which is almost impossible to locate:—I knew that I should never find Henry in that crowd because it was like looking for a needle in a haystack.

look forward to anticipate with pleasure:—We are all looking forward to your visit.

look high and low for look everywhere for:—We all looked high and low for Helen's pocketbook.

look in on visit, drop in on:—The doctor said that if he was in the neighborhood he would look in on his patient this afternoon.

look into investigate:—The police are looking into the records of all those involved in the crime.

look like resemble:—With his dark hair and light skin he looks just like his mother.

look on watch without participating, be an onlooker:—John took part in the games, but the rest of us, who were a little old for that sort of thing, just looked on.

look on with share in reading or looking at some printed matter:—The teacher told Helen, who had no book, to look on with me.

look out be careful, watch:—I was unwittingly about to step out in front of the oncoming truck when somebody yelled to me to look out.

lookout a guard, someone placed on watch:—A lookout was stationed at the approach to our camp to watch for the late arrivals.

look out for be on the alert for, watch for:—There were signs everywhere warning people to look out for falling rocks.

look out upon face, have a view upon:—Both of us have apartments which look out upon the Columbia University campus.

look over examine:—The auditors are looking over the bank's books.

look-see, have a look-see examine:—I'll have a look-see at your car and let you know how much I can offer you for it.

look to refer to, depend upon:—If you get into trouble, don't look to me for help.

look up (1) search for, consult a reference book for:—You should look up all unfamiliar words in a dictionary. (2) improve, prosper, become brighter:—Our sales are increasing daily, and business in general seems to be looking up. (3) visit, look for:—If you ever come to Chicago, be sure to look me up.

look up to respect, admire:—Jones had once played in a national tournament, so all of us kids who were crazy about tennis naturally looked up to him as some kind of god.

look upon consider:—It is quite unwise to look upon everyone who differs with us as a misguided fool.

lookout, be on the lookout be on the alert, watchful, in the market for:—I told him that I was on the lookout for a good used car.

looking-glass a mirror:—Some people believe that to break a looking-glass means seven years bad luck.

looking up, things are looking up circumstances are getting better:—At first my business was almost on the rocks, but now things are looking up.

looks, good looks, attractiveness of face and figure:—Character in a person is often more important than good looks.

looks, lose one's looks become less attractive:—After her long illness Rosa seemed to have lost most of her looks.

loose, at loose ends uncertain, indecisive, without direction:—She seems to have been at loose ends ever since her maid left.

loose, on the loose free, unrestrained:—The convention delegates roamed the streets singing and shouting like a bunch of schoolboys on the loose.

loose See also **cut** loose; **screw**, have a screw loose.

lose face lose prestige, suffer some disgrace or embarrassment:—They say that the Japanese soldier would rather die than lose face by retreating before the enemy.

lose one's balance to fall or nearly fall, lose one's equilibrium:—Henry slipped on the ice, lost his balance, and fell.

lose one's head become excited, lose one's normal self-control:—When her front tire blew out, Mrs. Harris lost her head and swerved into an oncoming car.

lose one's mind become insane:—Robert lost his mind and was committed to an insane asylum.

lose one's temper become very angry:—It was an accident; the child didn't mean to break the dish, so there is no reason to lose your temper.

lose one's way become lost, go astray:—I know that route so thoroughly that it would be impossible for me to lose my way.

lose out lose to another, fail to obtain:—Cramer applied for the job but lost out to a man who had much more experience.

lose sight of fail to see or keep in mind, forget:—"And don't lose sight of the fact," said our chairman, "that conditions in our profession were very different twenty years ago."

lose track of lose all contact with, fail to maintain current information about:—After Jones moved to the West Coast, we lost all track of him.

lose See also **heart**, lose heart; **looks**, lose one's looks; **shirt**, lose one's shirt; **thread** lose the thread of; **touch**, lose one's touch.

loss, at a loss (1) with a loss of money, suffering a loss rather than a profit:—He finally had to sell the business at a loss. (2) unprepared, unable, perplexed:—He was at a loss to explain where he had put the documents.

loss See also **stand** the loss.

lost cause a movement which has failed and has no chance of being revived:—With the repeal of the 18th Amendment, Prohibition became a lost cause.

lost, get lost remove oneself:—When Ruth's little brother hung around Ruth and her boy friend, the couple told him to get lost.

lost upon thrown away upon:—Your generosity is completely lost upon Williams, so don't expect any appreciation from him.

louse up (sl.) spoil:—The reporter felt that his story had been loused up by his editor.

love, no love lost existence of dislike, unfriendliness:—There is obviously no love lost between those bitter rivals.

love-sick languishing in love, deeply affected by love:—Each time Bill appeared, Jennie would get that love-sick expression on her face.

love See also **fall** in love; **make** love to; **platonic** love.

low, feel low feel depressed or in low spirits:—I don't know what's the matter with me, but I've been feeling low all day today.

low, lie low hide or conceal oneself, keep from getting public notice:—Brigg's lawyer told him to lie low for a while until he was no longer news.

lowbrow a non-intellectual, a person of limited culture:—Some people claim that only lowbrows read the comics.

lowdown, get the lowdown on get the facts on, obtain the essential information about:—The police are trying to get the lowdown on what he did before he came to New York.

luck, as luck would have it fortunately or unfortunately, as it turned out:—As luck would have it, I arrived in Chicago just when my sister got there.

luck, out of luck unlucky, unfortunate, without a chance:—I told him that if he was planning on borrowing money from me he was out of luck.

luck See also **down** on one's luck; **dumb** luck; **hard** luck; **pot**, take pot luck; **run** of luck; **streak** of luck.

lulu (n.) a boner, something remarkably bad:—When Tom makes a mistake, it's a lulu.

lump in one's throat a choking feeling caused by emotion, a feeling of sadness:—The story he told about his misfortunes brought a lump to my throat.

lump it suffer it, put up with it, go to the devil (sl.):—I told him that if he didn't like what I said he could lump it.

lump sum the complete amount, a total agreed upon and to be paid at one time:—The case was settled out of court with the plaintiff receiving a lump sum for damages.

M

McCoy, the real McCoy the real or genuine article:—This imported champagne is the real McCoy.

mad about (1) angry about:—What is Henry so mad about? (2) enthusiastic about, crazy about:—He is mad about horses.

mad money money carried by a woman to be used for expenses in getting back home if she quarrels with her escort:—Whenever she goes out on a date, Hilda carries some mad money with her.

mad, drive someone mad cause someone to go crazy:—His complete lack of responsibility is enough to drive me mad.

mad, like mad furiously, energetically:—We had to work like mad to finish the work by six o'clock.

maiden speech one's first public speech—usually before some legislative body:—It was the new Congressman's maiden speech, and all eyes were upon him.

maiden voyage the first trip of a boat:—On her maiden voyage across the Atlantic the new ocean liner broke the speed record.

mail order a purchase made by mail rather than in person or by telephone:—The company which has probably the largest mail order business in the United States is the Sears Roebuck Company.

main, in the main chiefly, principally:—In the main, his speech had to do with the dangers of inflation.

make a difference be of importance:—It doesn't make any difference to me whether we have our next lesson on Tuesday or on Wednesday.

make a fool of cause one to feel foolish or humiliated:—I refused to take part in the school play because I was sure that I would simply make a fool of myself.

make a go of make a success of:—He is energetic as well as intelligent and will make a go of any business he enters.

make a hit become popular with, please highly:—The special dessert which Emma prepared made a hit with everyone at the party.

make a killing win or earn suddenly a large sum of money:—He had bought up large quantities of the wanted fabric, and when the mills stopped manufacturing it, he naturally made a killing.

make a living sustain oneself economically, earn enough to live decently:—He has no ambition to become a rich man and is satisfied if he can make a good living for himself and his family.

make a match bring about an engagement or marriage:—Mrs. Barnes is anxious to make a match between her daughter and young Dick Williams.

make a monkey out of cause to feel or appear foolish:—In the debate which followed, the crafty old politician made a monkey out of his younger opponent.

make a night of it revel, make merry—often extending the merriment throughout the entire night:—It was already three o'clock, but instead of going home we decided to make a night of it and visit one or two more nightclubs.

make a point of give importance to, insist or place emphasis upon:—He makes a point of remembering each one of our birthdays.

make a practice of do habitually:—He makes a practice of telephoning a greeting to each of his friends on Christmas Day.

make a scene create a disturbance or otherwise attract attention unfavorably:—I had to give her the money; otherwise she was capable of making a scene right there before all those people.

make a train catch a train, arrive in time to get on a train:—Hurry, or we'll never make that train.

make after chase, run after:—The cat ran from the house, and the dog made after it.

make as if pretend:—He made as if to strike me, but then grabbed my purse and ran off.

make away with steal:—The robbers made away with all the money in the safe.

make believe pretend:—Sometimes when children play they make believe they are grown up.

make book serve as a bookmaker taking bets on horses (sl.):—The police have promised to prosecute anyone caught making book illegally.

make certain be sure:—Make certain that both doors are locked when you go out.

make clear clarify, explain:—I tried to make clear to him that we were not responsible for his mistake, but he refused to listen.

make do with manage with:—Since I didn't have the right size nails, I had to make do with smaller ones.

make eyes at flirt with:—She makes eyes at every attractive man who comes to the office.

make for (1) go in the direction of:—As it had begun to rain, we turned our boat around and made for the shore. (2) conduce toward, promote:—Secret treaties of that nature do not make for better understanding between nations.

make free with use freely, treat as one's own property:—The thirsty guests made free with their host's liquor.

make friends acquire friends, enter into friendship with:—Within two days Edna had made friends with everybody on the boat.

make good succeed:—John is hard working and conscientious, and I am sure he will make good in that job.

make (something) good exchange, repair, reimburse the buyer:—If the article is defective, you should take it back to where you bought it and ask them to make good.

make good time travel at a high average rate of speed, make fast, unimpeded progress:—There was little traffic, so we made good time on our trip to Washington.

make neither head nor tail of fail to understand, get a clear idea of—usually used in the negative:—The message which had been left on my desk was so badly written that I couldn't make head nor tail of it.

make headway move forward, make progress:—Because of the determined opposition of the owners the labor union made little headway in its efforts to organize the entire industry.

make known cause to become known, communicate:—Having temporarily lost the power of speech, he had to make his wants known by gestures and signs.

make like imitate (sl.):—The clown made like a bear and frightened the little tots.

make love to express physically one's love for another:—Although he tried desperately to make love to her, she repulsed his attentions.

make merry celebrate noisily, be gay:—Everyone likes to make merry occasionally and enjoy himself, but our neighbors have parties every night until three and four o'clock in the morning.

make much of be unusually attentive to, lay much emphasis upon:—The report made much of the fact that there had not been enough cooperation among the department heads.

make no bones about speak frankly or directly without fear of the consequences:—He made no bones about telling us that if we failed to deliver the goods on time he would bring suit against us for breach of contract.

make of understand by, interpret:—What do you make of John's sudden decision to join the Army?

make off with steal, run away with:—As soon as my back was turned, he made off with my umbrella.

make one's way open one's path, proceed forward:—As soon as he saw us, Henry made his way through the crowd to greet us personally.

make oneself at home feel as one does in one's own home, make oneself comfortable:—We were asked to make ourselves at home during the brief absence of our hostess.

make or break bring complete success or failure, victory or defeat:—Mother felt that all those houses Father was building in that undeveloped community would either make or break him.

make out (1) succeed, do:—How did you make out in your last French examination? (2) identify, distinguish, decipher:—In the dark it was hard for us to make out the numbers on the houses. (3) prepare, execute a paper, or legal document, write out:—He immediately sat down and made out a check for the money he owed me. (4) understand, interpret:—Frankly, it was difficult for me to make out what he was saying. (5) pretend:—When I passed him on the corner, he made out as though he had not seen me.

make someone out to be charge someone with being something other than he is:—Don't make me out to be such a terrible ogre; I am really quite harmless.

make over (1) alter, change:—After she finished the dress she didn't like it, so she decided to make it over. (2) transfer to another:—Just before his death he made over all his property to his wife.

make passes at flirt with, caress, make amorous approaches:—A witty American writer once remarked that men never make passes at girls who wear glasses.

make ready prepare, get ready to, set up:—The women made ready the table for the refreshments at the bazaar, while the men were very busy making ready the display booths.

make room for create space for:—There were already three people sitting on the sofa, but I tried to make room for her.

make short work of do quickly, finish rapidly:—If the enemy dares to attack us in these entrenched positions, we will make short work of them.

make something do adjust to what one already has since nothing better is possible or available:—I would like to buy a new car, but I am afraid that I will have to make this one do for another year.

make sure be certain:—Make sure to turn off the radio before you go out.

make the most of take advantage of, exploit to the greatest possible degree:—It was their last night in the city, and they decided to make the most of it by going to the theater.

make the rounds go from place to place in some regular or customary manner:—The night watchman makes the rounds of the building every hour.

make tick motivate, cause to operate:—Peter is so unresponsive that I confess I don't know what makes him tick.

make up (1) constitute, form:—The committee is made up of seven members. (2) invent, fabricate:—Not having a good excuse for being late, Sally made one up. (3) renew cordial relations, become reconciled:—After their quarrel, they shook hands and made up. (4) apply cosmetics:—I don't like to see women make up in public. (5) arrange the bedclothes in proper order:—The maid knocked at the door and asked whether we wanted her to make up the bed. (6) prepare, produce:—They didn't have exactly the kind of bracelet she wanted, but they told her that they could make one up for her within a few weeks. (7) compensate for:—His intelligence made up for his lack of personal charm. (8) complete:—She had been absent from school for two weeks, so she naturally had a lot of homework to make up.

make up for atone for, compensate for:—He mistakenly thought that a string of pearls would make up for his harsh treatment.

make up one's mind decide:—He has made up his mind to go to Mexico for his vacation.

make up to flirt with, flatter, try to please:—The way she tries to make up to the boss is distasteful to us.

make way for clear a path for, prepare the way for:—A half dozen policemen were elbowing their way through the crowd trying to make way for the mayor and his party.

make, not to know what to make of something or someone be puzzled or perplexed by, be unable to classify or understand:—I had never met my boss's wife before, and I didn't know what to make of the off-color stories she told. Jim was an old friend, and I didn't know what to make of his indifference at last night's party.

make, on the make bent on attracting and attaching oneself to another:—Watch out for that divorced lawyer at the party. He is always on the make.

make See also, **best,** make the best of; **clean,** make a clean breast of; **ends,** make both ends meet; **eyes,** make eyes at; **faces,** make faces at; **fun,** make fun of; **hay,** make hay while the sun shines; **hit,** make a hit; **hum,** make things hum; **land,** make land; **light,** make light of; **little,** make little of; **money,** make money; **money,** made of money; **pile,** make one's pile; **play,** make a play for; **racket,** make a racket; **ready** made; **scarce,** make oneself scarce; **secret,** make no secret of; **self** made; **sit,** make one sit up; **stand,** make a stand; **showing,** make a showing; **snappy,** make it snappy; **splash,** make a splash; **stab,** make a stab at; **stir,** make a stir; **sweep,** make a clean sweep of; **touch,** make a touch; **water,** make one's mouth water.

making, be the making of account for the success of:—The strict discipline which he had to undergo in the army was the making of William.

makings, have the makings possess the ingredients, have the basic qualities:—He is young, but he has the makings of a first-class salesman.

makeshift a temporary substitute:—During the storm we used an old piece of canvas as a makeshift tent.

man about town a sophisticate, an idler, a member of cafe society:—Though he rarely goes anywhere, Smith reads all the society news and gossip columns and thinks of himself as quite a man about town.

man Friday (girl Friday) an assistant who aids one in every way:—They gave me the title of Sales Manager, but I was really a sort of man Friday to the director of the company.

man in the street the common man, the average citizen:—In the last analysis, it is the man in the street who will decide which of the several candidates shall be president.

man of his word a reliable person who fulfills his promises:—If Bill said he would help us, you can depend upon him to do so, because he is a man of his word.

man of letters an author, a writer:—Cronin gave up his career as a doctor to become a man of letters.

man of the world experienced, traveled, liberal in attitude:—You could tell by his conversation and his interesting references to many countries that he was a man of the world.

man-of-war a large battleship:—We sent out a call for help, and shortly a large man-of-war appeared on the horizon.

man-to-man (adj.) frank, direct:—My boss and I had a man-to-man talk about my future with the company.

man, as one man unanimously:—The audience rose as one man to applaud the newly elected president.

man, be one's own man be independent:—Unhappy at being led by a domineering boss, Carl resigned in order to be his own man.

man, to a man without exception, unanimously:—The entire outfit supported the commanding officer to a man.

man See also **best** man; **feel** like a new man; **middle** man; **working** man.

manage to do succeed in doing, arrange to do:—After several unsuccessful attempts, I finally managed to get an appointment with the person who had charge of all the personnel work.

manhunt usually an organized hunt for a criminal:—Fifty men and several dogs went on a manhunt for the killer.

manner, to the manner born reared in an atmosphere of privilege and refinement:—That ambassador is to the manner born.

many a man (also **many a person, many a child,** etc.) many men:—Many a man has had the same experience as I.

many a time (also **many a day, many a week,** etc.) many times, frequently:—Many a time I have had to wait half **an** hour for that bus.

many's the time, many times, frequently:—Many's the time that he and I went fishing together.

many, a good (great) many very many:—A great many people feel as concerned as you do about our city parks.

many, one too many one more than necessary, excessive, not needed or wanted:—I soon realized that they considered the game complete without me, and that I was one too many.

map out plan, arrange, lay out:—He will meet this week with his managers to map out his election campaign.

mark down lower the price of:—The advertisement states that all the store's summer suits will be marked down fifty per cent.

mark off lay out in sections, mark with lines:—The field will be marked off in accordance with the special track events which will take place tomorrow.

mark one's words pay close attention to what one says—an emphatic expression indicating prophecy:—Mark my words, he will never be appointed to that position.

mark time delay, wait, be kept immobilized, go through the motions of marching without moving forward:—The delegates had to mark time until the chairman arrived.

mark, make one's mark achieve one's ambition, attain a position of importance:—Despite the help given to all of them by their father, Henry was the only one of the five brothers who made his mark in the world.

marry off succeed in one's efforts to achieve matrimony for one's child:—Of their four daughters the only one they were able to marry off was Agnes, the youngest.

master key a key so constructed as to open a set of different locks:—The superintendent used his master key to open our apartment door.

master of ceremonies one who has charge of introducing the various participants in a show or entertainment:—The most amusing character was the master of ceremonies who, with his ribald jokes, was a whole evening's entertainment in himself.

mastermind (v.) to supervise, direct, create:—The police believe that it was Sutton himself who masterminded the robbery.

matter of course a question of normal routine:—We expected him to get quite excited over the news of his firstborn, but he took it as a matter of course.

matter, for that matter as far as that is concerned, as regards that:—For that matter, we can just as well go by bus and save ourselves some money.

matter, no matter (1) regardless of, in spite of:—No matter whether it is light or dark at that hour, we have decided to leave at five o'clock in the morning. (2) of no importance:—I was going to discuss this with you, but since you must leave it's no matter.

matter, something (nothing) the matter See also **what's** the matter:—The doctor says that there is nothing the matter with John, but I can't help worrying about that constant pain in his side.

matter, what's the matter what is the trouble, what is the difficulty—What's the matter with Helen? She hasn't spoken a word all day.

matter See also **fact,** matter of fact; **mince,** not to mince matters.

mean well have good intentions:—Henry generally means well, but he has a genius for being tactless.

means to an end an action leading to some end or purpose:—Money with him was just a means to an end: what he really wanted, after becoming rich, was to be able to dominate and control the political life of his city.

means, a man of means a man of wealth:—From his manner of dress and style of living, I gathered that he was a man of considerable means.

means, by all means (1) definitely, certainly—an expression indicating consent and agreement:—When I asked whether I might go in and talk with him a moment, he said, "By all means." (2) using every possible way, at all costs:—We must get there by all means before he has a chance to break the news to her.

means, by no means (1) not at all, definitely not—an expression indicating dissent and disagreement:—I was by no means convinced by his arguments. (2) not in the slightest degree:—Though he didn't say anything, we could see that he was by no means pleased with Hal's behavior.

measure off mark by measuring:—She measured off two and a half yards with which to make the dress.

measure up to reach the standards set by another:—It will take a long time before they will find someone who can measure up to that man's ability and brilliant record.

measure, have one's measure evaluate correctly, size up; also, take one's measure:—Though she had never met Harvey before, Mrs. Bates soon had his measure.

measure, in great measure largely, to a great extent:—The attack on Pearl Harbor was in great measure a factor in our decision to enter the war.

measure, without measure abundantly, unstintingly:—Her devotion without measure to our cause was something no man could deny.

medicine, give someone some of his own medicine treat someone the way he treats others:—That fellow had beaten up an old man, so that when he resisted, the policeman decided to give him a little of his own medicine.

medicine, take one's medicine accept one's punishment gracefully:—The accused, on being sentenced to such a long term, took his medicine like a man.

meet expenses be able to pay one's bills:—In order to meet his expenses, he had to do extra work at night.

meet half-way compromise:—He asked a thousand dollars for the car; I offered him five hundred, so I suppose we will end up by meeting each other half-way.

meet one's death die:—He met his death in a plane crash.

meet the eye come into view:—As one turns the corner, a large statue meets the eye.

meet with (1) have, encounter:—He met with a serious accident while driving to Chicago. (2) agree with, be in accord with:—The plan you submitted seems to meet with the committee's ideas on the subject.

melting pot a large metal receptacle used to melt down various metals, thus a vessel for fusing many different elements:—The United States has been described as the melting pot for many of the races of Europe.

mend one's fences repair the weaknesses and smooth over the difficulties and dissatisfactions that have developed among one's political supporters during one's absence—a political expression:—While Congress is in recess, most Congressmen avail themselves of the opportunity to go back home to mend their political fences.

mend one's ways reform:—Young MacDonald had better mend his ways or he is going to end up in prison like his older brother.

mend, on the mend improving in health:—The doctor says that Jim is definitely on the mend.

mention, not to mention. See **not** to mention.

mercy killing intentionally causing the death of another person, often a patient, in order to put him out of his suffering or misery:—Jenkins was indicted for the mercy killing of his incurable son.

mercy, at the mercy of dependent upon, in the power of:—After the earthquake the inhabitants of the town were at the mercy of all kinds of thieving gangs and looters.

mess around with become involved with, fool around with:—I told the child to stop messing around with that bonfire if he didn't want to get burned.

mess up soil, disarrange, upset:—Bill certainly messed up our plans when at the last minute he refused to lend us his car.

method in one's madness have some idea or plan in mind which is not so mad as it first appears:—We all thought he was crazy to threaten to leave his job; but when he was offered a partnership, we realized there had been method in his madness.

mill around move impatiently:—The crowd milled around, waiting for the arrival of their favorite actor.

mill, through the mill experienced:—You could see at a glance that the man had been through the mill.

mill See also **run** of the mill.

milquetoast (milk toast) said of a timid man:—That milquetoast never questions any of his wife's statements.

mince, not to mince words be brutally frank and direct:—My employer did not mince words in telling me he was not satisfied with my work.

mincemeat, make mincemeat of literally, chop up into fine pieces, destroy completely:—The opposing lawyer made mincemeat of the argument that a woman of her refinement could not commit such a heinous crime.

mind (v.) (1) have some objections against, object to:—Do you mind my smoking? (2) take care of, tend:—Mary has promised to mind the baby while we go out. (3) obey, pay attention to:—That child should be taught to mind his parents.

mind one's own business not to interfere in the affairs of others:—I finally got tired of his criticism and told him to mind his own business.

mind one's p's and q's act with propriety, observe all the rules of etiquette and good conduct, be wary:—It was his first experience at such a formal dinner, so he was naturally careful to mind his p's and q's.

mind the store be in charge, be responsible for the running or care of a business, store, or library:—When Dick saw three of his fellow workers also on a coffee break, he cried: "Say, who's minding the store?"

mind, give someone a piece of one's mind say exactly what one thinks, express one's opinion clearly and frankly, censure:—If she continues to slander me, some day I'm going to give her a piece of my mind.

mind, have a (good) mind to consider doing, probably intend to:—I have a good mind to turn my old car in and buy a new one.

mind, have in mind intend, plan, select:—I don't know whom he has in mind for the job.

mind, never mind (1) don't bother:—Never mind! I can do this by myself. (2) pay no attention to; it is without importance:—Never mind what John says. I am sure you and I can solve that problem by ourselves.

mind, of the same mind of the same opinion:—They are both of the same mind in not wanting to take part in the tournament.

mind, on one's mind be preoccupied with, think about constantly:—Henry has nothing but girls on his mind.

mind, out of one's mind insane:—He went out of his mind and had to be put into an institution.

mind, to one's mind in one's opinion:—To my mind that mishap to the car was as much her fault as his.

mind See also **bring** to mind; **bear** in mind; **call** to mind; **change** one's mind; **eye**, in one's mind's eye; **keep** in mind; **know** one's own mind; **lose** one's mind; **make** up one's mind; **mastermind**; **open**-minded; **presence** of mind; **prey** on one's mind; **put** in mind; **right**, in one's right mind; **set** one's mind on; **slip** one's mind; **sound**, of sound mind; **turn** over in one's mind.

mint of money a great deal of money:—We spent a mint of money on our trip to Mexico.

minute, up to the minute up-to-date:—I get the up-to-the-minute news each night on the eleven o'clock radio broadcast.

miss a trick fail to see or hear something of even the slightest importance:—When it comes to gossiping, Mrs. Williams never misses a trick.

miss out lose out, fail to be present at and to enjoy:—It's too bad you couldn't have come earlier. You missed out on a wonderful dinner.

miss, a miss is as good as a mile an escape or failure, no matter by how slight a margin, is just as effective as one where the margin is greater:—When the bullet struck just a few inches above his head, I couldn't help saying to myself: a miss is as good as a mile.

miss See also **fire, misfire; hit** or miss.

mix up (1) prepare—by mixing various ingredients:—Dinner will be ready as soon as I finish mixing up this salad dressing. (2) confuse one person or thing with another:—The teacher always mixes me up with another student of the same name. (3) be confused, perplexed:—We were clearly mixed up in our directions and at least ten miles off our route.

mixed, get mixed up See **mix up**:—We got mixed up in our directions and drove far out of the way.

mod (rhymes with sod) said of current extreme fashions in clothes, etc.:—That folk singer was wearing a mod psychedelic leather jacket.

money, for one's money as regards one's endorsement or support, as far as one is concerned:—For my money the best candidate in the field is Senator Williams.

money, in the money rich, supplied with plenty of money:—To be able to buy a home of that size one has to be in the money.

money, made of money rich:—Let's ask Mr. Jenkins to contribute. They say he is made of money.

money, make money earn money, become rich:—They say that he is making money hand over fist in the plastic business.

money, one's money's worth a fair return on money spent or invested:—I wouldn't say that the cruise was a great bargain, but I feel that we got our money's worth.

money See also **coin** money; **pin** money; **raise** money; **ready** money.

monkey business foolishness, treachery, intrigue, crime, unethical dealing:—I don't know what they are planning, but I feel that they are definitely up to some monkey business.

monkey with meddle with, fool with. Also expressed as **monkey around with**:—Stop monkeying around with that electric plug; the first thing you know you will get a shock.

month of Sunday for a very long period:—I haven't seen Jacob in a month of Sundays.

mooch (sl.) beg, solicit a cigarette, etc.:—Randy is always mooching cigarettes from me.

moonlighting having two or more jobs at different times of the day or night:—That school teacher moonlights after school in a cafeteria.

mop up (1) clean by using a mop:—The porter came and mopped up the water which had spilled on the floor. (2) disperse or liquidate isolated groups or detachments:—Our troops have captured considerable enemy territory but there still remains much mopping up work to be done.

moral support aid and comfort, good wishes:—I'll go along with you to the dentist's and give you moral support.

more or less (1) somewhat:—Naturally, I am more or less tired after such a long trip. (2) approximately:—The trip will take ten days, more or less.

more, no more (1) no longer:—They used to live at this address but no more. (2) dead:—Poor old Tom is no more.

more, what's more in addition, furthermore:—Not only did he not write the letter but, what's more, I don't believe he ever intended to.

most, for the most part in general:—I found them, for the most part, a happy contented group of people.

most See also **at** most; **make** the most of.

motion picture moving picture, a movie, **a** cinema:—Certainly motion pictures

have had a great influence upon the young people of our time.

motion, go through the motions of pretend to be doing something by making the normal motions or procedure associated with it:—Although they were going through the motions of choosing a candidate, everyone knew that Smith had already been selected in a pre-convention conference.

motion, make a motion propose in any committee meeting or legislative group that a certain action be taken:—Everyone was tired, so Bill got up and made a motion that the meeting be adjourned.

motion See also **put** in motion.

mouth, by word of through the speaking of one person with another:—Even before the newspapers had a chance to announce it officially, news of the defeat had spread everywhere by word of mouth.

mouth, down in the mouth seem depressed:—Ever since he failed to get that promotion he has been pretty much down in the mouth.

mouth, from mouth to mouth from one person to another:—Though the government tried desperately to suppress it, information about the progress of the fighting passed quickly from mouth to mouth.

mouth, have a big mouth talk too much, be too outspoken and indiscreet:—Why did you have to have such a big mouth and reveal all our private affairs?

mouth, shoot off one's mouth talk too much, talk without thinking:—Everything had been planned very carefully; then Bill had to shoot off his big mouth and tell everyone in the office that I was planning to leave.

mouth See also **bread**, take the bread out of someone's mouth; **laugh** on the other side of one's mouth; **look** a gift horse in the mouth; **poor** mouth; **straight** from the horse's mouth; **take** the words out of one's mouth; **water**, make one's mouth water.

mouthful, say a mouthful say something important, significant (sl.):—You certainly said a mouthful when you remarked that Williams is not worth half the salary we are paying him.

move away move to another home, change one's place of residence:—They used to live around here, but they moved away years ago.

move heaven and earth do everything possible, do the impossible:—He moved heaven and earth to please her, but she just did not want to stay there with him.

move in on attack, descend upon:—At a given hour detachments of troops moved in on the town from three different sections.

move on proceed on one's way, leave:—We tried to see who had been hurt, but the policeman told us to move on.

move, make a move show evidence of action, move:—The robber said that if any of us made a move he would shoot.

move, on the move active, moving:—John likes selling rather than office work because it keeps him on the move.

move See also **get** a move on.

moving, keep moving an order to pedestrians not to loiter or congregate:—In order to prevent a disturbance, the police told the people stopping near the scene of an accident to keep moving.

much the same almost the same:—The doctor says that Helen's condition is much the same.

much, not to say much for not to have a high opinion of, hold in low esteem:—The movie at Radio City this week is good, but I can't say much for the stage show.

much See also **make** much of.

mud in your eye a popular toast when drinking, meaning "Good Luck," "Good Wishes":—Each time John raised his glass he would say, "Well, here's mud in your eye."

mud See also **stick**-in-the-mud.

muff mishandle, fumble with subsequent failure:—Jack had a good chance of becoming assistant to the general-manager, but he muffed it.

mug attack from behind with intent to rob, strangle:—The newspaper reports

that two more men were mugged and robbed last night.

mull over think over, consider:—He mulled over the offer for some time but finally rejected it.

muscle in penetrate, intrude, force oneself into another's business:—Our sales fell off when our competitor's men began to muscle in on our territory.

must, a must a necessity, a requirement, something which one must see, do, or hear:—They say that the new show at the Royal Theater this week is an absolute must.

N

name dropping the habit of mentioning celebrities' names in order to give the impression that the speaker knows them intimately:—I'm tired of listening to Ted's continual name dropping.

name, by name according to name:—I probably know him by sight but not by name.

name, go by the name of, be called:—In Europe that spy went by the name of Block.

name, in the name of invoking the name of—expressing exasperation:—Why in the name of common sense did you ever say such a thing?

first name, on a first-name basis asked or permitted to call an associate or client by his first name:—Soon after he was employed, Gilbert was on a first-name basis with all his fellow workers.

name, one's good name one's personal reputation:—She was worried that the scandal might affect her good name.

name, take someone's name in vain use a name in form of a curse or oath:—The Bible says that one should not take the name of the Lord in vain.

name, to one's name belonging to one:—He hasn't a cent to his name.

named after having been given the same name as:—He was named after his father.

name See also **call** one names; **given** name; **proper** name.

narrow down limit within very strict margins:—Of the twenty applicants who originally applied for the position, the choice has now been narrowed down to three.

narrow escape an escape by a very slight margin:—It was a narrow escape; had the bullet struck one inch higher it would have penetrated his heart.

narrow-minded bigoted, limited in outlook:—Though in general a liberal, easygoing fellow, Smith is very narrow-minded when it comes to politics.

natural, come natural to be easy for:—Since several members of his family have been literary people, writing comes natural to John.

nature, by nature innately:—He is by nature a kind, generous fellow.

nature See also **second** nature.

near at hand (1) close by:—Fortunately the baby's mother was near at hand when the accident occurred. (2) soon to happen:—With my vacation near at hand, I decided to get some new clothes.

near miss See **call**, close call.

nearby not far away, close by:—They live nearby—less than a block from us.

neat job a task done well or clevely:—Janice did a neat job on that poster announcing our Christmas party.

neck (v.) kiss and hug, caress:—Bill and Helen spent the evening necking in a corner of the porch.

neck and neck even, equally distant, running even in a race:—The horses ran the whole race neck and neck.

neck, break one's neck overextend oneself, make a superhuman effort:—I broke my neck trying to get there on time and then had to wait almost an hour for them to show up.

neck, get it in the neck suffer, be punished, sustain a serious blow:—The big corporations complain about the high taxes, but in the final analysis it's the little fellow who really gets it in the neck.

neck, stick one's neck out make a move or statement that might have unplea-

sant consequences:—Perhaps Jones was unjustly fired, but I'm not going to stick my neck out and complain about such ill-treatment.

neck, up to one's neck overwhelmed with, almost submerged in:—I am up to my neck in work and won't be able to leave the office before six or seven o'clock.

need, if need be if the necessity exists:—If need be, I can come early tomorrow and work ten hours instead of the usual seven.

need, in need destitute, having need of:—He is seriously in need of medical attention. Those children from that broken home are in need.

needle (1) (v.) joke, nag, criticize (sl.):—We kept needling Bill about his new girl friend, but apparently we went too far because he suddenly got angry. (2) nag, insist on one's doing something:—Mr. Scott is being needled by his wife to buy an expensive car.

needle in a haystack See **look** for.

negative, in the negative expressed negatively, no:—I knew that his answer would be in the negative.

neither here nor there See **here.**

nest egg savings set aside for use in one's old age:—He says he doesn't have to worry about his old age because he has a nice nest egg deposited in the First National Bank.

nest, feather one's nest avail oneself of an opportunity to make oneself very comfortable, enrich oneself:—The old man always treated her generously, and she was wise enough to feather her nest well while she worked for him.

never do used in such an expression as, That will never do—and meaning: that something one has done is bad form or that some article, idea, etc., won't be suitable:—When Mr. Crane found that his young daughter had been telling family secrets to the neighbors, he said that would never do.

new blood vigor, inspiration, new leadership:—The directors chose a new president, feeling that the organization required some new blood.

new deal literally, a re-shuffling of the cards in order to effect a fairer distribution; a new and more equitable policy for remedying social and economic abuses:—President Roosevelt always referred to his program of governmental reform as "The New Deal."

new-fangled newly invented or contrived, excessively complicated:—He felt that many of the new-fangled gadgets in the modern kitchen weren't absolutely necessary.

newshawk a newspaper reporter:—There are always several newshawks hanging around those public buildings.

next door to (1) in the house alongside of:—They live next door to us. (2) close to:—Nevins had been next door to death for several weeks.

next to alongside of:—Mrs. Smith sat next to me in the theater last light.

next to nothing practically nothing, almost nothing:—On the trade-in, they gave me next to nothing for my old car.

nice try a complimentary expression used to praise a performer or athlete who has failed skillfully or artistically:—That tennis champion once failed to return his opponent's serve, but it was a nice try.

nick, in the nick of time at the last possible moment, just in time:—John arrived with the oil for our camp stove in the nick of time.

nightcap a drink taken just before bedtime, also a good-night drink:—Let's have a nightcap and then go to sleep.

night, one-night stand a single performance given by a traveling theatrical company while on a tour of widely separated cities:—Having been featured on Broadway for many years, the aging star found the succession of one-night stands somewhat beneath her dignity.

night, overnight (1) from one evening until the next morning:—By driving rapidly we could get there in one day, but we think it will be better if we stay overnight in some town along the way. (2) rapidly:—When oil was discovered on the land which he owned, he became a rich man overnight.

night See also **make a night of**; **spend the night**.

nip in the bud quell or stop at the start:—The political revolution was nipped in the bud before even a single shot was fired.

no account (1) worthless:—His opinion is of no account in this matter. (2) a person of low social station:—At first everybody considered him just another no account, but he soon proved himself to be a man of great ability and integrity.

no end greatly, without limit:—We enjoyed the concert no end.

no go without success, negative in result:—He tried several times to start the car, but it was no go.

no picnic not easy, involving many difficulties:—I assure you that working on that report and getting it ready on time was no picnic.

no-show a person who doesn't come or show up at the airport for a plane reservation he has made:—Since there were several no-shows, I was able to get a plane seat at the last moment.

no two ways about it no alternative, no other choice:—Our boss said there were no two ways about it—we would all have to work late, if the job was to be finished on time.

no wonder naturally, it is not surprising:—No wonder he plays so well. They have their own private tennis court on which he practices every day.

no, on no account absolutely not, under no circumstances:—The children were told that on no account were they to open the door to strangers.

no See also **doubt,** no doubt.

noise about (abroad) make public, to spread widely:—His many large-scale business ventures were noised about in the newspapers.

none too not at all, not very:—The doctor arrived none too soon, as Mary's high fever was very alarming.

none, have none of want no connection with, refuse to participate in:—We told him all about our plan, but he would have none of it.

nonetheless nevertheless, however:— Despite his disappointing record this year, I nonetheless feel that he is the best man we have in the department.

nope a common American pronunciation of "no":—"Nope!" he said. "I won't go with you."

nose out outdistance, win by the margin of a nose:—Just before the finish line, the horse I was betting on managed to nose out the favorite.

nose, by a nose said of a very close contest finish in which one competitor barely wins:—The horse we bet on won by a nose.

nose, follow one's nose go forward, straight ahead:—If you follow your nose you can't miss it. It's the big red house right on the corner.

nose, on the nose directly, completely accurate:—All of our estimates about the costs were a little off, but George's was right on the nose.

nose, under one's nose in one's very presence but undetected:—The thief took Mrs. Dale's pearls right from under her nose.

nose See also **cut** off one's nose to spite one's face; **lead** by the nose; **look** down one's nose; **pay** through the nose; **turn** up one's nose at.

nosey tending to interfere in other people's business, inquisitive:—Grace is one of the nosiest persons I know; she isn't happy unless she knows everyone's business.

not a few many:—Not a few readers wrote letters of commendation to the magazine.

not in the least not at all:—I was not in the least tired after the long trip.

not on your life by no means, definitely not:—Not on your life would I risk putting money into that type of business.

not the thing socially improper, not the accepted form of action:—It is simply not the thing to wear sport clothes at a formal dinner.

not to mention without mentioning, besides, in addition to:—He owns much property in New York, not to mention a large summer estate in Connecticut.

nothing doing an expression of refusal:—When I asked him to lend me his car for the afternoon, he said, "Nothing doing! I want to use it myself."

nothing short of completely, thoroughly, absolutely:—His performance in the role of the king was nothing short of (nothing less than) marvelous.

nothing, for nothing free, gratis:—I can't believe that that book club gives you one book each month for nothing.

nothing, good for nothing worthless:—While she works hard each day, her good-for-nothing husband hangs around the local bars.

nothing, there is nothing to it it's easy:—Driving a car is not difficult. There is really nothing to it.

now and then occasionally:—I see him now and then at lunch time walking along Broadway.

now that since, inasmuch as:—Now that you know exactly how he feels about it, what do you plan to do?

now, from now on from this time continuously into the future:—From now on Henry will work in another office.

number among consider to be a part of, consider as one of:—I number George among my very best friends.

number one oneself:—If you don't look after number one, then who else is going to do it?

number, have someone's number know someone well, understand his motives:—He may think he is fooling me by his friendly manner, but I have his number.

number, without number in great quantity, limitless:—Patriotic citizens without number poured their savings into government bonds.

nut, a hard nut to crack a person or thing difficult to understand:—I never knew Bill very well. He was not very communicative and always seemed to me a hard nut to crack.

nut, off one's nut crazy (sl.):—He's off his nut if he thinks that I am going to lend him that amount of money.

nuts, be nuts crazy, foolish (sl.) also often expressed as **nutty:**—You're nuts to let him use your car so often.

nuts, be nuts about enthusiastic about, keen about (sl.):—He's nuts about baseball.

nuts, go nuts become crazy (sl.):—I'll go nuts if he doesn't turn off that radio soon.

nutshell, in a nutshell briefly:—And that, in a nutshell, is the story of his hunting expeditions.

O

oar, put in one's oar interrupt, interfere, meddle:—He is prejudiced against you, and if you put in your oar, it will spoil everything.

oars, rest on one's oars stop working, rest:—He explained that if we expected to finish in time we couldn't rest on our oars.

obliged, be obliged to have to, must, be required to:—She was obliged to go back to work in order to help meet the family expenses.

obliged, be obliged to one be in someone's debt, an expression acknowledging a favor received:—We are very much obliged to you for your help.

occasion, have occasion for have need for:—We had no further occasion for her services and therefore lost track of her.

occasion, have occasion to have reason to:—I haven't seen him in months, because I have had no occasion to call at his office.

occasion, on occasion occasionally, now and then:—I meet him on occasion at the club, or on the golf links.

occasion, take the occasion to avail oneself of the opportunity to:—Let me take this occasion to thank you publicly for all you have done for our church.

occasion See also **equal** to the occasion; **rise** to the occasion.

occupy oneself be busy with, make oneself busy with:—Having retired from business he now occupies himself with his garden.

occur to come to one's mind, suggest itself:—It just occurred to me that if we want to go to the seashore for our vacation we had better make reservations in advance.

oceans of lots of, very much:—In her letter she sent him oceans of love.

odd ball eccentric person:—No wonder Wilson isn't married. He's too much of an odd ball to appeal to any woman.

odd jobs work which is not steady or regular in nature, small isolated tasks:—He does odd jobs for people in the neighborhood and in that way earns enough to live on.

odds and ends remnants, miscellaneous items:—From the various odds and ends of information which he picked up, the reporter was able to piece together the whole story.

odds are against the chances or probabilities are not favorable:—The odds are strongly against his getting here before Saturday.

odds, at odds with at variance with, angry with, in disagreement with:—The partners have been at odds with each other over hiring a new manager.

off, be off (1) be in error, miscalculate:—The contractor was off at least a thousand dollars in his estimate. (2) leave:—He stayed only long enough to eat and then was off. (3) crazy:—I'm sure she is a little off; no one in her right mind would ever say such things. (4) canceled, terminated:—He told me that the trip was off. cf. **call off** (5) free from work, having time off:—It was true that we were off for the afternoon, but it rained too hard for use to go out.

off and on occasionally, now and then:—we don't go to the theater regularly, just off and on.

off-beat not in the regularly traveled routes, different, unusual:—Jess took us to an off-beat restaurant in the Village.

off-Broadway said of theaters located away from New York's central theatrical district and where the admission prices and overheard are lower:—"Man of La Mancha" was originally an off-**Broadway** production.

off-color risque, salacious, vulgar:—I felt that some of the jokes which the speaker told were a little off-color.

off day a period when one is not functioning at his best:—Bill was obviously having an off day; otherwise he would have been able to defeat Jenkins at tennis.

off guard unalerted, unpoised:—The lawyer cleverly caught the witness off guard and forced him to admit several damaging facts.

offhand (1) unprepared, impromptu, speaking generally:—Offhand, I would say that there were about two hundred people present. (2) casual, lacking formality, careless:—I could see that his rather offhand manner was annoying to the others.

off one's rocker crazy:—There is no question that he is off his rocker, but he is not sufficiently violent to be placed in an institution.

offshoot a derivative, a side shoot:—The development of the atomic bomb was an offshoot of discoveries in nuclear physics.

off the cuff from memory, impromptu:—That reporter told me about the next day's lead story off the cuff.

off, go off the deep end go to an extreme, do something radical in nature:—Just because the couple quarreled was no reason for the husband to go off the deep end and leave town.

off See also **get** something off one's chest: **see** one off; **well** off.

office, carry or have one's office in one's hat have no regular office, keep all business memoranda in one's pocket:—That magazine salesman carries his office in his hat.

offspring children:—If his offspring are anything like him, I pity them.

oil, burn the midnight oil work late at night:—Only by burning the midnight oil will I be able to finish writing my thesis before the end of the semester.

oil See also **pour** oil on troubled waters; **strike** oil.

O.K. satisfactory, acceptable:—He said it would be O.K. to leave the packages here.

okay, to okay approve put one's O.K. upon:—The company finally okayed our plan.

old country some part of Europe as distinct from the United States:—His wife was born here, but he is from the old country.

old maid an unmarried woman no longer young, a spinster:—If she doesn't find someone to marry soon, she'll be an old maid before she knows it.

old-timer an old person who reminisces about his youth:—There was an old-timer present who told of his experiences as a boy in the Pacific Northwest.

old world Europe, the continent—also continental in manner, courtly:—He had an old-world manner that quite charmed all the ladies in our group.

old, of old of ancient times:—The book contained many tales of knights of old.

old See also **hand,** old hand.

olive branch a symbol of peace, an overture of peacemaking:—Tired of the constant quarreling, Robinson finally extended the olive branch to his neighbor.

on and on continuously, without limit:— She talked on and on telling us all about her farm in the country.

on edge nervous, in a state of anxiety:— With so much depending upon the decision of the court, the litigants naturally felt on edge.

on one's own dependent upon one's own resources for support, independent:— "From now on you are on your own. You can expect no more help from me," his father told him.

on, be on in operation, being presented:— The feature picture is on now. It will go off in an hour.

on, be on to understand one's real motives, be undeceived:—He brags a great deal about how influential his family is, but we're all on to him.

on See also **bring** on; **call** on; **hand,** on the other hand; **purpose,** on purpose; **take** on; **time,** on time; **toes,** be on one's toes.

once and for all definitely, finally, permanently:—She told him that he must stop, once and for all, telephoning her at such late hours.

once in a while occasionally:—They go out together once in a while but not very often.

once-over an appraising look, a survey:—Everyone in the office gave the new secretary the once-over.

once over lightly superficially:—Our cleaning woman dusts all our furniture once over lightly. See **lick** and a promise.

once upon a time once (a conventional beginning of a story):—Once upon a time there were three bears.

one and all everyone, unanimously:—The party was enjoyed by one and all.

one and the same the same, identical:—Mark Twain and Samuel Clemens were one and the same person.

one at a time each separately:—He asked them to come to his office one at a time.

one by one separately, in single file:—The jury filed back into the courtroom one by one.

one-horse small, insignificant, provincial:—It's a one-horse town that doesn't boast of even one good motel.

one of these days sometime in the future:—One of these days I'm going to drive through Yellowstone National Park.

one, at one with in agreement with:—I am at one with Chester in his belief that the Supreme Court will find that law unconstitutional.

oneself, be oneself act naturally:—If she would only be herself instead of putting on so many airs, she would be more liked by the other girls.

one-shot a single try for something, said of an advertisement, a mailing, etc.:—That paid advertisement pleading for peace moves by Congress was a one-shot insertion.

open air outdoors, in the open:—On Wednesday, we attended an open-air concert at the Hollywood Bowl.

open and above board without concealment, open, honest:—I don't know why, but I had the feeling that they were not entirely open and above board with us.

open and shut case a legal case having few complications, obvious in outcome:—The lawyer had felt all along that it was an open and shut case in favor of his client.

open country unenclosed terrain, flat sparsely populated country:—After a half hour's ride on the train, we emerged into open country.

open-handed generous, liberal:—Although he himself never had much money, he was always very open-handed with those who needed help.

open house See **keep** open house.

open letter a public message in the form of a letter, addressed to a particular person or to a group:—This morning's newspaper printed an open letter to the President in which the Senator from our state criticized some of the provisions of the new tax law.

open market goods or securities available for purchase by all:—All stock in that family corporation is held privately and is not available on the open market.

open-minded liberal in attitude, fair, not prejudiced:—He is not a very religious man, but he is open-minded and respects the religious beliefs of others.

open on to give upon or have a view of:—Our hotel bedroom had a rear door which opened on to a long porch.

open question an undecided, debatable issue:—Whether mercy killing is justifiable is still an open question despite the recent prosecutions which have been concerned with such killings.

open secret something not officially announced or disclosed but nevertheless known to everyone:—That Mr. Miller earns much of his money through gambling is an open secret in our town.

open sesame an easy access, an immediate means of entrance:—He mistakenly supposed that his wealth would prove an open sesame to Washington society.

open shop a factory employing both union and non-union labor:—Throughout the negotiations the company insisted on its right to continue with its policy of an open shop.

open up (1) intensive form of "open":— After we had opened up the package, we found that it had nothing in it of importance. (2) disclose, reveal, become articulate, talk:—We tried to question him about the purpose of his new mission abroad, but the ambassador refused to open up.

open, leave open remain undecided, temporarily unsettled:—He said that the matter of salary would be left open and would depend upon the qualifications of the man selected for the job.

open, out in the open See **come** out in the open.

open See also **arms**, with open arms; **eye** opener; **fire**, open fire.

operator businessman, sometimes with the inference of tricky or dishonest:— That vice-president is a smart operator.

opportunity shop a store where second-hand merchandise donated for charity is sold:—We bought that used Oriental rug in an opportunity shop.

opposite sex the sex different from the one being discussed or mentioned:—He had never displayed any interest in the opposite sex.

order around (about) domineer, dictate arrogantly to:—He orders his assistants around in a way that is very offensive.

order, made to order prepared according to measurement, opposite of ready made:—He has all his suits made to order.

order See also **apple** pie order; **call** to order; **large** order; **mail** order; **out** of order; **standing** order; **take** orders; **under** orders.

other day recently, one day in the past:— I met Tom on the street the other day.

other than except:—They were given nothing other than dry bread and water for their evening meal.

other, every other every second one:— The doctor visits her every other day.

other, just the other way just the opposite. Also sometimes expressed as **the other way around:**—You would think that John would have been the courageous one and Janet the timid one, but it was just the other way (the other way around).

out-and-out complete, thorough:—That law is an out-and-out infringement of our civil rights.

out from under clear of, released from:— Henry was greatly in debt due to his illnesses, and it took him years to get out from under.

out of for reasons of, from:—He did it out of gratitude for all she had done for him.

out of action inactive, useless, so crippled or damaged as to be harmless:—With one torpedo the heavy cruiser was put completely out of action.

out of breath, breathless, without breath, panting:—After running up so many flights of steps, she was completely out of breath.

out of commission not working, out of order:—It was only a slight jar, but apparently it was enough to put the radio out of commission.

out of date (fashion) not in style, having passed from the current mode:—The streetcar is now definitely out of date.

out of doors outside, in the fresh air:— The doctor says that John should spend more time out of doors.

out of keeping with not consistent with, incongruous, not in harmony with:— The one modern chair seemed to be out of keeping with rest of the room, which was in the Victorian period.

out of order not in working condition:— Our refrigerator is out of order.

out of place (1) not in its proper position: —I saw at once that someone had entered my office because several of the chairs were out of place. (2) tactless, in bad social form:—Bill's smoking-room stories were decidedly out of place in that mixed gathering.

out of pocket suffer a loss of, poorer by:
—Not only did I fail to enjoy the evening, but I was out of pocket more than twenty-five dollars.

out of practice lacking in practice and skill:—Henry was badly out of practice and consequently gave his tennis opponent little competition.

out of print no longer available, not being published at present:—The book I was looking for was out of print.

out of season (1) not growing abundantly in the season described:—Peaches are expensive in winter, because they are out of season. (2) protected against hunters and fishermen:—The fisherman knew that trout were out of season, but he landed such a beautiful specimen that he was strongly tempted to keep it.

out of shape (1) having lost its original shape or form:—My hat was so out of shape after the rain that I decided to have it blocked. (2) in poor physical condition; also expressed as **out of condition:**—Due to long inactivity, that heavyweight boxer is so badly out of shape that he needs at least three months' training before he can fight again.

out of sight not within the field of sight:—Slowly the airplane flew out of sight.

out of sorts irritable, cross:—We were all tired and out of sorts the next day because of lack of sleep.

out of step not in unison with:—In their refusal to modernize their office, they are out of step with the times.

out of the ordinary unusual:—The restaurant was handsome, but the dinner itself was nothing out of the ordinary.

out of the question impossible:—He said that it was out of the question for them to commit themselves to such a large expenditure at this time.

out of the way not within the ordinary route of traffic, isolated, unusual:—We often go to a little out-of-the-way restaurant on Second Avenue which we find quite charming.

out of the woods no longer in danger, in the clear:—The doctor says that Jean is much better but is still not out of the woods.

out of touch with not in communication with:—We have been out of touch with each other ever since we left college.

out of wedlock not in the married state, of unmarried parents:—The child was born out of wedlock.

out of work unemployed, without work:—John has been out of work for several months.

out to intent upon doing, planning to do:—The police feel that, having been so successful here, the gang may be out to commit a series of similar robberies in nearby towns.

out, be out (1) suffer a loss of, be poorer by:—Unless more people came to the dance, we saw that we were going to be out at least two hundred dollars. (2) not at home or at one's place of business:—When I telephoned, they told me that Jack was out. (3) impossible, not acceptable, not to be considered:—I suggested that we put on more salesmen, but the boss said that such a thing was positively out. (4) published, in circulation:—He says that his new book won't be out for another two or three months. (5) a baseball term indicating that a player has been declared out of play:—Everyone thought he was safe at third, but the umpire said he was out.

out, have an out have an excuse, or a means of escape:—I despise Sam, and when he invited me to his birthday party, I was glad that I had an out—a previous engagement.

out of, be out of lacking a supply of. See also **run** out of:—I believe that we are out of gas.

outs, be on the outs (with) in disagreement with, not to be on speaking terms with:—They have been on the outs ever since they had that dispute over the damage to the fence.

out See also **hand,** get out of hand; **have** it out with; **head,** be out of one's head; **limb,** out on a limb; **mind,** out of one's mind; **stick** out; stick it out; **throw** out.

outer-directed said of persons who act according to outside influences, opposite of inner-directed:—Most salesmen are outer-directed.

outside of excepting:—Outside of psychology, there isn't a single subject in my present program which I don't enjoy studying.

outside, at the outside at the maximum:— The trip will not cost you more than two hundred dollars at the outside.

over again once more, again:—The teacher suggested that I write the composition over again.

over and above besides, in addition to:— I had to give the lawyer one hundred dollars for expenses over and above the fee agreed upon.

over-all comprehensive, all inclusive:— What is needed is an over-all plan to improve the operation of that department.

over and over many times, repeatedly, often expressed as **over and over agair** —He kept playing the same record over and over until I had to leave the room.

over one's head beyond one's comprehension:—He tried valiantly, but calculus was simply over his head.

over the counter said of securities not listed and handled on the big stock exchanges:—There are many speculative penny stocks sold over the counter.

over the hump past the dangerous or disagreeable part of a recovery:—Last year at this time that lunch-counter proprietor was nearly bankrupt, but now he is over the hump.

over, be over be finished, ended:—The meeting was over before ten o'clock.

overplay one's hand overextend oneself, reveal one's strategy through over-eagerness:—Though our prices were lower and our product better, we overplayed our hand, so that our competitors were awarded the contract.

own up confess, admit:—Little William finally owned up to having taken his brother's ball.

own, be on one's own be independent, self-supporting:—Ever since her father's death, Mary had been on her own.

own See also **hold** one's own.

P

pace, set the pace establish the speed at which others must follow:—He was accustomed to hiking and had set a pace which none of the rest of us could maintain.

pace See also **keep** pace with; **put** one through his paces.

pack off send away, usually hurriedly:— When September arrives, we will pack off the children to boarding school and then we'll have a little more time to entertain.

pack up prepare as in a package, pack one's trunk or suitcase for traveling:— Without giving us a chance to explain, he suddenly packed up and left.

pack, a pack of a lot of:—What he **told** you was a pack of lies.

package deal a sale or contract in which several items are sold together:—We bought two cars and a truck in a package deal that saved us a lot of money.

packed crowded:—By the time we arrived the movie theater was packed with schoolchildren.

paddle one's own canoe be independent, direct one's own course of destiny:— Living so far away, he could no longer depend upon his parents and had to learn to paddle his own canoe.

pain in the neck someone or something extremely disagreeable, unpleasant:— As a friend he is not bad, but as an employer, he is a pain in the neck.

pains, be at pains to taking the trouble to, extremely desirous to:—He was at pains to see that no one was left out.

pain, on pain of subject to the penalty of: The conspirators had to promise, on pain of death, not to reveal the plot.

pains, take pains put forth great effort, proceed with great care and attention: —It was clear that our hostess had taken great pains with the preparations for the party.

paint the town red celebrate, indulge in riotous fun through a visit to nightclubs, cabarets, etc.:—Every time he comes to New York, he wants to paint the town red.

pair off separate in pairs or couples:—After dinner the boys and girls paired off and went to the dance.

palm off foist upon, cheat, pass something spurious to another:—He tried to palm off the painting as a genuine Cezanne, but the dealer's suspicions were aroused by the low price he asked.

palm, grease the palm bribe:—Apparently, he obtained that road contract by greasing the palms of a few officials.

palm, have in the palm of one's hand control completely:—Langer felt that if he could gain control of the dissatisfied elements, he would have the organization in the palm of his hand.

pan criticize severely:—Despite the fact that all the critics had panned it, the show continued to attract theatergoers.

pan out develop, result, turn out:—His plans to remodel our house did not pan out very well.

pan See also **flash** in the pan.

pant for desire deeply:—The comedian's antics left the audience panting for more of the same.

paper the house give away many free tickets to a play or concert:—Since that pianist was not very well-known, his agent papered the house.

par, up to par up to standard, approaching a normal standard or degree. See **below par**:—I haven't felt up to par ever since I had that bad cold last winter.

parallel, draw a parallel make a comparison:—It is easy to draw a parallel between the careers of, say, Hitler and Stalin, but that doesn't mean that all dictators are alike.

parcel out divide into smaller sections:—The territory was too extensive for any one purchaser, so it was parceled out among a dozen or so small buyers.

pare down reduce, limit, economize:—With less money coming in, they had to pare down their household expenses.

park (v.) to align and station an automobile along the curb:—You can't park within fifteen feet of a fire hydrant.

parlay increase the amount of one's wealth by investing and reinvesting:—That broker parlayed $1,000 into $20,000 by investing in rising stocks.

Parkinson's Law a humorous but plausible "law" stating that as an organization's inefficiency increases the number of its employees increases also:—That country handled a million pieces of mail with 500 employees in 1930. Today it handles less mail and employs over 1,000 workers, in accordance with Parkinson's Law.

parrot-fashion through memory or imitation—to learn as does a parrot without regard to meaning:—It was a speech which had obviously been prepared for him, and he read it parrot-fashion.

part and parcel a basic portion, an integral part:—His stinginess is part and parcel of his nature.

part by part one part after another:—The mechanic examined the motor part by part.

part company separate from one another:—After their quarrel they parted company and didn't see each other again for years.

part with relinquish, give up, separate oneself from:—Though we offered the old farmer more than the chair was worth, even as a genuine antique, he refused to part with it.

part, do one's part perform one's share, do what is expected of one:—If everyone will promise to do his part, the program will certainly be a success.

part, for my part as far as I am concerned, to the extent of my interest:—You can go with them if you like, but for my part I prefer to save my money by staying at home.

part, in part partly, to an extent:—The responsibility was in part mine.

part, on the part of by, from:—I don't think we need fear any interference on the part of those who objected to the proposal.

part, play a part in be concerned with, have a role in:—Lincoln's stepmother played a great part in his life and in his ultimate success.

part, take in good part accept in good spirit, be a good sport:—Although the principal and some of the teachers were lampooned in the school play, they took it all in good part.

part, take part in participate in:—John takes part in many school activities.

part, take the part of (1) act the role of: —William will take the part of Hamlet in the school play. (2) defend, stand up for:—When the teacher began to complain about John's bad conduct at school, John's mother naturally took his part.

parts of speech the various grammatical categories into which words are grouped:—The eight parts of speech in English are as follows: noun, pronoun, verb, adverb, adjective, preposition, conjunction, and interjection.

part See also **most, for the most part.**

partial to favorable toward, having a weakness for:—Bill seems to be partial to blondes, while his brother is partial to brunettes.

particular, in particular especially:—I enjoyed in particular the singing of Miss Hamilton.

party to a participant in, concerned with: —The government is now trying to prove that Spencer was a party to the irregular practices it was investigating.

pass a law approve a law in some legislative body:—The law against lotteries has already been passed and is now awaiting the President's signature.

pass a remark make some derogatory statement or remark:—He passed a remark about Bill's religious affiliations that I found quite objectionable.

pass around distribute among a group, circulate from one to another:—Why doesn't he pass around the cake to the guests?

pass away die:—Our director passed away at eight o'clock last night; it was a great shock to all of us.

pass by (1) pass alongside of:—I passed by your house last night at about ten o'clock. (2) pass alongside of without noticing, ignore:—He passed me by as though he had never in his life seen me before.

pass for be considered as, be taken for:— With his dark skin Frank could easily pass for an Italian or a Spaniard.

pass judgment judge, express an unfavorable opinion about:—I don't believe we should pass judgment in this matter until we have all the facts.

pass muster be satisfactory, acceptable in accordance with some standard:—I should say that his work in French up to this point would hardly pass muster.

pass off (1) disappear gradually:—I often get headaches, but they seem to pass off in a little while. (2) ignore, treat as inconsequential:—Though the drop in sales was serious, the sales-manager passed it off with a shrug, saying that it was nothing but the usual seasonal decline. (3) deceive, cheat, pass something spurious to another:—The forger was caught by the police trying to pass off some counterfeit money to an unsuspecting storekeeper.

pass on (1) go to another through inheritance:—At his death all his property will pass on to his son. (2) give or convey to another:—The money was passed on from one to another until it reached the conductor's hands. (3) die. See **pass away:**—He passed on quietly at his home last night.

pass out faint, lose consciousness:—I knew that if he took one more drink he would pass out on us.

pass over ignore, disregard:—We decided that it was wiser to pass over his insulting remark rather than call further attention to it.

pass the time spend one's time:—Confined to his bed for a whole week, Smith passed the time catching up on his reading.

pass the time of day greet, chat with briefly:—I really don't know him very well because, although I have spoken to him a number of times, it was only to pass the time of day.

pass up forego, reject:—It was a good offer, and Bill naturally didn't feel like passing it up.

pass upon judge, express an opinion upon. See **pass judgment**:—He said that he wanted his wife to pass upon the car before he bought it.

pass, a pretty pass a critical state, an unfortunate condition:—While he was away, things at the office had come to a pretty pass.

pass See also **buck**, pass the buck; **come to pass**; **hat**, pass the hat; **let** pass; **make** passes at.

past See also **put**, not to put it past someone.

past master an expert, one with a complete mastery of an art:—Helen is a past master at bridge.

pat, have something down pat to know or to have memorized something perfectly:—Everyone except Tim had his part down pat.

pat See also **stand** pat.

patch up mend, reconcile:—We decided to patch up our differences and become friends again.

patch, not a patch on not to be compared with:—His playing is not a patch on that of Heifetz.

pave the way for lead up to, prepare the approach to:—Harriman's withdrawal from the campaign paved the way for Stevenson's nomination.

pay a call visit:—We have to pay a call on an old friend of ours tonight.

pay attention to heed, be alert to:—If he paid more attention to what the teacher says, he might make better progress.

pay (one's) attentions to court, woo:—The newspapers report that at the moment he is paying his attentions to an Italian countess.

pay court to shower with attentions, woo:—He paid court to her for at least two years before she agreed to marry him.

pay dirt something extremely profitable, that which gives sudden riches:—When he invested in that property in Texas, he really struck pay dirt.

pay down give as a deposit on some time payment:—How much did you have to pay down on the car?

pay lip service to agree with, or endorse outwardly but secretly to disdain, be insincere:—Naturally, they must pay lip service to the policy of the organization; otherwise, they would find themselves very unpopular.

pay off (1) give one's final pay and discharge:—After we had come to terms, we discovered that we didn't have enough money in the bank to pay him off. (2) discharge a debt completely:—It took him six years to pay off that judgment.

pay-off the climax, culmination point:—They had been quarreling all evening, but the pay-off came when she accused him of starting the quarrel.

pay one back in his own coin retaliate:—He once refused me help when I needed it, and I hope that some day I may have the chance to pay him back in his own coin.

pay one's own way pay one's own expenses:—Each of us paid his own way on the trip.

pay one's respects to discharge one's social obligations by calling upon:—One of these nights, we must go and pay our respects to our new neighbor across the road.

pay out disburse, make payment:—During this month, we have paid out more than two thousand dollars in commissions alone.

pay the piper suffer for one's fun and extravagances:—No one can live the wild kind of life he has lived for years without expecting some day to pay the piper.

pay through the nose pay dearly, pay for more than value received:—Going into that business at such a time was a costly error, and Smith has been paying through the nose ever since.

pay up settle one's bill, pay all arrears:—It has taken us two years to settle that loan, but at last we are paid up.

pay, the devil to pay severe penalty, great commotion and abuse:—If we don't have this work ready before five o'clock, there will be the devil to pay. See also **take-home** pay.

payola (sl.) money paid secretly for unauthorized or illegal favors:—That radio station will play a certain manufacturer's recordings as often as he likes provided he comes across with the payola.

peace, hold one's peace remain quiet, refrain from speaking out:—He told one lie after another, and it was only with the greatest effort that I was able to hold my peace.

peace, keep the peace retain order, refrain from riotous brawls:—The judge warned them to either keep the peace, or be prepared to go to jail.

peace pipe a sign of peace-making, the pipe of friendship smoked by Indian tribes after making peace:—It is about time that both groups got together and smoked the peace pipe.

pearls, cast pearls before swine waste by lavishing something of value on those who cannot appreciate it:—They are very unappreciative guests and to serve them so lavishly is to cast pearls before swine.

peas, as like as two peas exactly alike, closely similar:—In both appearance and manner, the two brothers are as like as two peas in a pod.

peel off (1) fall off in flakes or layers:—The paint on our house is peeling off in several places. (2) remove an outer covering:—As the sun grew hotter, Frank peeled off his coat first and later his shirt.

peeled, keep one's eyes peeled be alert, watch carefully:—Keep your eyes peeled and see if you can find out who owns that car parked in front of our house.

Peeping Tom one who peeps furtively into the bedroom or home of another, one having prurient curiosity:—Several women have complained to the police about the presence in the neighborhood of a Peeping Tom.

peg away work hard at, persevere:—To write a book or a novel one must keep pegging away at it consistently, day after day, week after week.

peg, take down a peg to humble, lower in esteem:—It certainly took her down a peg to be transferred to that small office.

peg See also **square** peg.

penny-wise and pound foolish careful about small amounts, but careless in large amounts:—Isn't he penny wise and pound foolish to buy that expensive automobile, and yet claim he can't afford a good pair of shoes?

penny See also **pretty** penny; **turn** a pretty penny.

per se in itself:—Alcohol per se is harmless enough: it is only when taken in excess that it becomes dangerous.

perfect sometimes used in the sense **of** "complete" as in the expressions **perfect stranger, perfect fool,** etc.:—That man was a perfect stranger to me.

perfect See also **letter** perfect.

period! used for emphasis or finality:—I'm not going to take you to the theater, period!

perk up regain one's confidence and usual good spirits:—For several days our dog lay in a corner, listless and inactive, but yesterday he began to perk up.

person, in person personally, in the flesh:—The announcement says that Bing Crosby will appear in person at the Paramount Theater next week.

personal, become (get) personal make personal, inquisitive, abusive remarks:—No one paid any attention to him until he began to get personal; then Helen promptly told him to keep his remarks to himself.

pet name an abbreviated or special name indicating affection:—He never addressed his wife by her real name, but always with such pet names as "Honey," "Sugar," "Doll," etc.

peter out die down, diminish, fail:—For a while that record was very popular, but suddenly the demand just petered out.

Peter, rob Peter to pay Paul take from one to give to another:—He took money from the fund for his daughter's education to send his son to a more expensive school; to me this seemed like robbing Peter to pay Paul.

petty larceny a theft of property valued at less than five hundred dollars:—When it was proven that he had taken only a watch, he was convicted of petty rather than grand larceny.

petty See also **cash,** petty cash.

pew, in the wrong pew in the wrong location:—We took our seats in the church, but soon the usher told us there was a mistake and that we were in the wrong pew.

phony fraudulent, dishonest, not genuine. Sometimes spelled **phoney:**—As soon as I saw him I knew that he was a phony, and that the business deal he offered was as phony as he.

photo-finish a close finish in a race where the camera must decide the result:—The brown horse won in a photo-finish.

pick a bone with See **bone,** have a bone to pick with.

pick a lock open a lock without the regular key, open illegally, burglarize:—They got into the apartment by picking the lock.

pick a quarrel seek the opportunity for a quarrel or fight:—When he gets a little drunk, he begins to pick a quarrel with whoever is at hand.

pick holes in criticize severely, find the weak spots in:—As presented, the bill was poorly drawn, and the Republican opposition in the House immediately began to pick holes in it.

pick-me-up a drink or other stimulant taken to relieve weakness or fatigue:—He obviously needed a pick-me-up, so we mixed him a good stiff highball.

pick off shoot or kill one by one:—Two of our snipers, hidden in the brush, kept picking off enemy soldiers as they emerged from the dugout.

pick on (1) nag, criticize insistently, annoy:—She makes his life miserable, picking on him for the slightest thing.

(2) choose, select as a victim:—Why doesn't he pick on someone his own size?

pick one's teeth clean one's teeth with a toothpick:—It is bad form to pick one's teeth in public.

pick one's way walk carefully amid obstacles:—Only someone knowing the terrain intimately could have picked his way through all that underbrush.

pick out choose, select:—My wife is going with me to help me pick out a new suit.

pick over handle, sort and select:—When I arrived at the bargain counter, the best items of merchandise had already been picked over.

pick to pieces analyze, criticize, find fault with:—As soon as she left the room, the other girls began to pick her to pieces.

pick up (1) lift or raise with the fingers:—He picked up the ashtray and put it on the table. (2) improve:—After a slow summer season, business began to pick up. (3) offer or give a ride to someone:—The motorist picked up a couple of servicemen along the highway and took them as far as Buffalo. (4) become acquainted with, make friends with, without having been formally introduced:—The police question whether the murdered man knew the girl previously; they feel that she is someone he picked up somewhere in a bar. (5) learn, acquire:—He never studied French; what he knows he picked up while living in France. (6) begin again, start afresh:—His wife had carried on his business while he was in the army so that when he came back he was able to pick up exactly where he had left off. (7) gain speed:—This car has a very rapid pick-up. It picks up speed with just a touch of the accelerator. (8) find, locate, secure:—Can you tell me where I might pick up a good used car?

pickle, in a pickle in a quandary, in a difficult situation:—With no spare to use as a replacement, I was certainly in a pickle when my front tire blew out.

picture window a large unpaned glass window, usually in the living room, that frames a natural scene:—From our neighbor's picture window you can see the lake and the hills surrounding it.

picture, get the picture understand, have sufficient information:—Tell me why Jacob left that good job. I don't get the picture.

picture, out of the picture rejected, no longer a possibility or in the running:— From the very beginning I felt that the tall girl was out of the picture, and that Joan would win the prize.

pidgin English simplified form of English used as a language of trade:—It is said that the amount of formal business carried on in the Far East through the use of pidgin English is enormous.

piece by piece one piece at a time, part by part:—The first step is to dismantle the bookcase piece by piece.

piece out combine with, extend by use of a substitute:—Lacking sufficient new lumber to finish the shed, we had to piece out what we had with boards from an old fence.

piece together assemble, form a whole from various component parts:—From the bits of scattered evidence he had picked up here and there, the detective was finally able to piece together the whole story of the crime.

piecework work paid for in accordance with the quantity produced:—Ellen says she prefers to work on a piecework basis because she earns more in this way than if she were given a regular salary.

piece, of a piece consistent with, connected with:—Her recent indifference to her work is of a piece with her troubled mental state.

pieces, in pieces broken:—The crystal vase was shattered in pieces when it fell off the shelf.

piece See also **fall** to pieces; **go** to pieces; **mind,** give someone a piece of one's mind; **pick** to pieces; **pull** to pieces.

pig-headed stubborn:—He is so pig-headed that it is useless to try to reason with him.

pig in a poke something purchased without being examined beforehand:—When I tried to use the percolator the man

had sold me, I regretted that I had bought a pig in a poke, because it was defective.

pigeon-hole one of the small compartments in a desk or cabinet—also, to set aside, defer consideration of:—He learned that the plan he submitted had been pigeon-holed till next year.

pigskin the leather used in making a football, therefore, a football:—When Bill picked up the pigskin and ran ninety yards for a touchdown, the crowd roared.

pile up grow greatly in quantity, assume the proportions of a pile, accumulate:— I almost regretted having gone away, because my work had piled up to such an extent that it took me days to catch up.

pile, make one's pile make one's fortune: —He made his pile in stock-market investments.

pill, a bitter pill for one to swallow a disappointing and humiliating situation which one must of necessity accept:— To see his worst enemy get the position which Bill had tried so hard to obtain was a bitter pill for him to swallow.

pin back someone's ears chastise, defeat completely, best (sl.):—Maybe the Mets won today's game, but tomorrow we'll pin their ears back.

pin down (1) bind to an agreement:—He tried to pin me down to a definite promise to write that letter. (2) confront with evidence admitting of no further evasion:—When they finally pinned him down, he admitted having been born in Germany.

pin money extra money used for incidentals:—She has a regular job, but she earns pin money by selling Christmas cards.

pin one's faith on trust, depend upon:— We pinned our faith on Mary Winslow from our town to win the scholarship, and she did.

pin something on another person assign or transfer the blame for a mistake or crime to another:—John's boss made an error that cost the firm a large sum, and he tried to pin it on John.

pin up raise or attach with pins:—Each time my wife buys a new dress and the skirt is too long, I have to pin up the hem for her.

pin-up girl an attractive girl whose picture is tacked or pinned to the wall by an admirer:—Hollywood actresses are naturally popular pin-up girls among our soldiers.

pins, on pins and needles in a state of great excitement or suspense:—I was on pins and needles all evening until he finally telephoned.

pinch hit for substitute for:—Last night at our club meeting I had to pinch hit for our chairman, who happens to be out of town on business.

pinch, feel the pinch suffer from lack of money:—Ever since our neighbor's husband lost his job, his family has been feeling the pinch.

pinch, in a pinch in an emergency:—He is a good Spanish teacher, and in a pinch he can even teach German.

pine away waste away with grief:—After her son went into the army she pined away for him to such an extent that her health began to suffer.

pine for long for, desire, think fondly of: —During these hot summer spells I begin to pine for the cool Maine woods and those evenings spent out in the open.

pink, in the pink at the highest point of perfection:—Both fighters claim to be in the pink. He seems to be in the pink of health once more.

pipe down be quiet (sl.):—Though several people in the audience yelled to him to pipe down, Jones kept interrupting the speaker every few minutes.

pipe dream a reverie, fantastic or impractical notion:—His plan to spend next year in Europe is just one more of his usual pipe dreams.

pipe up speak up:—She is such a timid person that I was surprised to hear her pipe up for a better seat.

pipe, put that in your pipe and smoke it an expression indicating defiance and meaning: think that over carefully, consider well:—Whether my boss likes it or not, I am going to take my vacation in June, and he can put that in his pipe and smoke it.

pipe See also **peace** pipe, **pay** the piper.

pit against place in competition with, fight against:—It was foolish on the part of his manager to pit him against a fighter with so much more experience.

pitch a tent erect a tent:—We pitched our tent as close to the river as possible.

pitch dark extremely dark. Also expressed as **pitch black**:—When I got up at five o'clock this morning, it was still pitch dark.

pitch in join in with enthusiasm, work energetically:—We all pitched in, and within an hour the whole camp was set up.

pitch into attack vigorously, devour:—It was a wonderful meal, and we all pitched into it as though we hadn't eaten in a month.

pity, for pity's sake an expression of annoyance:—For pity's sake, please stop making so much noise.

pity, take pity on feel sorry for, aid:— My sister always takes pity on some stray cat or dog.

pity, what a pity what a shame, how unfortunate:—What a pity that he couldn't join them on that trip.

place, give place to be succeeded by, be replaced by, give way to:—As the war went on, Hitler's sense of elation and superiority gradually gave place to a feeling of despair and defeat.

place, in place in correct order or position. See also **out** of place:—We instructed the maid to leave everything in place, just as she found it.

place, in place of instead of:—The Chinese use chopsticks in place of knives and forks.

place See also **know** one's place; **out** of place; **put** someone in his place; **take** place; **going** places.

plain Jane a girl without beauty:—Esther certainly is a plain Jane, and yet she is quite popular.

plain sailing an easy, uncomplicated course:—For a man of Harry's ability, that assignment was plain sailing.

plain speaking direct, frank speech:—If you don't mind my plain speaking, I want to tell you that we do not consider your work entirely satisfactory.

plan on count upon, depend upon:—Don't plan on my going with you, for I expect to be busy this weekend.

plank down pay, put, or lay down somewhat noisily; pay an excessive amount:—I had to plank down six dollars for a theater ticket.

plant oneself station oneself firmly:—The policeman planted himself directly in the runaway's path.

plaster down slick down:—During that period, the style for men was to wear their hair plastered down on their heads.

plastered, get plastered get drunk:—That laborer gets plastered regularly every payday.

platonic love non-sexual love:—She maintained on the witness stand that theirs had been a case of platonic love.

play along with cooperate with—with the idea of gaining some advantage thereby:—We felt that the best way to get what we wanted was to play along with them.

play around with (1) keep thinking about (an idea):—I've been playing around with your idea for opening an office in Chicago. (2) to spend time with a person of the opposite sex without serious intent:—He's been playing around with a number of girls, but I don't think he is serious about any one of them.

playback the replaying of a recording from a tape recorder, etc.:—After recording the new song, the vocalist listened to the playback.

play down (up) minimize the importance of, place small emphasis on:—In the election campaign, the party in power naturally played down some of the scandals that had occurred during its administration.

play fair act justly, honorably, fairly:—He doesn't know how to play fair; with

him business is a game in which he tries to beat the other fellow by every means possible.

play fast and loose with abuse without regard for the rights of others, act irresponsibly:—For years, he had played fast and loose with her affections.

play favorites show partiality:—That teacher is unpopular with most of the students because she plays favorites.

play into the hands of be maneuvered into giving the advantage to another:—Many people believe that in agreeing to the East-West division of Germany, we played right into the hands of the Russians.

play it by ear improvise, handle a situation without a plan or instructions:—Since I had had no experience in dealing with troubled persons, I decided to play it by ear when I was suddenly left alone with a mental case.

play off to play a game previously canceled or postponed:—The Yankees have at least three previously canceled night games which they must play off before the season ends.

play off one against the other place in competition two opposing elements in order to gain a personal advantage thereby:—It is not uncommon strategy in politics to play off the conservatives against the radicals.

play on (upon) exploit, stimulate, utilize:—He tried to play on her sympathies by telling a long tale of his hard luck.

play on words a pun, a joke utilizing the double-meaning or similarity in sound of certain words:—When closely analyzed, many jokes depend for their effect upon a play on words. Example: She gazes at my son and moons.

play one's cards right (wrong) maneuver efficiently, make the most of one's resources:—The competition is strong, but if we play our cards right, we may yet win that contract.

play possum pretend to be dead or asleep:—The dog was actually playing possum, and, though apparently asleep, was aware of every move his master made.

play second fiddle to be subordinate to, hold a secondary position to:—We don't think he realizes that, with all those changes in his department, he may have to play second fiddle to his former subordinate.

play someone dirt do someone a dirty trick, treat unfairly or treacherously:—He played his employer dirt by resigning, and then going into competition with him.

play the fool act foolishly, squander one's time and money on trifles:—It is about time he stopped playing the fool and began to settle down.

play the horses to bet on horse races:—No wonder his wife is penniless; he is always playing the horses and losing his money.

play to the gallery show off, attempt to captivate the attention of the audience:—Several times during the trial the district attorney seemed less concerned with the furtherance of justice than with playing to the gallery of visitors and newspaper reporters.

play tricks on someone make another the victim of some joke or trick:—Fred got very angry when the other boys played a trick on him and hid his clothes while he was in swimming.

play up maximize the importance of:—In its ads that night club plays up the TV stars that entertain there.

play up See also **play down.**

play up to make oneself agreeable to another person, fit in with his moods:—Marie knows how to play up to her rich old uncle.

play, at play playing:—I like to watch the children at play in the schoolyard.

play, bring into play put into action, introduce:—He is very resourceful and knows how to bring into play all the knowledge and experience he has accumulated.

play, make a play for attempt to win the favor of:—With their talk about higher farm prices, both parties are naturally making a play for the agricultural vote.

played out exhausted:—The work was too strenuous for John, and each day he would arrive home all played out.

play See also **child's** play; **dirty,** play dirty; **false,** play one false; **field,** play the field; **grandstand** play; **hooky,** play hooky; **part,** play a part in; **safe,** play safe.

pledge allegiance swear to uphold, promise to adhere to:—We all had to pledge allegiance to the flag.

pledge, take the pledge swear to give up drinking:—Frank's family finally prevailed upon him to take the pledge.

plough (plow) through pass through laboriously:—In order to gather material for my lectures I had to plough through dozens of old books on economics.

plug (sl. v.) publicize, promote:—If it is plugged properly, this song should become very popular.

plug, pull the plug remove the bottom, withdraw support, cause disaster:—When those stock promoters pulled the plug, hundreds of investors lost their entire savings.

plume oneself on pride oneself on, take pride in:—She plumes herself on the fact that she was educated in Europe rather than here in the United States.

plump for favor, be in favor of, support:—The Mayor plumped for Evans for Councilman.

plunge, take the plunge venture, take a fatal or decisive step:—When I asked him when he planned to get married, he said he was going to take the plunge next month.

pocket money money for incidentals:—She was given ample allowance for household expenses, but very little for pocket money.

pocket one's pride suffer or conceal one's feeling of injured dignity:—Although he had not received an invitation to the wedding, Henry pocketed his pride and asked whether he might not attend.

pocket, air-pocket empty spaces, partial vacuums existing in the atmosphere:—Each time it struck an air-pocket the plane would drop suddenly.

pocket, pick a pocket steal by removing from the pocket of another:—While in the subway someone picked his pocket of the last five dollars he had to his name.

pocket See also **out** of pocket.

point a moral show by example, indicate some moral truth or concept:—The story of the dictator's downfall points a moral for all those who seek to dominate the lives of others.

point blank directly, bluntly, straightforwardly:—He refused point blank to have anything to do with the plan.

point of view attitude, viewpoint:—From the point of view of the capitalist, increased government spending is wrong.

point, a case in point an applicable situation, example:—In support of his argument the lawyer cited the recent Supreme Court decision as a case in point.

point, be on the point of be about to, ready to:—We were on the point of telephoning you when your telegram arrived.

point, come (get) to the point arrive at the important or crucial part:—We were there to ask for an extension of time on our note, but I thought George would never come to the point.

point, one's strong point one's forte, that which one does best:—He is a good novelist, but character portrayal is not one of his strong points.

point, stick to the point adhere to the subject at issue. See also **come** to the point:—His speech was weak because, instead of sticking to the point and discussing the tax issue, he digressed frequently and discussed matters that had nothing to do with the subject.

point, stretch a point make some slight concession or exception:—The bank told us that on this occasion they would stretch a point and give us an extra ten days in which to meet our note.

point, to the point relevant, germane:—He asked us to be brief and to the point as he had little time to spare.

point See also **beside** the point; **make** a point of.

poke around (about) dig around, investigate:—The detectives kept poking around among old records and finally found the evidence they were looking for.

poke fun at laugh at, make fun of:—Everyone in the office kept poking fun at Jim because of his new haircut.

pokey slow:—Give that work to someone else. Grace is so pokey she'll never get it done in time.

poke See also **pig** in a poke.

polish off finish quickly:—We were all so hungry that it took us only a few minutes to polish off that big steak.

pool, dirty pool taking an unfair advantage of another, cheating, lack of sportsmanship, etc.:—I call Allan's trying to take a client away from us dirty pool.

poop out (sl.) become exhausted, drop out,—fail to appear:—All but one of our group came back to our class reunion, the other pooped out.

poor farm a publicly supported home for the indigent:—Since he had no family to support him, he was obliged to spend his declining years at the county poor farm.

poor-mouth said of a person who is always insincerely pleading poverty:—Although he earns a good salary, that poor-mouth won't even chip in to buy flowers for our hospitalized fellow employee.

poor white the poor, underprivileged white man in the southern part of the United States; a destitute group distinguished chiefly by color from poverty-stricken blacks:—The poor whites in the South are often sneeringly referred to as white trash.

pop in appear or enter suddenly:—He pops into my office for a short visit once in a while.

pop the question make a proposal of marriage:—He has been trying for weeks to get up enough nerve to pop the question.

pop up appear suddenly and unexpectedly:—I haven't seen Jim for several months, but I'm sure he will pop up one of these days.

pore over study carefully:—He has to spend a great deal of time in the library, poring over old historical manuscripts.

port, any port in a storm in an emergency, any substitute must serve:—The hotel that we stopped at left much to be desired, but we were so tired after driving all day that it was a matter of any port in a storm.

post, left at the post left waiting, beaten badly by one's competitors:—If Jack doesn't hurry up and ask Helen to marry him, he may find himself left at the post, because she has several other admirers.

pot calling the kettle black criticizing another for faults or errors of which one is also guilty:—Jane claims that Mary is deceitful, but knowing Jane's faults, as I do, I would say that it is a case of the pot calling the kettle black.

pot shot a direct shot at an easy, stationary target; to twit, slander:—That newspaper columnist likes to take pot shots at political and social celebrities.

pot, take potluck accept whatever is available as a meal:—I told him that we had nothing special prepared, but that if he would like to take potluck we would bee glad to have him dine with us.

pot See also **go** to pot.

pound a beat said of a policeman who is a foot patrolman in a certain section of the city:—Casey has pounded the same beat for twenty years.

pound away at work industriously at, attack, criticize:—In his campaign speeches, he kept pounding away at the weakness of the government's foreign policy.

pound of flesh the maximum payment authorized by law:—We had hoped that he would be lenient regarding the interest on the money, but he demanded his full pound of flesh and we could do nothing about it.

pour in enter or arrive in great quantity:—After the President's speech, protests poured in from all sections of the country.

pour oil on troubled waters pacify, calm:—The situation was very tense, but the Prime Minister tried to pour oil on the troubled waters by promising some changes in policy.

pour See also **rain,** it never rains but it pours.

powder, take a powder leave suddenly and unceremoniously, disappear (sl.):—Several of the witnesses decided that it might be wiser, instead of testifying, to take a powder.

power, more power to you an expression of encouragement:—If he decides to run for the office, then I should say more power to him.

powers, the powers that be those in authority, constituted authority:—We have done all we can; the rest is up to the powers that be.

practical joke a hoax, an elaborate trick played on a person:—Being fond of practical jokes, Bill sometimes makes a nuisance of himself in the office, pulling chairs out from under people, messing up their papers, etc.

practice on use as a subject for practice or experience:—In our first-aid class, the students had to practice on one another.

practice what one preaches do what one advises others to do:—If cold showers are so good for the health, why don't you practice what you preach and take one yourself each morning?

practice See also **make** a practice of; **out** of practice.

praise, damn with faint praise give or pay another lukewarm compliments that detract rather than add:—When Frank told his boss that Helen was adequate as a typist, he damned her with faint praise.

presence of mind quick and effective thinking in time of crisis:—Fortunately Leo had the presence of mind to throw a rug over the burning basket of waste paper.

present oneself appear:—He has been asked to present himself before the draft board at once.

present, at present now, at the present time:—At present he is working in Washington.

press forward push in a forward direction:—The crowd pressed forward to get a better look at the President.

press into service make use of, utilize:—So many people came to the party that Helen had to press several of her women guests into service to help with the refreshments.

press, go to press start to print, begin the process of being printed:—The news arrived too late to catch the morning edition because the paper had already gone to press.

pressed, hard pressed harassed by many debts:—With his wife in poor health and a new baby to care for, my brother is rather hard pressed to meet all his expenses.

presume upon impose upon, take advantage of, take liberties with:—We certainly need the money, but, on the other hand, I don't want to presume upon your generosity.

pretty often used colloquially in the sense of "rather," "somewhat." Compare **pretty good, pretty busy, pretty late,** etc.:—I thought the show was pretty good, but Elsie didn't care for it.

pretty kettle of fish a difficult and annoying situation, a mess:—When Jackson saw the various electrical appliances which his wife had succeeded in burning out, his only remark was: "This is a pretty kettle of fish."

pretty penny a large sum:—That imported car must have cost Davis a pretty penny.

pretty See also **pass, a pretty pass.**

prevail upon induce to do, persuade:—The hostess finally prevailed upon her distinguished guest to play the piano.

prey on one's mind worry, afflict:—The fact that he owed everyone so much money kept preying on his mind.

prick up one's ears listen eagerly, become closely attentive:—Whenever our dog hears someone coming he pricks up his ears.

pride oneself on be proud of, feel important because of:—She prides herself on her knowledge of home decorating.

pride, take pride in be proud of, gain satisfaction from:—She takes pride in her home and likes to keep it looking clean and neat.

probability, in all probability very likely, probably:—In all probability you will get back before us.

problem, no problem easy and simple to do:—You want to open a checking account for your under-age daughter? No problem.

progress, in progress in process, going on:—The construction of that new state highway is now in progress.

promise, show promise give indication:—He shows promise of being one of the best chess players our club has yet produced.

promise See also **lick** and a promise.

proof against resistant to. Compare **fireproof, rust-proof, rain-proof,** etc.:—The application of this paint makes the metal rust-proof (proof against rust).

proof of the pudding is in the eating only through actual experience can the worth of something be actually tested:—Those elaborate menus in the ladies' magazines look very tempting, but of course, the proof of the pudding is in the eating.

proper name one's first or given name:—Her proper name is Helen; her surname is Smith.

proper noun the name of a particular person, place, or thing—always capitalized:—Names of individual cities are all proper nouns.

protest, under protest unwillingly, against one's wish:—I know I have to go with you, but I want it clearly understood that I do so under protest.

proud, do someone proud cause someone to feel proud, to honor:—The competent way in which his wife looked after his business while he was away did Mr. Phillips proud.

public enemy a criminal:—John Dillinger was known for some time as Public Enemy No. 1.

public school in the United States any free village or municipal school; in England a privately owned school:—At least ninety-five per cent of the children in the United States attend public schools.

puffed up conceited, proud, elated:—Just because they gave him a slightly better position is no reason for him to get so puffed up.

pull (1) (n.) influence which can be used to one's personal advantage:—He got the job because his father has a lot of pull in that company. (2) (v.) commit, perpetrate:—The police feel that the same gang pulled this job as pulled the Brinks robbery in Boston.

pull a fast one deceive, trick, gain the advantage over another unfairly:—When he heard that they were about to give us a big order, he rushed down there and pulled a fast one by obtaining the order for himself.

pull a long face become sullen, dejected, express facially one's disapproval or annoyance:—Grace pulled a long face when she heard that we were behind in the work and would have to stay longer.

pull down (1) raze, demolish:—All those old buildings were pulled down to make way for a new housing project. (2) earn, have as a salary:—He pulls down more than five hundred dollars a month in that job.

pull in (1) draw inward, tighten:—The thinner I got, the more I had to pull in my belt. (2) arrive. See also **pull** out:—The train was just pulling in as we got to the station. (3) pick up, capture, take:—The police have already pulled in a half dozen people whom they suspect. (4) drive into a place:—Just as it got dark, we pulled into our motel.

pull off (1) remove:—He pulled off his sweater and threw it into a corner. (2) perpetrate, perform with a certain amount of underhanded cleverness:—What does he think he is trying to pull off here anyway?

pull one's leg make fun of, victimize someone:—He kept telling me how beautifully I spoke Spanish, and it was only much later that I realized he had been pulling my leg.

pull one's (any) punches limit or restrain one's full power, proceed gently:—The Senator didn't pull any punches when he attacked the system of lobbying in Washington.

pull one's rank assert one's self by reason of one's superior rank or position, have one's way:—At first, in the debate, the General treated Holmes very cordially, but Holmes felt all along that the General would sooner or later pull his rank, and then the discussion would end.

pull out (1) leave—said particularly of trains. See also **pull** in:—The train pulled out of the station just as we got there. (2) retreat, withdraw:—One detachment after the other pulled out under the heavy enemy fire, until only the men under Lieutenant Hearn were left to hold the center line.

pull someone's chestnuts out of the fire injure oneself in order to get someone else out of a difficulty:—If they got themselves into this trouble, why should we have to pull their chestnuts out of the fire?

pull something on someone deceive, do something prejudicial:—He pulled a very dirty trick on her when, after going with her for five years, he suddenly married another girl.

pull strings (wires) use influence with others, manipulate:—His uncle pulled all sorts of wires to get John placed with that organization.

pull the wool over someone's eyes deceive:—They certainly pulled the wool over her eyes when they sold her that fur coat as genuine mink.

pull through recover from some difficulty or illness:—He is still quite sick, but the doctor is sure he will pull through.

pull to pieces destroy, dismantle:—While we were out, our dog pulled to pieces two of our good sofa cushions.

pull together cooperate, work together harmoniously:—If they can only forget their differences and pull together, they may have a chance to win the election.

pull up (1) remove, uproot:—He pulled up the plant by its roots. (2) bring close:—Pull up a chair and sit here with us at this table. (3) draw near, approach:—At that moment a police car pulled up at the curb, and two policemen jumped out.

pull up short stop suddenly:—When he realized that he had been rather tactless, he pulled up short and began to discuss an entirely different matter. See also **stop short**.

pull up stakes leave, make preparations for leaving:—He would work in one town for a few months, then pull up stakes and move on to another.

pull See also **boner,** pull a boner; **plug,** pull the plug; **punches,** pull one's punches.

pump (v.) to extract private information from:—He kept pumping me until finally he found out everything he wanted to know.

punches, pull one's (any) punches treat less harshly than possible or desirable:—In taking his accountant to task for carelessness, the president of the company didn't pull any punches.

purpose, answer (serve) the purpose be useful as a means of achieving some end or purpose:—What I need is a pair of scissors, but, since you don't have one, this penknife will have to serve the purpose.

purpose, on purpose intentionally:—She broke the dish on purpose just to show her anger.

purpose, to little (no) purpose to no avail, without success:—We all argued with him not to sign that contract, but to no purpose.

push off depart, leave:—If you have nothing more for me to do here, I think I'll push off.

push on go forward laboriously, press forward:—We pushed on through the woods until we reached an open road.

pusher a person who distributes and introduces others to narcotics:—Being a pusher is a criminal offense.

pushover something easy to accomplish or overcome:—Using a tractor is a pushover for Jack as he was brought up on a farm.

put a stop (end) to terminate rather abruptly, cause to cease:—We ought to find some way of putting a stop to that noise.

put about turn around, turn in the opposite direction:—When we saw the storm clouds gathering, we put about and sailed back to our port.

put across accomplish, carry through in the face of some opposition or difficulties:—He is the kind of speaker who puts across his arguments through sheer physical energy, rather than by the brilliance of his reasoning.

put all one's eggs in one basket place all of one's faith or money in one single enterprise:—I don't want to invest all my money in this business; it would mean putting all my eggs in one basket.

put aside (1) place at one side:—The teacher told them to put aside their books and get ready for the weekly drill. (2) save, put to one side for a special purpose:—Joseph puts ten dollars aside every week.

put away put or store something in its proper place:—If you have finished with those tools, I wish you'd put them away.

put back return:—Please put this plate back on the shelf where it belongs.

put down (1) cease to hold, place down somewhere, lay aside:—Put down that book and help your mother with the dishes. (2) suppress:—The troops had little trouble putting down the rebellion. (3) write down:—Please put your name and address down on this pad. (4) attribute to:—A good part of his shyness can be put down to the dominating influence of his mother.

put-down (n.) a humiliating treatment, a squelching or belittling:—The president's refusal to see one of his aides was a severe put-down.

put forth issue, send out, grow:—At this time of the year all the chestnut trees put forth blossoms.

put heads together confer:—I am sure that if we put our heads together, we can find some solution to the problem.

put in a word for speak in favor of:—If only someone would put in a word for John, I am sure he would get that promotion.

put in an appearance appear, make an appearance, attend:—We put in only a brief appearance at the party because we had a theater engagement.

put in black and white put in writing:—They made us various proposals orally, but I suggested that it would be better if they put everything in black and white.

put in mind recall, remind one of:—That joke you just told puts me in mind of an experience I had last summer.

put in motion start or cause to move:—The Archduke's assassination put in motion a whole train of events that led directly to the beginning of the First World War.

put in order place in proper form or order:—Please put these folders in alphabetical order.

put in shape place in good form or condition:—A few months in the country will put him in good physical shape again.

put in (into) use begin to use, use:—In his present job, he will be able to put in (into) use everything he studied at the university.

put in writing express in written form. See **put** in black and white:—We asked him to put in writing the various points we had agreed upon.

put into practice use, put into effect, carry out:—It is one thing to have theories, and another thing to put them into practice.

put into words express in words, describe exactly:—Only a poet could put into words the deep affection which that couple seem to feel for each other.

put off (1) postpone:—The meeting has been put off until next week. (2) prove indefinite or evasive, evade:—They have apparently decided to buy our house, but each time I ask them about it, they keep putting me off.

put-on (n.) an unfair trick or deception:—The ad said that there would be a live band playing for the dance, but there was only recorded music—what a put-on!

put on (1) to don, place upon oneself—said of clothes:—He put on his hat and coat and went out. (2) pretend, feign:—That modesty of Ralph's is all put on; at heart he is very vain. (3) add, schedule:—They always have to put on extra flights to handle the holiday travel.

put on airs act in a superior and affected manner, show conceit:—The fact that she spent the summer in Europe is hardly reason for her to put on such airs.

put on paper See **put** in writing.

put on weight gain in weight:—Since getting married, Bill has put on a lot of weight.

put one in mind of remind one of, cause one to remember:—He puts me in mind of a boy I used to room with in college.

put one on his feet revive one, reestablish one firmly:—What you need is a good stiff drink to put you on your feet.

put one out of the way murder, dispose of:—Apparently, she was not the first victim he had put out of the way in order to collect the insurance money.

put one through his paces test one's abilities, train and discipline:—The men were certainly put through their paces at that training camp.

put one up supply living or sleeping accommodations for the night:—Why go to a hotel? We can put you up here in our apartment for the night.

put one up to instigate, cause another to do something:—I am sure that it is Bill who put the child up to doing all those tricks.

put one wise inform one, explain, bring one up to date:—The accountant put us wise to the fact that someone was taking money from the cash box.

put (turn) one's hand to work at, show skill in:—He is a very useful employee because in an emergency he can put his hand to anything and do it well.

put out (1) exclude, dismiss, eject:— They were both put out of the restaurant for causing a disturbance. (2) extinguish:—Be sure to put out the light before you go to bed. (3) disturb, inconvenience:—It won't put us out a bit if we drive you home. (4) annoyed, indignant:—She was very much put out because we hadn't invited her to the party.

put out of action cause to become useless or inactive:—Anti-aircraft fire put two of the planes immediately out of action.

put out of one's head cease to think about, forget:—I told him to put out of his head any ideas he might have about a vacation because we need every worker we can get.

put over carry out successfully:—We knew that to put over a deal of that sort we would have to send our best man.

put someone in his place scold, humble:— When the student asked her her age, the teacher had to put him in his place.

put something over on trick, deceive, gain the advantage over:—It is our impression that our neighbors put something over on us when they got us to share the expense of pulling up those tree stumps.

put through (1) arrange, carry out:—If he can put through one more good deal like this, he will more than have earned his salary for this year. (2) effectuate, carry to a successful end—often said of telephone calls:—We spent all evening trying to put through a call to some friends in Jamaica.

put to bed place in bed:—We usually put the children to bed about eight o'clock.

put to death kill, bring about the death of:—The murderer was put to death in the electric chair.

put to flight cause to flee:—The sudden appearance overhead of our planes was enough to put the enemy to flight.

put to rights See **rights, put to rights.**

put together assemble:—It is easy to take a watch apart but rather difficult to put it together again.

put to shame embarrass, belittle, put in the shade:—His wife's politeness put her crabby husband to shame. Smith's new Cadillac rather put to shame our old Ford station wagon.

put to sleep cause to fall asleep:—One of these pills will put you to sleep in an hour.

put to use utilize, make use of:—You can be sure that the money you give them will be put to good use.

put two and two together deduce, draw conclusions from observable data:—Seeing Tom in the florist shop, I put two and two together and naturally figured that he was buying flowers for Edna.

put up (1) erect, build:—They are putting up several new houses on our street. (2) supply or contribute money for:— The church itself will put up half the money, and it is relying on wealthy parishioners to put up the rest. (3) preserve, put in glass jars:—Each summer my mother used to put up great quantities of fruits and vegetables. (4) stay, pass the night as in a hotel:—We put up at a small hotel just on the edge of the town.

put up a fight offer resistance:—He put up a good fight, but he lacked the experience of the older boxer.

put up for sale offer for sale:—The building was put up for sale about a year ago.

put-up job something fraudulently prearranged or concocted:—The police feel sure that the robbers worked in cooperation with someone inside the building, and that the whole robbery was a put-up job.

put up to one refer a decision to someone. Also expressed as **leave up to someone:**—In that divorce action, the question of the custody of the children was put up to the judge.

put up with tolerate, stand:—I refused to put up with his carelessness any longer.

put upon impose upon, burden unfairly:—He feels put upon because he has to work overtime so often, without any extra pay.

put, not to put it past one consider someone capable of doing something discreditable:—Knowing his character as I do, I wouldn't put it past him if he tried to break the contract.

put, well put well defined or expressed:—His remarks about Hollywood's unconcern with artistic integrity were well put and drew applause from the audience.

put See also **airs**, put on airs; **cart**, put the cart before the horse; **dog**, put on the dog; **foot**, put one's foot down; **foot**, put one's foot in it; **foot**, put one's best foot forward; **front**, put up a front; **hard** put; **heads**, put heads together; **pipe**, put that in your pipe and smoke it; **oar**, put in one's oar; **rights**, put to rights; **shoulder**, put one's shoulder to the wheel; **stay** put; **teeth**, put teeth into.

Q

q.t., on the q.t. secretly, on the quiet:—He had been going out with her on the q.t.

qualms, have qualms about have hesitation in doing, be uneasy about:—I had no qualms in telling him that his behavior had been very thoughtless.

quarter, give (ask) quarter give consideration, show mercy toward:—They announced that they would fight to the bitter end and would neither ask nor give quarter.

queer oneself act so as to offend others and thus injure one's own chances or position:—He has queered himself with many prospective clients by his foolish insistence on full payment in advance.

question, beside the question not relevant, not pertinent to the subject under discussion:—What you are saying may be true, but in this case it is completely beside the question.

question, beyond question not subject to doubt or dispute:—He may be a little careless in his work, but his loyalty to the company is beyond question.

question, call into question examine, doubt, investigate:—Tom's loyalty to his firm was never called into question.

question, in question under discussion:—This is the document in question.

question, without question undoubtedly, unquestionably:—He is without question the best player on the team.

question See also **beg** the question; **open** question; **out** of the question; **pop** the question; **raise** a question; **shoot** questions at.

quick on the draw alert, ready, having a quick reaction time:—Jack is quick on the draw and has a ready answer to almost every question.

quick, a quick one a short drink, a drink taken rapidly:—What do you say to a quick one before the train pulls in?

quick See also **cut** to the quick; **touch** to the quick.

quiet down become quiet, calm:—At first the children made a lot of noise, but later they seemed to quiet down.

quiet, on the quiet secretly:—They were married on the quiet in a little town in Connecticut.

quite a rather, somewhat:—We had quite a busy day.

quite a few many, a lot:—There were quite a few students absent from class today.

quite the thing the socially proper thing to do:—It has become quite the thing to send your date a corsage before taking her to any formal dance.

quits, cry quits accept defeat, admit to having had enough, terminate a dispute:—We were ready to cry quits and discontinue selling those stoves because we had had so many complaints about them.

quits See also **call** it quits.

R

R's, the three R's reading, (w)riting, and (a)rithmetic, which comprise the basic elements of primary education:—He had completed the study of the three R's, but otherwise had had little formal education.

rack and ruin a condition of decline, complete decay:—The entire farm, including the barn and stables, had gone to rack and ruin.

rack one's brains strive desperately to devise or remember something:—We both racked our brains for hours trying to figure out where we might have made the mistake in our accounts.

rack up total, add up, acquire, gain, win: —That bright student racked up ten scholarships during his college years.

racket (1) an illegal business, a form of doing business whereby one gains quick and easy profits by deceiving or exploiting the customer:—Horse racing may be a sport to some, but others feel that it is just a big, legalized racket. (2) any easy, lucrative job or business:—They pay her $150 a week just for sitting in an office and reading novels. What a racket!

racket, make a racket cause a lot of noise or disturbance:—I wish the neighbor's small boy wouldn't make such a racket while I'm trying to sleep.

rage, all the rage popular:—Guitar players are all the rage today.

railroad (v.) to push through by force, force through:—A number of the very large manufacturers were interested in the bill, so it was railroaded through the Legislature with little show of protest.

rain check (1) a special ticket entitling one to attend a later performance when the original performance has been canceled:—It began to rain during the third inning and the baseball game was called off. Everyone received a rain check. (2) a request for an invitation at some future date in place of one you received but are unable to accept:—I can't come to your house for dinner tonight, but I'd like to have a rain check for some later date.

rain or shine in any event, regardless of climatic conditions:—The meeting has been announced for tomorrow evening, rain or shine.

rain out force to close because of rain:— The Yankees were rained out yesterday.

rain, it never rains but it pours troubles never come singly:—First Bill lost his job, then his wife had to go to the hospital; it never rains but it pours.

rainy day a period of scarcity or want:— Each week they have made it a practice to put aside a few dollars of Henry's salary for a rainy day.

raise a question ask, present a question:— A question was raised at the meeting as to the chairman's right to take part in the debate.

raise a row (rhymes with how) cause a disturbance, scene, or fuss:—Paul raised quite a row when he found that someone had damaged his bicycle.

raise a stink complain or protest strongly, cause a disturbance:—There was quite a stink raised in our office when it was discovered that several of the staff had left for the day without permission.

raise Cain (1) behave violently, cause a disturbance:—Bob came to the house and raised Cain with me because I had kept the news from him. (2) protest vigorously:—Your brother will raise Cain if he ever finds out that you didn't feed his dog on time. (3) roister, celebrate, make a night of it:—Let's step out tonight and raise a little Cain.

raise hell See **raise** Cain.

raise money borrow or solicit money for some project:—Our church is trying to raise money for a new organ.

raise money on pawn, obtain by pledging an article to a pawnbroker:—How much money do you think I can raise on this gold watch?

raise one's voice speak loudly, shout:— Father could get pretty angry, but he never once raised his voice to any of the children.

raise the devil See **raise** Cain.

raise the roof (1) cause so much noise as to blow off the roof:—When the President appeared, the audience burst into such applause that I thought it would raise the roof. (2) protest vigorously, cause a disturbance:—She knew that her husband would raise the roof as soon as he saw the bills for the month's expenses.

raise, get a raise obtain an increase in salary:—They promised he would get a raise the first of the year.

rake in take in lots of money, realize great profits:—Because of the continued hot spell, beach concessionaires have been raking in money this summer.

rake-off a special commission or cut, a discount:—In some of the slot-machine rackets, everyone, from the local gangster to the policeman on the corner, gets his special rake-off.

rake up gather, bring to light, expose:—In telling the story, I don't think it necessary to rake up the past.

random, at random haphazardly, without special plan or purpose:—The professor picked several students at random from the class and asked them to help him with the experiment.

rank and file common soldiers, ordinary people:—It will be the rank and file, not the newspapers or the newspaper editors, who will finally decide who is to be elected.

ranks, from (through) the ranks from the masses, from the basic group:—He began as a mechanic and rose from the ranks to become president of the company.

rank See also **pull** one's rank.

rap, not to care (give) a rap not to consider important, place little value upon, show indifference:—Apparently, he doesn't give a rap whether we get there or not.

rap See also **beat** the rap; **take** the rap.

raspberry, give (get) the raspberry ridicule, laugh at, mock:—Feeling against him was so strong at the meeting that they gave him the raspberry every time he started to speak.

rat, smell a rat be suspicious, suspect treachery:—George began to smell a rat when they started to say the contract wasn't valid.

rate (v.) to be held in a high opinion or in affection:—How George rates with the boss!

rate, at any rate in any case, nevertheless:—At any rate, even if he doesn't stay there permanently, he will get some valuable experience.

rate, at this (that) rate at this speed:—At this rate, we won't get to Chicago before Wednesday.

rate See also **cut** rate; **second** rate.

rather, would rather prefer to:—Naturally, we would rather have taken the cruise for our vacation than have stayed at home.

rattle off say or recite rapidly:—Bill has a remarkable memory and can rattle off every item on the price list.

rattled, get rattled become nervous and confused:—Mrs. Watkins got so rattled when she saw the policeman that she drove the car up over the curb.

rave about become very enthusiastic about:—Helen liked the picture very much, but I didn't think it was anything to rave about.

rave notice or review a very enthusiastic critic's account of a play, movie, book, etc.:—That Book-of-the-Month Club selection for January got rave notices.

raw deal unfair treatment:—It was a raw deal assigning Jim's territory to another salesman and giving Jim a less profitable territory.

raw, in the raw naked:—Hal stepped out of the shower in the raw.

razz (v.) ridicule, make fun of:—The fans kept razzing the young pitcher, hoping to get him rattled.

read aloud read in a speaking voice:—It is excellent practice, when studying a foreign language, to read aloud each day from some book or newspaper.

read another understand another person:—Tired of his partnership, Bill said to his partner: "I want out. Do you read me?"

read off read in a speaking voice from some list:—The teacher read off the names of those students who were going to take part in the play.

read into deduce from, consider to be implicit in:—Just because Bill's letters were friendly was no reason for Mary to read into them a promise of marriage.

read one's fortune predict one's future:—Let's go to a fortune-teller some night and have our fortunes read.

read over read hurriedly, in a rather superficial manner:—The teacher said that she had not had time to correct my examination, but that she had read it over.

read the riot act censure severely, threaten with punishment:—After catching several students smoking in the halls, the Principal called us to his office and read us all the riot act.

read up on study carefully in preparation for an examination or other special purpose:—Since he had never paid much attention to either history or economics, Robert now has to read up on both subjects before taking the examination.

read, well-read (rhymes with head) said of a person who has read widely and discriminately:—As you might suppose, that professor of literature is very well-read.

read See also **lines,** read between the lines; **sight** read; **well**-read.

ready-made machine-made, mass produced, not made to order:—I buy all my suits ready-made.

ready money money on hand and immediately available:—He would purchase that land if he had the ready money.

ready, make ready make preparations for, get ready to:—Just as they were making ready to leave, a messenger brought them the telegram canceling the arrangements for the trip.

real property land, real estate:—In that state one has to pay taxes on both real and personal property.

reality, in reality actually, really, in point of fact:—She gives the impression of being generous, but in reality she is a very selfish woman.

rear its head appear, raise its head:—At that point in the play, jealousy, in the form of the rejected lover, reared its ugly head.

reason, within reason within sensible limits, reasonable:—I think he would buy the property if he could get it for a price within reason.

reason See also **listen** to reason; **stand** to reason.

receipt, on (upon) receipt upon receiving:—Upon receipt of your check we will send you the merchandise.

reckon with consider, allow for, take into consideration:—We had failed to reckon with the fact that the weather would change so suddenly.

record, break the record set or establish a new mark or record:—Smith broke the record in both the high jump and the one-hundred meter dash.

record, go on record state publicly one's views, express oneself publicly as being for or against some issue:—The Mayor said that he wished to go on record as favoring a larger appropriation for new schools.

record, off the record confidentially, expressed in confidence, not for official publication:—The Governor spoke to the reporters about his plans, but emphasized the fact that everything he said was off the record.

Red Book the classified telephone directory:—See **Yellow** Pages, its more common name.

redcap a railway-station porter:—Why don't you get a redcap to help you carry your bags?

red carpet, roll out the red carpet:—Treat an important person or dignitary with ceremony:—When the Emperor of Ethiopia visited New York the city officials rolled out the red carpet.

red cent a penny, a copper coin:—He doesn't have a red cent to his name.

red-handed in the very act, while committing some evil action:—The thief was caught red-handed just as he was putting the watch in his pocket.

red herring something designed to deceive, a false scent laid down to mislead pursuers:—The charge that he had mishandled the funds was just a red herring designed to discredit his standing with the committee.

red ink loss or indebtedness:—There's too much red ink in that company's present financial state. They need a more profitable year.

red-letter day a memorable and important occasion, those days on the calendar printed in red, to indicate their importance:—It was a red-letter day for Pete when he won first prize in three different track events.

red-light district that section of a town or city inhabited by prostitutes, a district of brothels:—Most large American cities have done away with their red-light districts.

red tape bureaucratic routine, needless but official delay:—There is so much red tape involved in obtaining a government contract that it is sometimes almost not worth the time and expense.

red, in the red showing a loss rather than a profit, showing liabilities in excess of assets:—They had to sell the building because for years they had operated it in the red.

red See also **paint** the town red; **see** red.

reel off name or recite quickly:—Harry can reel off the names of all the Presidents of the United States in less than a minute.

reel See also **right** off the reel.

refusal the privilege of exercising acceptance or refusal, usually regarding the purchase of property:—We have a month within which to exercise our refusal of the property.

regard, with (in) regard to regarding, with reference to:—With regard to your request for a refund, we have referred the matter to our main office.

rein, give rein to give free play to, remove all restrictions or limitations:—It was the type of writing which he enjoyed, because it permitted him to give free rein to his imagination.

reins, take the reins assume the control or direction of:—When the president of our company goes on vacation, the vice-president takes the reins during his absence.

relative to referring to, relating to, with reference to:—He said nothing relative to his plans about returning.

relief, on relief receiving public assistance because of low income:—When Mrs. Jack lost her husband, the city had to put her and her five children on relief.

relieve of lighten the load of—also, jocularly, to rob:—Gross was given an assistant to relieve him of some of his onerous duties. Some thief in the subway relieved him of his briefcase.

relieve oneself go to the toilet:—After dinner Father went into the bathroom to relieve himself.

relish, have no relish for dislike, have no liking for:—I have no relish for the type of gossip that tends to injure another's reputation.

remember someone to another convey one's greetings to a mutual friend:—Be sure to remember me to Smith if you happen to see him in Chicago.

resort, as a last resort as a final expedient:—Having tried to raise the money by every means possible, we decided, as a last resort, to ask my aunt if she would lend it to us.

respect, with respect to regarding, with reference to:—With respect to the President's views on the matter, nothing has yet been published in the press.

respect See also **pay** one's respects.

rest on one's laurels rely or depend upon one's past achievements to sustain one's prestige:—Since winning high honors in his junior year, Oscar has done little studying, apparently with the idea that he could rest on his laurels.

rest-room a public washroom or toilet:—Can you please show me the way to the men's (ladies') rest-room?

rest, set (put) one's mind at rest relieve someone's anxiety:—You can set your mind at rest; the train makes only one more stop before our destination.

rest See also **lay** to rest; **oars,** rest on one's oars.

retreat See beat a hasty retreat.

return a visit call upon someone who has previously called upon you:—One of these nights we must return the Lodges' visit.

reverse, put in reverse an automobile term meaning to put the car in reverse speed, to go backwards:—Being very excited, she put the car in reverse rather than in first and backed into a telephone pole.

rhyme, neither rhyme nor reason without any sense whatsoever:—As far as I am concerned, his proposal has neither rhyme nor reason.

rib (v.) make fun of another, kid, chaff:—We all kept ribbing him about his new girl friend.

rid, get rid of discard, eliminate, dispose of:—It took me a month to get rid of my cough.

ride for a fall tempt danger or misfortune, act recklessly:—Gambling every night and losing money at his present rate, Jones is certainly riding for a fall.

ride herd on dominate, force performance, drive hard:—In order to get the annual report out on time, the boss rode herd on all his employees.

ride one be severe with someone, pursue and annoy constantly, criticize continually:—He is the kind of man who is always riding someone for one thing or another.

ride roughshod over treat with little consideration, disregard feelings of those around one:—Mrs. Bates always rode roughshod over the objections of her husband to the rather meager meals she served.

ride something hard overdo or over-emphasize something:—An avid stamp collector, John rides the subject pretty hard whenever it is introduced.

ride, let something ride let something pass, accept or put up with:—Since there is nothing we can do just now, why not let things ride for a while?

ride, take for a ride (1) an expression from the gangster period when rival gangsters were frequently taken for a ride in an automobile and murdered:—The body was found lying along the road, and the police assume the victim had been taken for a ride by some of his enemies. (2) make fun of, victimize:—Don't pay any attention to what he says about reporting you to the boss; he's just trying to take you for a ride.

ride See also **bum** a ride; **thumb** a ride.

rig out fit or dress in special clothes or equipment:—Janet arrived all rigged out in her new spring outfit.

right and left on all sides, freely, without restraint:—He spent his money right and left until he didn't have a penny remaining.

right away immediately, at once:—He said that he would be back right away.

right-hand man a valued and indispensable assistant:—The Governor never goes anywhere without Smith, who is his right-hand man and for whose judgment he has great respect.

right here (there) exactly here, on this spot:—It was right here that the accident happened.

right itself shift to the correct position, reestablish its proper balance:—Although our boat started to tip over, it soon righted itself.

right off without hesitation, right away, straightforwardly:—She told him right off that he was wasting his time proposing to her.

right off the reel Same as **right off.**

right, all right satisfactory, acceptable, O.K.:—He said it would be all right if I paid him next week instead of today.

right, be right be correct:—You are right when you say that he is overly generous.

right, in one's right mind sane, sensible:—I couldn't have been in my right mind when I lent him so much money.

rights, by rights in all justice, rightly, justly:—By rights the property should have gone to him rather than to his sister.

rights, put to rights put in orderly shape, arrange:—Our apartment certainly looked a mess when the maid arrived, but she soon put it to rights.

rights, stand on one's rights insist on one's privileges:—He said he would stand on his rights as a citizen and would not speak before he consulted his attorney.

right See also **serve** one right; **set** one right; **set** to rights; **strike** it right.

ring a bell remind, recall to mind, sound familiar (sl.):—I don't remember him personally, but the name Wilson seems to ring a bell.

ring in come or participate without being invited:—Nobody invited him, but he works in our office and somehow managed to ring in on our party.

ring out to sound sharply:—Two shots rang out in the night.

ring true be convincing, have a tone of genuineness:—I believed the tramp's story because somehow his words rang true.

ring up to telephone:—Why don't you ring up Bill and ask him to go with us?

ring, give someone a ring to telephone. Sometimes expressed as **give someone a buzz:**—Let's give Helen a ring and ask her to come over.

ringer a person who joins a group that he is not really an accredited member of:—That college football team was disqualified because they used a ringer who was not enrolled in the college.

ringleader the chief of an unsavory group, a higher-up:—The police finally caught the ringleader of the smugglers.

rise to the occasion prove to be adequate for the purpose or situation:—When the campaign to raise funds for the church fell short of the goal, a number of the wealthier members rose to the occasion and, with a large contribution, covered the deficit.

rise up revolt, rise in rebellion:—The people finally rose up and dethroned the unpopular monarch.

rise, get a rise out of provoke, induce a reaction or reply:—If you want to get a rise out of Dick, just mention that time he missed the train.

risk, run a risk expose oneself to chance of injury or loss:—In some states you can drive a car without being covered by insurance, but who wants to run such a risk?

road-hog a driver who takes more than his share of the road, making it difficult to pass:—Road-hogs are responsible for a good proportion of serious accidents.

road, on the road working as a traveling salesman:—He has always been on the road and enjoys the work very much.

road, one for the road a final drink before leaving a party:—Let's have one for the road before we say goodnight.

rock rock-and-roll music, popular music with a monotonous loud beat and little harmonic variety:—A rock band played at the wedding.

rock-bottom the lowest point, the absolute bottom:—They advertised that all the furniture would be sold at rock-bottom prices.

rocks (be, go) on the rocks become stranded, broken, destroyed:—They lived happily together for a few months, but then their marriage went on the rocks.

roll out the carpet to welcome with ceremony:—They rolled out the red carpet for the Minister when he arrived at the airport.

roll up make into or form a roll:—He rolled up his sleeves and set to work at once.

room and board a room with meals included:—A room alone in that boarding house costs ten dollars a week, but room and board together run twenty dollars a week.

room service the service supplied in most hotels, whereby food and drinks may be delivered directly to one's room:—As soon as we were settled in our room, we called up room service for some sandwiches and coffee.

room with live with in a furnished room, be a roommate to:—I roomed with Jack in college for two years.

room See also **elbow** room; **ladies'** room; **make** room for; **rest** room; **smoking** room; **waiting** room.

root for support, applaud, cheer for:—In the World Series I was rooting for the Red Sox and my wife for the Yankees.

root out remove, destroy, eradicate:—He has promised to root out any evidence of disloyalty in his department.

root See also **take** root.

rope in secure, capture, maneuver one into:—That barker at the fair was so persuasive that we were roped into buying a lot of things we didn't really want.

rope off isolate or divide into sections by the use of rope:—The section of the street which had caved in was immediately roped off by the police.

rope See also **know** the ropes.

rot, talk rot talk nonsense:—He's talking rot when he says that the company is almost bankrupt.

rough often used in the sense of "preliminary" or "approximate" as in such expressions as **rough copy, rough guess, rough estimate, rough idea,** etc.

rough and tumble violent, disorderly, noisy, scuffling:—It was a rough and tumble fight in which no holds were barred and no quarter given.

rough-house riotous play or commotion; horse-play:—I told the children that I would allow them to play in the barn on condition that there would be no rough-house.

rough it live primitively in the woods without any of the modern conveniences:—I like to get away to the woods for a month or so each year and really rough it.

rough-neck a low, coarse fellow:—The only boys in the neighborhood were a bunch of rough-necks, and she didn't want her son to associate with them.

rough, be rough on be hard on, injurious to and destructive of:—This kind of stone pavement is rough on tires.

roughly speaking speaking in general, approximately:—Roughly speaking, I would say that about a hundred people attended the exhibit.

round-about indirect:—He told me in a rather round-about way that he planned to go into business for himself.

round numbers approximate figures:—In round numbers there are about twenty-thousand people now living in that area.

round off terminate, make complete:—He decided to round off his trip to Europe with a brief visit to Yugoslavia and Greece.

round out make whole, complete:—He needs only one or two more stamps to round out his collection of post-war Central-American stamps.

round-trip passage to and back from a place:—The ticket agent asked me whether I wanted a one-way or a round-trip ticket.

round up capture, bring in:—The police have promised to round up every criminal in the city with a past record of dope addiction.

round, in the round said of a theater where the audience sits on all sides of the stage:—We saw an interesting play in the round.

round See also **go** around.

rounds, go the rounds See **make** the rounds.

royal road an easy path, a quick means of accomplishment:—There is no royal road to learning.

rub it in tease or annoy by constant reference to some irritating fact or incident:—I know that it was a foolish thing for me to do, but you don't have to keep rubbing it in.

rub off on (1) pass from one thing to another by rubbing, come off on:—Some of that chalk has rubbed off on your coat. (2) said of some personal quality or attainment that one has acquired:—Her father was a great actor and a little of his magnetic personality has rubbed off on his daughter.

rub one the wrong way annoy, irritate:—She may be a very nice person, but everything she says seems to rub me the wrong way.

rub out (1) erase:—He rubbed out his name and wrote hers in its place. (2) murder—a gangster term:—One by one members of the rival gang were rubbed out.

rub up polish:—If the plate tarnishes, you can rub it up a little and bring back its shine.

rub up against have contact with:—In his type of business, you naturally have to rub up against all kinds of people.

rub See **elbows,** rub elbows with.

rubber stamp signify official approval uncritically or automatically:—That state legislature rubber stamps all the bills sent to them by the Governor.

rule out refuse to allow, reject:—The proposal to give special bonuses to war heroes was ruled out on the grounds that it was discriminatory and unconstitutional.

rule the roost (originally roast) dominate, control:—Although at the office he is regarded as a forceful and stern executive, at home it is his wife who rules the roost.

rule, as a rule, generally, customarily:—As a rule, he arrives at the office about nine-thirty in the morning.

rumpus room a room, usually in the basement, used for indoor games, etc.:—Our neighbors have a rumpus room where their kids can play table-tennis.

run (1) operate, manage:—He and his wife own the business; she runs the office, he is in charge of the purchasing. (2) fail to hold fast—said of colors in a textile:—Will the colors in this dress run if I wash it? (3) campaign as a candidate for political office:—He is running for mayor on the Democratic ticket. (4) continue to function—said of theatrical plays, movies, etc.:—The show "Tobacco Road" ran for several years on Broadway. (5) continue in effect—said of legal documents, leases, contracts, etc.:—Our contract with them runs for another two years. (6) average, fall into a category:—Those eggs seem to run to about a pound per dozen. (7) place an advertisement or announcement in the newspaper during several successive editions:—I think the best way to sell your car would be to run an advertisement for a few days in the Times.

run a chance See **risk,** run a risk.

run a temperature continue to have a body temperature above normal:—The little girl ran a temperature and had to be put to bed.

run across meet or find unexpectedly:—I ran across an old friend of mine in the library.

run after pursue:—Instead of devoting himself to his studies, he wastes his time running after girls.

run around in circles be confused, waste time in repetitious movements:—There was such a crowd in the lobby that I kept running around in circles trying to find my group.

run around with associate with, go out frequently with:—Recently, Frank has been running around with a girl from the office.

run away leave home, escape:—He ran away as a boy, and his family has never heard from him since.

run away with escape in the company of, leave with, elope with:—He was never any good, and the fact that he ran away with another woman, leaving his wife and children unprovided for, only proves it.

run counter to be opposed to, be the opposite of:—All his ideas about how to run a farm run directly counter to ours.

run down (1) slow down, stop—said of a watch or clock:—My watch is run down. I must have forgotten to wind it. (2) criticize, speak disparagingly of, slander:—She not only gossips about her friends but seems to enjoy running them down. (3) trace, track down, follow to a source:—I spent two weeks in the library trying to run down some facts about the early voyages of Columbus. (4) strike and pass over—as with an automobile or other fast moving vehicle:—The child was found unconscious at the side of the road, having been run down by a car. (5) in poor condition, having deteriorated badly:—The whole place was run down and in need of repair. Sue is quite run down and needs a vacation. (6) pass over, check, review:—Let's run down this list of names to see whether everybody is present.

run dry become dry, dry up:—One day, after several years of use our well ran dry.

run errands carry messages or perform similar minor tasks for another:—Jimmy runs errands for all our neighbors.

run for one's money a close race, a contest causing thrill and excitement:—We were chased by a police car, and although it did not catch up with us, it certainly gave us a run for our money.

run in (1) visit informally:—Why don't you run in to see him some day and talk with him personally about it? (2) arrest, put in jail:—The man was making a nuisance of of himself, and the policeman told him that if he didn't behave himself, he would run him in.

run-in (n.) a disagreement, quarrel:—They had a violent run-in and are not speaking to each other now.

run in the family be a characteristic of various members of the family, be inherited:—They say that musical talent runs in his family.

run into (1) meet unexpectedly:—I ran into our old friend Marie Dodd the other day at the grocer's. (2) reach, approach:—They say that the cost of remodeling the building will run into thousands of dollars.

run into debt get in debt, acquire debts:—I prefer to make sacrifices and pay my bills, rather than run into debt.

run its course terminate its normal period, fulfill its normal development:—The health authorities predict that by the end of the summer, the epidemic will have run its course.

run low become scarce in supply:—We had to return to camp because our food supply was running low.

run of luck a period of good luck:—I had a run of luck last night at bridge and won several dollars.

run off (1) flee, run away:—When he heard our dog barking, the trespasser ran off. (2) print, publish:—On the first edition, they ran off only three thousand copies of the book.

run-of-the-mill average, ordinary, not outstanding:—They had only run-of-the-mill entertainment at that nightclub.

run on continue speaking without pause:—He kept running on and on, telling me the same story over and over again.

run out (1) terminate, become exhausted:—We decided it would be best to go home before our money ran out. (2) eject, throw out:—The Mayor has warned that all vagrants will be run out of the city.

run out of exhaust one's supply of:—On our way to Washington yesterday we ran out of gas.

run out on forsake, abandon, leave in the lurch:—I suspected that he was the type of employee who might run out on us if he got a better offer from someone else.

run over (1) knock down and pass over with an automobile or other moving vehicle:—While trying to avoid running over a child, the driver swerved and ran into a tree. (2) review, rehearse:—Let's run over these questions once more so as to know the answers well. (3) exceed:—The amount collected in taxes ran well over the estimate.

run short of develop a shortage in supply:—Since we didn't want to run short of food on the trip, we each carried extra rations in our knapsack.

run the streets roam the streets unsupervised:—That careless mother lets her small children run the streets all day.

run through (1) spend completely, exhaust the supply of:—He ran through his entire inheritance in less than a year. (2) go through, review, rehearse:—Let's run through the first scene once more in order to be sure that we all know our parts perfectly.

run to approximate, reach:—It is expected that the casualties may run to more than a hundred thousand killed and wounded.

run to seed deteriorate completely:—Though it had once been a prosperous business, it had, through neglect and bad management, run completely to seed.

run up to sew a garment, etc.:—I ran up this dress on my machine in less than forty minutes.

run up a bill incur, accumulate:—Pete is a generous man, but he doesn't like his wife's running up such large bills each month.

run up against meet, encounter, have contact with:—Being a pawnbroker, he naturally ran up against some rather strange characters.

run wild grow without restraint, be without limitation or control:—Since there was no one at home to care for them, the children were allowed to run wild in the streets each day.

run, get the run of understand the management and operation of:—As a new worker, it may take him a few weeks to get the run of things.

run, have a long (short) run show for a long (short) time—said of a movie or theatrical performance:—The play had a long two-year run on Broadway before being made into a movie.

run, have the run of have permission to use freely:—While his parents are in Florida each winter, Charles has the run of the house.

run, on the run (1) active, moving:—With three young children to take care of, Helen is kept on the run every minute

of the day. (2) without stopping or pausing:—We are so busy at the office these days that I generally have to eat my lunch on the run. (3) in flight, running away:—The reports say that on the southern section of the front we now have the enemy on the run.

run See also **long,** in the long run; **show,** run the show.

runaround, get (give) the runaround be sent fruitlessly from place to place, fail to receive proper attention:—Jack felt that he was given the run around when he was sent to four different floors of the department store before he found the tennis racket he wanted.

runner-up a competitor who is beaten in the last or final round of a contest:—Bill won two tennis tournaments this season and was runner-up in a third.

running commentary a continuous series of remarks:—Though his subject was European history, our professor used to give us each day a running commentary on current political events.

running, for a certain time running successively, continuously:—He has made inquiries about her for three days running.

running, out of the running not in the race or contest:—It was clear from the start that Coster was out of the running in the Congressional race.

rust away disappear gradually through the process of rust or corrosion:—If you don't paint those metal trimmings on your windows, they will soon rust away to nothing.

S

sack, get (give) the sack be dismissed, discharged, fired:—He was so unconcerned about doing his work that we were sure he would get the sack sooner or later.

sack, hit the sack go to bed (sl.):—We had been hiking all day, and by nine o'clock we were ready to hit the sack.

sack, in the sack in bed (sl.):—I'm usually in the sack by ten-thirty.

saddle, in the saddle in command, in control:—As dictator of his country he had been in the saddle for fifteen years, but the people were beginning to tire of his autocratic methods.

saddled with burdened with:—The business was so saddled with debts when Holmes took it over that he had a difficult time of it for several years.

safe and sound unharmed in mind or body:—Despite the fact that the ship had passed through a virtual hurricane, all the passengers arrived at port safe and sound.

safe, be on the safe side be well prepared, provided for against a possible emergency:—Though Miami is rarely very crowded during the summer months, we decided to be on the safe side and write for hotel reservations.

safe, play safe be prudent, cautious:—Instead of risking his inheritance in the stock market, Harry decided to play safe and invest it in corporate bonds.

sail close to the wind Said of one's actions that are on the borderline between legality and illegality:—Most people believe that in all those big business enterprises of his he must have been sailing quite close to the wind before the crash came.

sail into (1) enter suddenly, majestically:—Just at that moment Marjorie sailed into the office, all decked out in her new coat and hat. (2) abuse, scold:—I couldn't understand why Ellen sailed into her sister so harshly. (3) attack vigorously and efficiently:—He and his secretary sailed into the large stack of mail and disposed of it very quickly.

sail, set sail leave by boat, prepare the sails of a boat for sailing:—They will set sail for Le Havre on Wednesday.

sails See also **trim** one's sails; **wind,** take the wind out of someone's sails.

salad days the period of one's youth, a period of inexperience:—Hal had been quite a playboy in his salad days.

salt away save, store up:—Phillips had always salted away a good part of his earnings; consequently, when he reached fifty he was able to retire comfortably.

salt of the earth a basically good or precious person, one who helps to make society good and wholesome:—Everybody considered Jim and his wife the salt of the earth.

salt, not to be worth one's salt not to be worth what one is paid:—He was discharged because his employer felt that he was not worth his salt.

salt, take with a grain of salt accept with reservations, discount the full weight of:—John doesn't deliberately mislead, but I think what he says should be taken with a grain of salt.

sandwich (v.) to place or squeeze between two dissimilar things:—George was a little annoyed because his speech had been sandwiched in between two dull committee reports.

save sometimes used with the meaning of "except":—Everyone save John seemed affected by the news.

save face preserve one's dignity or prestige:—He tried to save face by claiming that the machinery had been defective to begin with and had not broken down because of his neglect.

save up intensive form of "to save," put money away in the form of savings:—He says that he is saving up to buy a home for his family.

saving grace a redeeming quality, a single good attribute:—Thrift might be termed the miser's saving grace.

save See also **breath,** save one's breath.

say-so (n.) permission, word, approval:—He was angry because she had taken his car without his say-so.

say the word give the signal, indicate approval:—Just say the word and I'll telephone and make the reservations.

say, have a say in participate in, have some authority in:—Although he has considerable money invested in the company, he has no say in its management.

say, you don't say an expression indicating surprise or incredulity:—"She was graduated from college at sixteen." "You don't say!"

say See also **grace,** say grace; **much,** not to say much for; **go** without saying.

scale, on a large (small) scale of great proportions:—They accept only government projects and similar construction work on a large scale.

scales See also **turn** the scales.

scalpers ticket speculators, those who buy up tickets to theatrical or sports events and resell them at a high price:—Since no tickets were available anywhere, we had to go to a scalper and pay him double the price.

scarce, make oneself scarce disappear, efface oneself, leave suddenly:—We had been smoking in front of our classroom, and when the school principal appeared we all promptly made ourselves scarce.

scare away (off) frighten away, cause to flee:—She is very stingy, so that the best way to scare her away is to begin talking about spending money.

scenes, behind the scenes in the background secretly—said of a controlling group:—You can be quite sure that there is a great deal going on behind the scenes of political conventions.

scene, make the scene appear, visit, arrive:—While we were visiting Rome, two of our dearest friends also made the scene. Thousands of young people made the scene when the summer jazz festival was held in Newoprt.

scene See also **make** a scene.

school, of the old school old-fashioned, belonging to an earlier period in manner or ideas:—Father was definitely of the old school and had some rather rigid ideas about the rearing of young daughters.

school See also **primary** school; **public** school; **tell** tales out of school.

scoop (n.) an exclusive news item:—The Times scored a scoop when it published the list of new ambassadorial appointments twelve hours before any of the other newspapers.

scorcher (n.) something very hot:—Isn't today a scorcher?

score (v.) win acceptance, affection, or compliance from a member of the female sex:—Did Harry score with Elsie last night?

score, know what the score is be alert, attentive, abreast of the latest events:—In this job we need someone who is hardworking and who knows what the score is.

score, on that score on that point, in that matter or consideration:—I can assure you that on that score you need have no further worry.

score See also **settle,** have a score to settle.

scot free completely free, without punishment:—Though he was apparently guilty, the jury finally acquitted him and he went scot free.

scout around look around, search for:—We spent all weekend scouting around for some antiques to use in furnishing our new apartment.

scout See also **talent** scout.

scram leave quickly and unceremoniously, get out (sl.):—Helen and Jim wanted to be alone, so they told her little brother to scram.

scrap (v.) destroy, break up, get rid of in the form of scrap:—After the war the United States scrapped many naval vessels.

scrape together gather or save with difficulty:—It took Jones more than six months to scrape together enough money to make the trip.

scrape up Same as **scrape together.**

scrape, get into a scrape get into trouble or into some predicament:—His police record shows that even as a boy he got into one scrape after another.

scratch the surface penetrate very lightly into something, not to go deeply:—Economists say that we haven't even begun to scratch the surface of the potential wealth of some of the countries that are not yet industrialized.

scratch, from scratch from an absolute beginning, with nothing:—After that tornado last year, we had to start from scratch rebuilding our house.

scratch, up to scratch up to standard:—Dean's playing, as a result of his illness, is not quite up to scratch.

scream, to be a scream be very funny and laughable:—Harry's a scream when he tells jokes in dialect.

screw, have a screw loose act strangely, show symptoms of insanity:—I am not surprised they finally put him in an asylum; for a long time I had suspected that he had a screw loose.

screws, put on the screws bring pressure to bear upon, force:—To make him do his best, you have to put the screws on him.

screwy odd, mad, illogical:—Dunn has the screwy idea that in order to make a lot of money you first have to spend a lot of money.

sea, at sea perplexed, confused. Sometimes as **all at sea:**—Having had poor preparation in mathematics in high school, Bill was all at sea for the first few months of his college calculus course.

sea, go to sea become a sailor:—He had run away from home and gone to sea when he was only sixteen years old.

sea, put (out) to sea set sail, leave on a sea voyage:—The report states that they put to sea on November 5, in a small sailing craft.

search me an answer meaning: I don't know.:—"Why did Elsa divorce James?" "Search me."

seat-belt a safety-belt worn by passengers in a car or in a plane:—As our plane took off we had to fasten our seat-belts.

second childhood dotage:—The old man, who was in his second childhood and therefore not responsible for some of the rather strange things he said and did, required constant attention.

second-hand used, not new:—There are some shops along Third Avenue selling second-hand men's suits.

second nature an acquired skill or tendency that has become almost instinctive, easy, natural:—Percy is perfectly at home in the water; swimming seems to be second nature to him.

second-rate inferior, not of the highest quality:—We disliked the movie and thought it second-rate.

second sight intuition, prescience:—How Joan's father learned about her secret marriage is a mystery; he must have second sight.

second thought upon reflection, after further consideration:—On second thought, I believe I will go with you to the theater.

second wind renewed strength:—I was very tired after dinner, but about nine o'clock I got my second wind and was able to play a good game of bridge.

secret, make no secret of show or reveal openly:—Jack makes no secret of the fact that he doesn't like his sister's friends.

secret See also **open** secret; **top** secret.

see (1) like, approve of:—I can't see Pearson at all; to me he is just a pompous old fool. (2) have the experience of:—I feel sure that old beggar has seen much better days. (3) attend to something, take steps to insure that something is done:—He said he'd see that I was paid before he left. (4) think over, consider:—When little Tommy asked his father whether he might go to the circus, his father replied, "We will see."

see about take care of, take steps to get or to arrange to get:—Will you see about getting some new shades for our front windows?

see after look after, take care of, take charge of:—Helen has promised to see after the children while we go to the movies.

see fit consider advisable, choose, decide:—For reasons best known to herself, Grace saw fit to exclude Mr. and Mrs. Carter from her invitation list.

see how the land lies investigate, reconnoiter:—Before asking him for the loan, we had better talk with Smith a while and see how the land lies.

see a lot (little) of be frequently (seldom) in the company of:—She has been seeing a lot of Henry Jones lately.

see one off accompany to the starting place of a journey, go to say goodbye to someone at a railway station, airport, etc.:—A group of us went to the airport to see Helen off on her trip west.

see one out (in, home, to the door, etc.) accompany someone as far as the door, etc.:—Just a moment, John will see you to the door.

see one's way find or consider possible. Sometimes expressed as **see one's way clear**:—He said he was sorry but that he couldn't see his way clear to allowing us to rent the house.

see red become incensed, angry:—I see red every time I hear him speak disrespectfully to the old man.

see service (1) be in use over a considerable period of time:—This overcoat of mine has already seen five years of service. (2) serve in a military sense:—Colonel Brown has seen service in Egypt, Bulgaria, and Japan.

see something through carry something to completion, ensure that something is completed:—We don't have to worry, she is very competent and will see the job through on time.

see stars become dizzy or unconscious as the result of a blow on the head:—For a moment, when I hit my head against the iron gate, I saw stars.

see through (1) penetrate, understand the real nature of, not to be deceived by:—My mother is a very astute woman; she saw right through John's seeming politeness. (2) support or pay the expenses of, ensure passage through:—Frank's uncle very generously offered to see him through college.

see to take care of, ensure that something is done:—I asked the superintendent of our building to fix the leak in our faucet, and he said he would see to it today.

see, long time no see We haven't seen you in a long time:—Hello, George! Long time no see.

see See also **eye,** see eye to eye; **light,** see the light.

seeing that inasmuch as (colloq.):—Seeing that you already have a good fur coat, perhaps it would be best for you to buy a lighter weight cloth coat.

seek a place look for work or for a position:—Our old cook is seeking a place with a childless couple.

self-conscious embarrassed, shy as a result of being unable to forget oneself:—Sometimes, when Grace is not comfortable, she has a tendency to stutter, and that makes her very self-conscious.

self-made having achieved success by one's own efforts and without outside help:—Abraham Lincoln was a self-made man.

self-possessed sure of oneself, confident:—For such a young girl, she is very self-possessed.

self-seeking selfish, ever alert to one's own advantage and aggrandisement:—In the pursuit of his ambition, John has become very self-seeking and indifferent to others.

sell (on) secure approval of, get one to agree to:—Let's try to sell John on the idea of going to Florida with us for the holidays. Cf. **be sold on.**

sell down the river desert or betray—from the manner of selling slaves "down the river" at a public marketplace:—Everybody knows that when he became so successful, he sold many of his friends down the river.

sell one a bill of goods defraud, persuade another to accept or buy something which cannot be readily utilized or disposed of:—That salesman certainly sold you a bill of goods when he induced you to buy that foreign-made car for which replacement parts are rarely available.

sell out (1) to dispose of the entire supply or stock of:—The advertisement says that Macy's is selling out their entire supply of last year's television sets at a great discount. (2) prove false to one's friends or supporters, betray for a price:—Many people still feel that Petain sold out to the Germans. (3) (n.) a great success:—The new musical play at the Cort Theater is a sellout. A sign on the box-office window each night says "All Sold Out."

sell short undervalue, disparage, or depreciate:—Don't make the mistake of selling the Democratic candidate short; he has a good chance of winning the election despite appearances to the contrary.

sell See also **hard** sell; **soft** sell.

send one about one's business dismiss another summarily:—When Mrs. Smith discovered that her daughter's suitor was simply a fortune hunter, she promptly sent him about his business.

send-off a demonstration of respect or affection at someone's departure:—One of the members of our staff was leaving on a six-months business trip, and we gave him a big send-off.

send one packing dismiss, send away summarily:—I happen to know that when she tired of him she just sent him packing.

send one up send or sentence to prison:—Upon being convicted for tax evasion, Grimes was sent up for five years.

send word advise, send notice to:—We sent word to Frank to come home immediately.

sense of humor capacity to appreciate humor, ability to laugh at oneself:—He is quite ready to laugh at the failings of others but has no sense of humor about his own.

sense, in a sense in one respect:—In a sense you are right in refusing to join that club.

sense, makes sense be intelligible:—What he told us about the situation simply doesn't make sense.

sense, make sense out of understand, decipher:—The letter was so badly written that I couldn't make any sense out of it.

senses, come to one's senses (1) regain consciousness:—She fainted when the car hit the pole, and when she came to her senses, she was in a hospital bed. (2) become reasonable, return to a reasonable state or point of view:—Helen was hysterical over the accident, but she came to her senses when her friends persuaded her that it was not her fault.

serve a sentence pass a definite and prescribed period of time in prison:—He served two years of his three-year sentence and was then released for good behavior.

serve notice advise, notify in a formal or legal manner:—They served notice upon all the tenants to vacate their apartments by the end of the month.

serve one right be a just and deserved punishment:—It would serve him right to get a ticket for speeding, inasmuch as he drives very recklessly.

serve the purpose Same as **answer the purpose.**

serve time pass time in prison:—Since it was well known that Brown had once served time, it was often difficult for him to find work in our town.

service station a gasoline station:—Let's stop at the next service station and get some gas.

service, at one's service at one's disposition or disposal:—We had a maid and a car at our service all the time we were visiting them.

service, be of service be useful, serve:—If I can be of any service to you, just let me know.

service See also **see** service.

set (1) place the hands of a watch or clock at the proper hour:—After winding the watch, he set it at eight o'clock. (2) arrange the plates and cutlery on a table:—While her mother prepared the dinner, Mary set the table. (3) arrange an hour or date for an appointment, meeting, etc.:—The date for the wedding was set for the first Sunday in March. (4) serve as a model:—Bill's fine performance set a good example for the rest of us. (5) arrange or place a broken bone in proper position:—The bone in Bill's shoulder had not been properly set, and therefore had to be reset. (6) disappear from the sky—said of the sun:—The sun at this season of the year rises at six o'clock and sets at about seven o'clock in the evening.

set about begin, take steps towards doing:—After supper Mary set about clearing the table.

set aside (1) place to one side, save:—
Each week he tried to set aside a few
dollars of his salary. (2) annul, disregard:—The judge set aside the jury's
award of a hundred thousand dollars as
being excessive.

set back (1) reverse the progress of, im-
pede:—Mussolini and his group set back
the progress of Italy many years. (2)
turn backwards:—As a joke, Bill set
back the clock a whole hour. (3) cost:—
How much did your new car set you
back?

set-back a reversal, relapse:—Just as she
was getting well, Helen suffered a set-
back and had to remain in bed another
week.

set down record, state in writing:—The
lawyer asked him to set down the facts
just as he remembered them.

set eyes on see:—It was one of the most
beautiful sights that I had ever set eyes
on.

set foot in enter:—He said he would never
set foot in that house again.

set forth (1) record, expound, present:—
In his preface the author set forth his
reasons for writing the book. (2) start
on a journey:—We set forth on our hike
immediately after breakfast.

set free liberate, free:—Following the
Civil War, the Southern slaves were set
free.

set in arise, take place, begin:—Just as he
was recovering from his attack of the
flu, pneumonia set in.

set loose cause, provoke, release:—His resignation set loose a flood of rumors as
to who his successor would be.

set off (1) begin a trip or journey:—With
their knapsacks on their backs, they set
off in the direction of Bear Mountain.
(2) ignite, touch off:—Since no one had
any more matches, there was nothing
with which to set off the firecrackers.
(3) enhance, act as a foil or contrast
to:—The platinum mounting tends to
set off the rich color of the rubies.

set on foot institute, begin, cause to start:
—The disappearance of the bank president immediately set on foot a general
investigation of the bank's operations.

set one's cap for seek to catch as a husband:—You'd better be careful; it looks
to me as though Grace is setting her cap
for you.

set one's mind on decide to, be determined to:—Jack has set his mind on going to college next year.

set one straight correct one, orient properly:—We had been experimenting and
making many mistakes, but when the
chief engineer arrived he set us straight
with his excellent suggestions.

set out (1) begin a journey:—He set out
on foot early the next morning with the
intention of reaching the next town before nightfall. (2) display, exhibit:—All
the better merchandise was set out on
shelves at the front of the store.

set out to begin with the intention of:—
Obviously he had set out to kill her but
was restrained by the presence of so
many people in the house.

set right to correct, discipline, indicate
the correct procedure. Sometimes expressed as **put right**:—He came to the
meeting with the intention of dominating it, but the chairman soon set him
right.

set store by place value upon, treasure
highly:—The lawyer for the defendant
said he didn't set much store by some
of the evidence the other side had produced.

set to music compose a musical accom-
paniment to verses:—Schubert set some
of Goethe's lyrics to music.

set to rights See **put** to rights.

set to work begin to work, arrange to
work:—As soon as he gets back from his
trip, he plans to set to work revising the
manuscript.

set up (1) begin, start:—They plan to set
up housekeeping right after they get
married. (2) put together, erect:—Let's
set up the tent first, and build the fire
later. (3) provide with the means of
starting a business or undertaking:—His
dad is sufficiently wealthy to set him up
in any business he chooses. (4) treat
someone to a drink:—After we had each
bought a round of drinks, the bartender
insisted that it was now his turn to set
them up.

set-up arrangement, structure:—When we got to the camp, we didn't like the set-up and decided to go elsewhere.

set upon attack:—That unlucky pedestrian was set upon by thieves.

set, be set be ready, prepared. Also frequently expressed as **be all set**:—We were all set to uproot some of the old trees, when my father suggested that we might wait until we decided on how the grounds were to be planted.

set, be set against opposed to. Frequently expressed as **be dead set against**:—His father and mother were both set against his marrying so young.

set, be set in one's ways fixed in one's ideas or habits, unyielding:—You know how set David is in his ways; he has been a bachelor so long that he'll never marry.

set, be set on (upon) be determined upon:—He is set upon leaving school and going to work because he feels responsible for the support of his mother.

set-to an argument, discussion, quarrel:—They had come to an agreement in the afternoon, but when they reached home in the evening they had a set-to about who was to be in charge.

set See also **dead** set against; **fire**, set fire to; **fire**, set on fire; **heart**, set one's heart on; **pace**, set the pace; **rest**, set one's mind at rest; **teeth**, set one's teeth on edge.

settle, have a score to settle with pay back for some wrong or injury, retaliate, get even with:—Michael didn't forget that he had a score to settle with that boy who had attacked him without provocation.

settle down adopt a regular mode of life, after one's youthful fling:—I think it is about time that Frank got married and settled down.

settle on agree on:—They have finally settled on the terms of the lease.

settle one's hash punish, put another in his place:—"Wait till your father comes home, you bad boys," said their mother; "he'll settle your hash for you."

settle up conclude money or other transactions, pay up:—Mr. Hicks owed us a balance of about $50, but he telephoned to say that he would come in next week and settle up.

seventh heaven the pinnacle of happiness:—We were in seventh heaven all through that beautiful sail down the river.

sew up tie together, win, accomplish, settle:—Smith is going to sew up that insurance deal with the bank tomorrow.

sewed up engaged, busy, unable to free oneself:—It was too bad that Tom couldn't go to the ball game with us; he said he would be sewed up all afternoon with some out-of-town customers.

shack up with (vulgar sl.) said of a man living with a woman to whom he is not married:—During the war many soldiers shacked up with native girls.

shadow (v.) to follow (trail) closely and secretly:—He testified that he was sure he had been shadowed by two men that evening.

shady unscrupulous, not quite legal or legitimate in nature, dubious:—There have been some rumors that it is a shady enterprise, and I personally would not do business with them.

shake avoid, desert, escape from:—We tried all afternoon to shake Claude, but he stuck right with us.

shake a leg hurry:—We'd better shake a leg or we'll miss the train.

shake hands greet another by a clasping of the hands:—When friends in America meet, they usually shake hands.

shake off (1) get rid of:—I can't seem to shake off this cold. (2) lose, escape from by disappearing:—Although two detectives were following him, the suspect managed to shake them off.

shake one's head move one's head from one side to the other in gesture of negation:—John simply shook his head when I asked him whether he had come home late.

shake the dust from one's feet leave or depart with some displeasure or disgust:—

Hal had been so unhappy here that he was glad to shake the dust of the town from his feet.

shake up mix by shaking:—Let me shake up a cocktail for you while you're waiting.

shake-up (n.) a reorganization, change:— He was very much depressed over the graft exposures and the general shake-up in his department.

shake, give one a fair shake be just or fair to another:—That dealer gave me a fair shake on my trade-in for a new car.

shake, in a shake quickly, immediately. Sometimes expressed as **in the shake of a lamb's tail:**—Wait just a minute. I'll finish this in the shake of a lamb's tail.

shakes, no great shakes of little importance, inferior:—He had been a great ball player, but as a team manager he was no great shakes.

shame, put to shame to cause a feeling of inferiority:—We felt we hadn't done badly at the audition, but when Frank began to sing, we were all put to shame.

shape up take form, progress towards fulfillment:—The plans for the new housing development seem to be shaping up nicely.

shape, in shape in form or condition:— The business was in very bad shape after he retired.

shape See also **lick** into shape; **out** of shape; **put** in shape; **shipshape; take** shape.

sheepskin diploma:—It was a happy day for us when John graduated and finally secured his sheepskin.

shelf, on the shelf inactive, discarded:— Since his enforced retirement at 65, he has felt rather on the shelf.

shell out pay for, produce the money for: —Father claims that all he does is shell out for our extravagances.

shelter, take shelter seek refuge, protection:—We took shelter from the storm in an old barn.

shift for oneself support oneself look out for oneself:—Kent lost both parents

when he was a small boy, and has had to shift for himself almost all his life.

shilly-shally to hesitate, be indecisive, waiver:—You ought to stop shilly-shallying and begin work on that thesis.

shine up to seek to impress, flatter, fawn upon;—It was amusing the way he tried to shine up to us when he realized that we were Kent's sisters.

shine See also **take** a shine to.

shiner a black (bruised) eye:—John appeared with a beautiful shiner which he resolutely refused to discuss.

shipshape in good order, in perfect condition:—At the end of the summer we left the cottage shipshape for the next occupants.

shirt, lose one's shirt lose everything, become penniless:—Everybody knows that John lost his shirt when that business he had invested in failed.

shirt See also **keep** one's shirt on; **stuffed** shirt.

shoe is on the other foot the situation is reversed, the opposite situation prevails:—His brothers used to tease him for being so small, but now the shoe is on the other foot, because he has grown much taller than they are.

shoe, where the shoe pinches where the trouble lies:—He has a fine income, but where the shoe pinches is that there has been so much illness in his family.

shoes, be in someone else's shoes be in the situation of someone else:—He has had so much trouble recently that we ought to be grateful we are not in his shoes.

shoestring, on a shoestring on an insignificant amount of capital:—It is said that Henry Ford started his business on a shoestring.

shoo away chase or frighten away:—A lot of small boys gathered around the house, but Mother shooed them away.

shoo-in a sure winner in a contest:—The Democratic candidate is a shoo-in for the Governorship.

shoot (v.) photograph, take pictures of:— The director ordered the cameraman to shoot the scene over again.

shoot ahead of (past, through, alongside of) drive or move ahead of rapidly:—As we slowed down for the turn, a low gray car shot ahead of us.

shoot it out shoot to a conclusion:—Many of the movies about pioneering life in the West show scenes where the outlaws shoot it out with the sheriff and his men, or with the townsfolk.

shoot one's bolt exhaust one's last resource:—History may judge that the Germans shot their bolt at the Battle of the Bulge; after that, their defeat was just a matter of time.

shoot questions at interrogate vigorously and rapidly:—The lawyer shot one question after another at the witness in an effort to confuse him.

shoot the breeze (sl.) talk or visit informally, chat:—After supper, Tom came over and we sat around shooting the breeze.

shoot up (1) grow rapidly:—It is amazing to see how that child has shot up in one year. (2) arise suddenly, burst forth:—When we arrived, flames were shooting up from the roof of the building. (3) engage in wild and indiscriminate shooting:—On Saturday nights the cowboys would get drunk and then shoot up the town.

shoplifter a store thief, one who steals merchandise from store counters:—Every large department store always has several detectives on guard against shoplifters.

shopworn said of an article slightly soiled or damaged and thus offered for sale cheap:—Though shopworn, the dress was still usable, and Grace considered it a good bargain.

shop, talk shop discuss common problems with one engaged in the same business or profession:—Our wives were annoyed because John and I spent the whole evening talking shop.

shop See also **open** shop.

shopping, go shopping go to a store to make purchases:—Men generally dislike going shopping while women enjoy it.

shopping, window-shopping the pastime of walking along the street looking at the merchandise displayed in store windows:—In the evening my friend and I often go window-shopping along Fifth Avenue.

short lacking in money:—I am a little short. Can you let me have ten dollars until payday?

short-cut a shorter route than that normally taken:—We can save at least ten minutes if we take this short-cut through the park.

short of (1) lacking in, in short supply:—The attack was delayed because several of the battalions were short of ammunition. (2) other than:—There doesn't seem to be any way of dealing with that student short of expelling him from college.

short of breath easily winded:—He has put on so much weight that, at the slightest exertion, he becomes short of breath.

short, for short as an abbreviation:—We call him Monty for short, his real name being Montgomery.

short, in short in brief, by way of summary:—He became, in short, the finest actor on the American stage.

short, stop short stop or pause suddenly:—The sudden appearance of the child directly in front of the car caused the driver to stop short. Similar to **pull up short.**

short See also **cut** short; **fall** short; **make** short work of; **run** short of; **sell** short.

shortchange give a customer less change than is due him, cheat:—The cashier shortchanged me, giving me eighty instead of ninety cents in change.

shorthanded insufficiently supplied with workers:—With three people on vacation the sudden rush of business found us shorthanded.

shot (1) (n.) a drink:—I told him that what he needed was several good stiff shots of whiskey. (2) (adj.) ruined, exhausted from long or excessive use, worn out:—I need a new car; my present one is pretty well shot.

shot in the arm literally, an injection into the arm; thus a stimulus of courage, enthusiasm, etc.:—The whole market needs a shot in the arm if stocks are to regain last year's levels.

shot in the dark an indiscriminate attempt with little chance of success, a wild guess:—The question was a shot in the dark on the part of the prosecutor, but the witness's answer gave him just the information he wanted.

shot to pieces ruined, exhausted. See **shot** above. Also sometimes expressed as **shot to hell**:—His health, as a result of his two years in a concentration camp, was naturally shot to pieces.

shot, half shot partially intoxicated:— Every day, after lunch, Bill would come back to the office half shot.

shot, take (have) a shot at try, experiment, take a chance at:—I told him that I didn't think I could do the work but that I would be glad to take a shot at it.

shot See also **by,** not by a long shot; **long** shot; **one-shot; snapshot.**

shots, call one's shots be frank:—When you called him a sneak, you certainly called your shots.

shots, call the shots direct, command:— The boss's son may tell you that the firm is going to buy a truck from you, but it's the boss who calls the shots.

shotgun wedding a compulsory marriage: —Shotgun weddings are not as frequent today as they were in the past.

shoulder, give someone a cold shoulder treat with indifference, ignore:—Grace had reason to give him a cold shoulder at the party.

shoulder, put one's shoulder to the wheel exert oneself in an effort to accomplish or to aid in accomplishing something, cooperate:—The lecturer said that if we would all put our shoulders to the wheel, we could accomplish a great deal toward increasing the cultural activities in our town.

shoulder, straight from the shoulder frank, direct, not roundabout:—The contractor told us straight from the shoulder that we would be making a mistake to build our house on that corner.

shoulder See also **chip,** carry a chip on one's shoulder; **head** and shoulders above; **head,** have a head on one's shoulders.

shouting, all over but the shouting a foregone conclusion, completed as regards the essentials:—By 10 o'clock we knew who had won, and that the election was all over but the shouting.

shove around push from one side to another, domineer over, maltreat:—He lost his temper and shouted that he was tired of being shoved around by everybody in the department.

shove off leave, depart (sl.):—I think it's about time for me to shove off.

show around conduct on a visit or tour, serve as a guide:—My cousin is visiting us next week, and I have promised to show him around New York.

show cause give a reason or explanation: —The judge required the defendants to show cause why they should not be held without bail.

show fight exhibit a tendency to fight, not to submit, resist:—We were pleased to see little Willie show fight; previously he had allowed the other boys to dominate him.

show-girl one who works as an entertainer or dancer in a night club, musical show, or the like:—Many famous Hollywood actresses began their careers as Broadway show-girls.

show in (out, up, to the door, etc.) conduct or lead in (or out):—The maid will show you in.

show of hands an exhibition of raised hands indicating a vote:—The chairman of the meeting called for a show of hands on the proposed measure.

show off (1) attempt to attratct attention by display of either one's abilities or possessions:—Grace speaks French well, and, whenever the opportunity arises, likes to show off in front of strangers. (2) display to advantage:—These pearls will show off well against your black velvet dress.

show one's hand (cards) exhibit or reveal one's true, and hitherto hidden, purpose:—It was only after Hitler became Chancellor that he really showed his hand.

show one's teeth exhibit one's pugnacity, show anger:—Each time I tried to pet him the dog showed his teeth.

show the door (to) ask one to leave, eject, dismiss summarily:—Exasperated by the man's insolence, Ted finally showed him the door.

show up (1) put in an appearance, appear:—Although we waited until ten o'clock, John never showed up. (2) reveal, expose:—The investigation showed up the inefficiency of the management, and indicated the need for better trained personnel. (3) exhibit to advantage:—The dark-toned furniture shows up well against the light walls.

show, give (get) a fair show allow a fair chance or opportunity:—The master of ceremonies promised to give each contestant a fair show in answering the questions.

show, give the show away reveal something hidden:—Mr. Allen wanted to surprise his wife with a new car, but her little son told her about it first and gave the show away.

show, goes to show proves, illustrates:—The fact that his novels have been so successful goes to show that he was right in turning to literature as a profession.

show, put on a show pretend:—She's not really ill; she's just putting on a show.

show, run the show be in charge, manage:—Mr. Allen is our President, but our Vice-President really runs the show.

showdown a final challenge necessitating a disclosure of one's actual resources:—Some authorities maintain that you can't know a country's military strength until a final showdown occurs.

showing, make a good (poor) showing acquit oneself well, make a good presentation:—The former champion made a poor showing in his attempt at a comeback.

shut down close, become idle—said particularly of a factory or plant:—The plant was shut down for two months as a result of the strike.

shut off stop, terminate—said particularly of anything which flows, such as water, electricity, gas, etc.:—The water was shut off for several hours while the plumber repaired the pipes.

shut up (1) be quiet, stop talking:—She told that noisy boy to shut up. (2) close completely—often said of a house:—We decided to shut up our town house and move to the country for the summer.

shut up shop close a business permanently, temporarily, or at the end of day:—Because of the extra holiday this Friday, we are going to shut up shop for three days.

shy away from avoid, act suspicious of:—After one term as City Councilman, Smith shied away from politics.

shy of short of, lacking in:—Being a little shy of money, Jack took his girl to a movie instead of the theater.

side-kick a close friend or companion:—Wherever you see Bill, you can be sure to see his side-kick Jack.

side-step avoid, step to one side so as to let something pass:—Several of the men tried to side-step the issue by ignoring the questions put to them.

side-track deflect, delay, postpone:—Although some Congressmen tried to side-track the issue, public opinion forced its immediate consideration.

side-trip a short trip taken from the central location of the main trip:—When we went to London we took several side-trips to the literary shrines of England.

side with favor, espouse the cause of:—I am inclined to side with Henry in that matter.

side, be on the side of support, favor, champion:—He expressed himself openly as being on the side of the poor rather than the rich.

side, get on someone's good side flatter, please, gain the favor of:—Whenever she wants anything, Janice knows how to get on her father's good side.

side, on the side (1) as a side-dish, something extra:—They served us fried chicken with peas, and corn on the side. (2) as something extra—apart from one's regular work or duties:—He earns a little something on the side by taking subscriptions to magazines.

side See also **wrong** side of the tracks.

sides, on all sides everywhere:—On all sides there was great enthusiasm over the President's speech.

sides, take sides show partiality, favor one person's views rather than another's:—Despite my friendship with Frank, I tried not to take sides with him in his argument with his brother.

sight for sore eyes a person or thing the sight of which causes pleasure:—We hadn't seen Jack in so long a time that when he dropped in the other evening we all felt he was a sight for sore eyes.

sight gag a joke or humorous skit that needs to show some article to the audience in order to be funny:—Sight gags do not succeed on the radio.

sight-read read and perform a piece of music at sight without previous study:—Jay cannot sight-read well, but he is nevertheless an excellent performer on the piano.

sight, at first sight at the first glance, upon being first seen:—It was clearly a case of love at first sight.

sight, at sight without previous sight of:—That pianist can read the most difficult music at sight.

sight, in sight in view, visible:—There was no one anywhere in sight.

sight, keep sight of retain in mind, remember, consider:—In judging his conduct, we must keep sight of the fact that he was under great strain at the time.

sight, know one by sight recognize through having seen, though not known personally:—I have never met the man, but I know him well by sight.

sight, not by a long sight virtually impossible, by no means, absolutely not, or unlikely:—I wouldn't feed bears out of their cages—not by a long sight.

sight See also **lose** sight of; **out** of sight; **second** sight.

sights, see the sights visit the notable places of a metropolis:—I explained to them that three days in New York was very little time to see all the sights.

sign, give signs of indicate, show:—The poor old man showed no signs of having heard us.

silver lining the hopeful part of an otherwise sad situation, the consoling or compensating element:—The fact that almost immediately John found a better job than the one he lost is further proof of the saying that every cloud has a silver lining.

silver wedding a couple's twenty-fifth wedding anniversary:—My mother and father will celebrate their silver wedding anniversary tomorrow.

sing someone's praises praise or extol continuously:—Everyone left the concert singing the young pianist's praises.

single out choose select one from among many:—There were very many pretty girls at the dance, but Elliott singled Mary out immediately.

sit-in the act of striking labor unionists sitting idly in their employers' offices or factories until their wage demands are met or settled:—After a week of sit-ins, the carpet company signed a new agreement with the union.

sit in on participate in, take part in as a spectator:—Though he had no vote the delegate from Hawaii was allowed to sit in on the conferences.

sit out wait inactively until a dance or other event is over, not participate, skip:—I'm pretty tired. Let's sit this dance out.

sit this one out not participate:—Thanks for inviting me to speak at your meeting. I'll just sit this one out.

sit tight make no move, await developments:—Instead of questioning the witness, our lawyer decided to sit tight and let the defense first present its case.

sit up (1) change from a lying to a sitting position:—The operation was performed only three days ago, but the doctor is going to permit William to sit up for a while. (2) refrain from going to bed at the usual time:—I sat up last night until three o'clock reading that novel you gave me. (3) assume an erect, upright sitting position:—As soon as the teacher appeared, all the students sat up in ther seats.

sit up for wait until after the usual bedtime for someone's return:—Mrs. Smith always sits up for her daughter no matter how late it may be.

sit up with be with, particularly to keep company with someone ill:—The mother sat up with her sick child all night.

sit, make sit up surprise, shock, interest:—Dorothy's sudden appearance at the party, and her sensational dress, made us all sit up.

sitting pretty be in a fortunate and enviable position:—With all those government contracts, our firm is sitting pretty.

sixes and sevens disorganized, confused:—We have been at sixes and sevens ever since we moved into our new offices.

size up estimate, evaluate, comprehend:—Some people have the ability to size up a situation at a glance.

skim the surface treat superficially:—This book only skims the surface of the political and economic problems facing Europe.

skin deep shallow, superficial:—It is often said that beauty is only skin deep.

skin game a fraud, something unethical and dishonest:—It was discovered, on investigation by the District Attorney, that they had been operating a skin game, and not a legitimate business.

skin, by the skin of one's teeth by a very narrow margin:—He just made the train by the skin of his teeth.

skin, get under one's skin irritate, annoy:—Several remarks he made got under my skin, but I tried not to show my annoyance.

skin, have a thin skin be unusually sensitive to imaginary or real slights, insults, etc.:—Don't make fun of Jones. He has a pretty thin skin.

skip it forget it, omit it:—I tried to thank him several times for his help, but he told me to skip it.

skip out desert, abandon, run away:—Just as the business was beginning to go well, his partner skipped out with all the money.

skip over omit, go past:—In reading a novel, I generally skip over all the long descriptive passages.

sky, out of a clear sky unexpectedly, suddenly:—He announced out of a clear sky that he was going to quit his job and join the army.

sky, to the skies highly, greatly:—Janet's former employer praised her to the skies.

slap in the face a rebuke, disappointment, slight:—It was quite a slap in the face to Helen when she learned that Bill had invited Grace to the school prom.

slated for scheduled for, intended for:—They say that their present ambassador to this country is slated for a diplomatic post abroad.

slave-driver a boss or employer who exacts the utmost from his employees, a severe disciplinarian:—Carpenter is such a slave-driver that no one wants to work for him.

sleep off sleep until the effects of some drug or liquor pass:—George had too many drinks last night and is now sleeping off the effects.

sleep in said of an employee or household worker who regularly stays overnight in his room at his or her employer's house or apartment:—That young couple wants a child's nurse who will sleep in.

sleep on something defer consideration of, consider carefully:—I'll sleep on your offer and give you my answer in the morning.

sleep See also **put** to sleep.

sleeve, have something up one's sleeve hold back or conceal something, have some hidden resource or intention:—The moment she came in, we knew that she had some mischief up her sleeve.

sleeve, laugh up (in) one's sleeve laugh or be amused at secretly:—All the time we were talking about who had eaten up the pie, George must have been laughing up his sleeve at us, because it was he who ate it.

slip away (past, through, off, out, etc.) leave unobtrusively or surreptitiously:—The couple slipped away through a side door without anyone seeing them leave.

slip of the tongue an unintended remark or word:—He meant no offense in mentioning her weight; it was just a slip of the tongue.

slip one's mind forget:—I meant to mail the letter, but it completely slipped my mind.

slip up make a mistake, miscalculate, fail to do that which is necessary:—We lost the contract because someone in our office slipped up and forgot to mail out the bid.

slip, give the slip escape from, get rid of:—By ducking into one subway train and out the next, the suspect managed to give the detective the slip.

slow down (up) reduce speed:—Be sure to slow down as you approach that dangerous curve.

slumlord a landlord or owner of rented property situated in a slum section of a city:—Our slumlord refuses to repair the plumbing.

sly, on the sly slyly, surreptitiously, secretly:—Helen has been seeing William on the sly, because her mother objects to their friendship.

smack of resemble, have a suggestive taste or flavor of:—His dealings with foreign agents, though supposedly legitimate, smack of treason.

smack one's lips reveal an appetite for, testify enjoyment of:—She smacked her lips over the rich dessert set before her.

small talk general, idle conversation:—At the party there was a good deal of small talk about literature and music.

small See also **feel** small; **fry,** small fry.

smash hit an extremely popular play or theatrical entertainment:—"My Fair Lady" was a smash hit.

smell have a disagreeable odor; figuratively, to be repulsive:—The third act of the play smells.

smell out detect:—As a result of his years of experience, the detective can actually smell out a burglary plot.

smell See also **rat,** smell a rat.

smoke out bring out into the open, unmask:—It took the police only a few weeks to smoke out the real criminal.

smoke screen a veil, something used to cover up or hide, camouflage:—He hides his real intentions behind a smoke screen of religious piety.

smoking-room a public room where smoking is permitted, often used exclusively by men:—During intermission the women stood in the lobby and chatted while the men all went to the smoking-room.

snack-bar usually a small counter restaurant where a limited variety of food can be ordered:—We stopped in a snack-bar and had a bowl of soup and a sandwich.

snag, strike a snag encounter a difficulty or impediment:—The negotiations struck a snag when the union leaders asked for sick benefits in addition to the usual wage increase.

snake in the grass a hypocritical and treasonable person, a hidden danger:—I had always suspected her of being a snake in the grass; and now that she had betrayed her best friend, my suspicions were confirmed.

snap to it hurry, go into action, address oneself to the task at hand:—He told us that if we didn't snap to it we would never finish the work on time.

snap one's fingers at treat with indifference or contempt:—He seemed unaware of possible consequences, snapping his fingers at the judge's admonition.

snap out of arouse oneself from one's lethargy, go into action:—Finding the men chatting idly, the sergeant yelled at them to snap out of it and get to work.

snap up seize quickly, buy hastily:—The bargains were quickly snapped up by the crowd of women shoppers.

snap, a cold snap a period of cold weather:—It's quite a cold snap we've been having lately.

snap, make it snappy hurry up, put on speed:—You had better make it snappy, if you want to catch that train.

snap, not to give a snap of one's fingers for scorn, consider of little importance:—I don't give a snap of my fingers for what she says about me.

snapshot a small photograph:—We took several snapshots of the children while at the beach yesterday.

snatches, in (by) snatches in brief spells, with interruptions:—The prisoner had worked at digging the tunnel in snatches over a period of many months.

sneak away (off, out, past, etc.) leave furtively:—The dog, with our expensive Sunday roast in his mouth, was sneaking away when my husband caught him.

sneak-preview the showing of a new unreleased movie as an extra bonus on a regular movie program:—We saw a sneak preview of a new Western last night.

sneeze at look upon with scorn:—He ought to know that such an excellent offer is nothing to sneeze at.

snow under overwhelm, burden with:—I have been snowed under with correspondence ever since my secretary was taken ill.

snow, be snowed in unable to leave or go out because of the abundance of snow:—After one particularly heavy storm, they were snowed in for more than two weeks.

snow, do a snow job on one cheat, deceive, misrepresent:—That dealer did a snow job on me by selling me a car that was a worthless piece of junk.

snuff, up to snuff up to standard:—That concert last night was hardly up to snuff.

so-and-so the term used as a substitute for the name of an unidentified person or for one whose name is temporarily forgotten:—Pick out furniture which you yourself like and forget what Mrs. So-and-So has in her parlor.

so as to in order to:—Go quietly so as not to wake the baby.

so far up to now:—So far he has done very well at school.

so far so good See **far.**

so to speak speaking in general terms, as it were:—He is, so to speak, the brains of the organization.

soap box the box used as a platform by political orators; therefore the symbol of such street oratory:—Hyde Park in London and Union Square in New York are well-known as the meeting places of soap-box orators.

soap opera radio or television serialized stories:—Soap operas are popular with housewives who listen to them while they wash dishes or clothes; generally, they advertise soap products.

so-called so termed, alleged:—Many so-called patriots do not hesitate to exploit their fellow citizens.

so-so fair, mediocre:—Mary liked the movie, but I thought it was just so-so.

so what? meaning: What difference does it make? What's wrong with it, if anything?—often an expression of defiance:—"Emma stays out pretty late nights." "So what?" You don't like my drinking? So what?

sob story a story provoking tears and pity (iron.):—The beggar told us some long sob story about having been victimized by an unscruplous older brother.

soft drink a non-alcoholic beverage:—Helen was afraid to drink whiskey and therefore ordered a soft drink.

soft-hearted sympathetic, generous:—Many street beggars gain good incomes playing on the sympathies of soft-hearted citizens.

soft-pedal minimize, hush up:—They thought it best to soft-pedal the fact that there had been carelessness in handling the merchandise.

soft sell advertising or salesmanship that doesn't pressure the customer:—The advertising for Volkswagens is of the soft-sell variety. Compare **hard sell.**

soft-soap flatter with the idea of gaining an advantage:—If you think you can soft-soap me into giving in to your plan you are mistaken.

soft touch said of a person who is an easy mark, or overly generous:—Let's ask Uncle Bill for a bicycle. He's a soft touch.

soft, have a soft spot for have partiality or affection for another:—The old man has always had a soft spot in his heart for Jack, possibly because he reminds him of his son.

sold on convinced of the value of, well disposed toward, approving of:—When we first moved in, our neighbors seemed cold and unfriendly, but now we are sold on them.

solid, be in solid with be in very good favor with:—Jules is in solid with all those wealthy people at the country club.

song and dance a usual routine, a story often repeated:—When I asked him to repay me the money, he gave me the usual song and dance about his having many crushing expenses.

song, for a song very cheaply:—The house, though built at an expense of more than one hundred thousand dollars, was finally sold for a song.

sonic boom heavy noise and vibration from an airplane going at a very rapid rate of speed:—Sonic booms broke our front windows.

sooner or later ultimately, inescapably:—If he continues drinking, sooner or later he will lose his job.

sore angry, annoyed (colloq.):—There was no reason for him to get so sore over such an innocent remark.

sorts, out of sorts in bad humor:—When we had to cancel our plans for the picnic because it rained, we naturally felt out of sorts.

soul food said of items of food typical of black cooking in the South:—That restaurant features a soul-food menu this week.

sound off express oneself loudly and dogmatically, talk for effect:—I hesitated to mention Russia because I knew that Smith would begin at once to sound off on the subject of communism.

sound out obtain one's views indirectly, test out, hint to:—Why don't you sound out your Uncle Ben? I am sure he might offer to lend you the money.

sound truck a truck equipped with loudspeakers:—The night before the election the streets were full of sound trucks.

sound, of sound mind perfectly sane:—A person cannot make a valid will unless he is of sound mind.

soup and fish a dress suit, formal male attire:—Everyone who attended the party wore soup and fish.

souped up given extra power:—A racing auto has its carburetors souped up.

sour grapes pretended dislike for something unobtainable:—His disapproving attitude toward color television is simply sour grapes; the fact is that he would like to have a set but can't afford to buy one.

sow one's wild oats dissipate, indulge in youthful excesses:—Having sowed his wild oats in Paris as a young student, James came back very much matured and ready to settle down.

space ship an interplanetary vehicle:—Three men in a space ship landed on the moon in 1969.

spades, in spades an expression to indicate emphasis:—I tell you that new employee is lazy in spades.

speak for represent, speak in behalf of:—He said that he was not speaking for himself but for the group which he represented.

speak of mention, be worth mentioning, notable:—I didn't think his performance was anything to speak of.

speak one's piece express one's ideas, say what one wishes to say:—He didn't say much during the meeting, but toward the end he got up and spoke his piece.

speak out express oneself boldly, freely:—We all agreed to speak out at the next town meeting about the poor bus service.

speak out of turn commit an indiscretion, say something tactless:—You spoke out of turn in criticizing Mrs. Reese's modern furniture; she considers herself quite an expert on home decoration.

speak up (1) raise one's voice to an audible degree, speak louder:—The judge asked the witness to speak up. (2) assert oneself, protest:—If you don't approve of what your associates are doing, why don't you speak up?

speak up for vouch for, defend:—Since he was a complete stranger in the town, there was no one to speak up for him when he was brought into court.

speak well of praise, approve of:—Everyone always speaks well of Bill Jackson.

speak well for serve as proof of the efficiency of, testify favorably to:—The speed with which the treaty was negotiated speaks well for the skill of our diplomatic staff.

speak, not to speak of besides, not to mention, in addition to:—They have two Cadillac sedans, not to speak of a Lincoln convertible.

speaking, on speaking terms on a basis or terms of friendship:—Ever since their quarrel last year they have not been on speaking terms.

speed trap a length of roadway used by the police to detect auto speeders:—We were doing sixty in a fifty-mile-an-hour zone and got caught in a speed trap.

speed up increase the rate of, accelerate:—Installation of these machines will speed up production fifty per cent.

spell out elaborate or explain, decipher letter by letter, spell slowly and carefully:—He had a long foreign-sounding name which I asked him to spell out.

spick and span very clean and neat:—She always keeps her kitchen spick and span.

spin a yarn tell a story of adventure, create or protract such a story:—That old man can certainly spin some fascinating yarns.

spin, go for a spin go for a ride in a car:—Jack has invited us to go for a spin in his new car tomorrow.

spirit away abduct, cause to disappear mysteriously:—We caught just one glimpse of him and then he was spirited away by his friends.

spit and polish very neat, excessive orderliness:—In came the Major, all spit and polish.

spitting image an exact resemblance:—That child is the spitting image of his father.

splash, make a splash cause a sensation:—The young heiress made quite a splash in Washington society.

split-level a house that has two levels on the first floor:—In their split-level house you go through the living room and then down a few steps into the dining room.

split the difference divide the difference between two suggested amounts:—After arguing as to whether the price should be ten dollars or five dollars, we decided to split the difference, and accordingly I paid $7.50 for that strange-looking knife.

split up divide, separate, get a divorce:—The hikers split up into two groups.

split See also **hairs**, split hairs.

spoil for desire, be in a pugnacious mood:—After a few drinks, it was evident that Harry was spoiling for a fight.

sponge on (off) live off of parasitically, depend shamelessly upon or for support:—He is too lazy to go to work and prefers to sponge off his brother.

sponge, throw in the sponge give up, quit:—After two years of unprofitable business, that storekeeper threw in the sponge and got himself a job.

spot (v.) to notice, pick out:—It was not difficult for us to spot Harry in the crowd, with his imposing height and red hair.

spot cash ready money, money paid immediately:—We were fortunate; we were able to get spot cash for the car.

spot check a sample check or investigation:—Our accountant asked us if a Government auditor had called to make a spot check on our books.

spot, on the spot (1) in a predicament, in trouble:—With the mortgage payment due and no money to meet it, George was on the spot. (2) immediately, at once:—Frank applied for the job and was hired on the spot. (3) at the particular place:—We telephoned, and within five minutes the ambulance was on the spot.

spot See also **hit** the spot; **soft,** have a soft spot for; **tight** spot.

spread abroad distribute widely, broadcast:—There is a rumor being spread abroad that Jackson is going to retire because of ill health.

spread the table set the table, lay the dishes upon the table:—While his wife prepared the meal, Jack helped her by spreading the table.

spring a leak develop a hole or opening through which water may enter a boat; figuratively, be threatened:—When our small boat suddenly sprang a leak, we all had to pitch in and help bail it out.

spring from come from, originate with:—His love of the sea can be explained by the fact that he sprang from a long line of seafaring folk.

spring something on one surprise, approach someone unexpectedly with some unpleasant idea or project:—Just as we sat down to dinner they sprang the news on me that I was scheduled to make a speech.

spring up arise suddenly:—Small yellow wildflowers are springing up all over our garden.

square accounts settle one's bill or obligations:—Each month, as soon as I get paid, I like to square all my accounts.

square deal fair treatment:—Even though we did not get the contract, we felt we had been given a square deal.

square meal a full, nourishing meal:—The poor fellow looked as though he hadn't had a square meal in months.

square off assume a threatening, boxing stance:—Before we knew it the two men had squared off and were throwing punches at each other.

square oneself with make amends, apologize, reestablish friendship with:—Helen is very angry with you for what you did, and it will take more than a few pleasant words to square yourself with her.

square peg in a round hole one unsuited for his occupation or environment:—That lad should study art; to train him to become a doctor is making him a square peg in a round hole.

square-shooter a completely honest and straightforward person:—You can trust Dean in any situation; he's a square-shooter.

square up settle, liquidate debts or other obligations:—I want to square up my dentist's bill before incurring any other debts.

square, call something square consider as a fair adjustment or division for both sides:—He had paid for my dinner and I had bought the theater tickets, so we decided to call it square.

square, on the square honest, trustworthy:—You need have no fear of Jack's honesty. He is completely on the square.

squawk complain:—Some people are always squawking about one thing or another.

squeak through manage to pass a barrier or a test by a very narrow margin:—Hal didn't fail his chemistry exam, but he barely squeaked through.

squeal give information about another, inform on:—One of the gang squealed and gave the police all the information necessary to solve the case.

stab, make a stab at try, attempt, perform:—Though she was not familiar with the piece of music, the pianist decided to make a stab at it anyway.

stack the cards arrange cards secretly before dealing, to secure an unfair advantage:—Fortune, Mr. Billings felt, had stacked the cards against him.

stack up compare with:—How does Bill stack up against the more experienced members of the team?

stack See **blow** one's stack.

stacked, to be well-stacked (sl.) of a graceful bodily build:—That blonde is certainly well-stacked.

stag, go stag (1) go to a dance or party without a female companion:—Henry decided to go stag to the college prom. (2) an affair for men only:—Mrs. Crosley's husband is at a stag dinner this evening.

stage fright the fear which possesses one when appearing before an audience:— One of the great stars of the stage once confessed that she always felt stage fright just before curtain time.

stage-struck anxious to become an actor or actress, enamored of the acting profession:—She has been stage-struck ever since she was a little girl.

stage whisper a loud whisper intended to reach other ears than those of the person addressed:—That actor has such a flexible voice that we could hear his stage whisper from the middle row of the orchestra.

stake, at stake seriously involved, in jeopardy:—He watched the stock market reports intently, since his whole fortune was at stake.

stake one to something lend or give aid to, provide the funds for:—Even though he might never be able to repay me, I decided to stake the poor fellow to the money he said he needed.

stall (v.) delay purposely, loaf:—Quit stalling and let's get going and finish the job.

stall for time See **stall.**

stamp out eradicate, suppress:—Medical men say that with this new drug many types of hitherto incurable diseases may soon be stamped out.

stamping ground familiar, home grounds, frequented location:—The local golf club is Herman's stamping ground during the summer months.

stand a chance have the possibility of gaining or winning:—With his lack of experience and smaller physique, we don't think he stands a chance of winning the fight.

stand a show See **stand a chance.**

stand by (1) help, support, give moral and physical support to:—Gerald's wife stood by him through all his difficulties (2) stand in readiness, or waiting:—A small launch stood by, waiting to take the tourists around the lake.

stand-by tested and reliable, a staple item:—The shopkeeper told me that the thick-soled, flat-heeled shoes had been a stand-by with hikers for many years.

stand firm (fast) be firm and immovable: —The newspaper stood firm and refused to retract the accusation that there had been gross incompetence in the organization.

stand for (1) tolerate, endure:—I won't stand for his insults any longer. (2) advocate:—I stand for freedom of speech for everyone regardless of color, race, or creed. (3) represent, signify:— What do the letters R.S.V.P. stand for?

stand good remain in effect, continue to be valid:—He says that his offer to buy us out still stands good.

stand in good stead prove to be useful, helpful—particularly in an emergency: —Frank's knowledge of Spanish stood him in good stead when his firm sent him to Mexico on business.

stand in (good) with be on friendly terms with, enjoy the favor of:—He should be able to do this favor for you, because he stands in good with that company.

stand on ceremony be formal, stiffly decorous:—Make yourself at home; there's no reason to stand on ceremony in our home.

stand on one's own feet be independent: —Early poverty had taught Sam to stand on his own feet.

stand one's ground hold one's position without surrender or retreat:—Despite the grueling cross-examination by the prosecutor, the witness stood his ground.

stand one up disappoint someone by failing to appear for an appointment, leave someone waiting indefinitely:—It was her opinion that any young man who stands up a girl is not a gentleman.

stand out (1) be prominent, outstanding: —One thing stood out in his career as a politician and that was his constant concern for the less fortunate. (2) **stand out against** resist, refuse to surrender: —Our troops stood out resolutely against the long siege of the enemy.

stand over another supervise closely:— Jones's boss is always standing over him.

stand pat remain static, adhere to one's opinion, be adamant:—The newspaper stood pat on its stated policy of not favoring the new zoning laws.

stand the loss (expense) suffer or pay the loss:—Fortunately for Walker, the insurance company stood the loss when his barn burned down.

stand to reason be perfectly clear and logical:—It stands to reason that a man with his experience should expect to be well pai⁻ᴵ

stand treat pay the cost of entertaining guests:—After the show our host stood treat to a late supper.

stand trial submit to court trial:—The case has been postponed, and he may not stand trial until November.

stand up for champion the cause of, support:—It made me feel good to see so many of his friends stand up for him when he was blamed for the loss.

stand up to challenge, show resistance to: —If you don't stand up to this man, he will abuse you unmercifully, because he is really a bully.

stand, make a stand, resist, take a defensive position against the enemy:— The retreating troops made a last futile stand at the bridge, just before they crossed it.

stand-offish stiff, reserved in manner, aloof:—It is hard to get to know Alex, because he is so stand-offish.

stand See also **gaff,** stood the gaff; **leg,** not a leg to stand on; **long**-standing; **rights,** stand on one's rights; **take** a stand; **take** the stand.

standing permanent, unchanging—as in the expressions **standing army, standing offer, standing invitation, standing** joke, etc.:—Every nation of any importance maintains a standing army.

standing order a permanent order for merchandise as it is issued and put on sale:—Our library has given a standing order to that publisher for all its forthcoming books.

start out begin a task, relationship, or journey—intensive form of "start":— They started out by quarreling and then became fast friends.

start the ball rolling begin an enterprise, give initiative or impulse to:—After a call for contributions, Holmes started the ball rolling by being the first to donate a thousand dollars.

start up resume operations:—That factory, closed since last winter, will soon start up again.

station wagon a model of passenger automobile having a long body with a back exit and accommodating more passengers than a regular sedan:—They have a Cadillac sedan and a Ford station wagon.

status symbol something that gives social consequence to a person:—To have two cars in our neighborhood is a necessary status symbol.

stave off to postpone, avoid:—They tried their best to stave off vacating the building, but to no avail.

stay in remain at home:—Let's stay in tonight and read, instead of going to a movie.

stay on continue to stay in a certain place, remain:—Although the Smiths' maid had decided to leave their employ, she agreed to stay on until a replacement was found.

stay out (1) remain away from home:— Jill stayed out last night until three o'clock. (2) keep away from, remain apart from:—Please stay out of my business and I will stay out of yours.

stay put remain in place or position:— Although I knot my tie carefully, it never seems to say put.

steal a march on forestall, arrive ahead of another:—Carl was going to invite Mary to the dance, but Bill stole a march on him and asked her first.

steal away (out, in, past, through, etc.) leave or depart secretly, unobtrusively:—We thought we'd steal away from the party for a few moments and get some fresh air in the garden.

steal home (or **steal first base**) said of a runner in baseball who reaches home-plate before he is tagged by the ball:—Archer drove a fast ball to left field, and the player on third base stole home.

steal one's thunder present an idea, etc. before another person who has already thought of it has a chance to present it:—Ernie was going to suggest a new way to cut down on overhead to the boss, but Phil stole his thunder and told the boss first.

steal the show win the applause and attention of the audience—especially as achieved by a minor actor in a play:—The young man who played the minor part of the butler really stole the show.

steal up on approach by stealth, sneak up on:—The thief stole up on his victim and struck him over the head.

steal, to be a steal to be a great bargain:—That $100 radio is a steal at $29.

steer clear of avoid:—Burt is such a bore that I always try to steer clear of him.

stem the tide hold back something of great strength or pressure, resist:—Educators claim that one of the ways to stem the tide of increasing juvenile delinquency is to improve our educational system.

step by step gradually, by slow, steady progress:—A foreign language cannot be learned rapidly; it must be learned step by step.

step on it hurry, make haste:—If you don't step on it, we will never get to the station in time.

step on one's toes offend someone:—Before such a large, mixed audience, the speaker had to be very careful not to step on anyone's toes.

step out (1) go out—particularly socially, on a date:—You're all dressed up; you must be stepping out tonight. (2) leave for a brief period during the work day:—Mr. Smith just stepped out of his office for a moment.

step up increase, accelerate:—Production in that particular industry could be greatly stepped up with more efficient methods.

step, be one step ahead of the sheriff be deeply in debt, be in a precarious financial condition:—Ever since they took over that business they have been just one step ahead of the sheriff.

step, keep step with maintain the same pace as:—In our armament production, there is no other course open to us except to keep step with our potential enemies.

steps, take steps do whatever is necessary in order to initiate or start a project, or to accomplish some result:—The citizens of that village took steps to improve their fire-fighting equipment.

step See also **side**-step; **in** step with; **watch** one's step.

stew in one's own juice brood, nurse a grievance:—Bob has been sulking ever since we had that argument, and I'm letting him stew in his own juice.

stew, be in a stew be upset, worried, harassed:—She has been in a stew ever since she got the news that her sister was going to marry that man.

stick (v.) cheat, defraud, take advantage of:—They stuck me plenty for this second-hand car; I have had nothing but repair bills ever since I bought it.

stick around stay nearby, not leave:—Are you going to stick around to see that movie twice?

stick by prove loyal, support:—All of George's friends stuck by him faithfully despite the serious charges brought against him.

stick out (1) protrude, project beyond:—I could see the letter sticking out of his pocket. (2) be plainly apparent:—His guilt stuck out all over him.

stick something out suffer or endure something, remain until the end:—Steve's job was not at all to his liking, but he decided to stick it out until something better turned up.

stick to (1) remain loyal:—His wife stuck to him throughout all his troubles. (2) persevere in, continue:—How can he expect to get ahead if he never sticks to any job more than a month or two?

stick to one's guns stand one's ground, hold one's position resolutely:—When questioned by the police, the suspect stuck to his guns and insisted that he had not been anywhere near the scene of the robbery.

stick to one's last do only what one is qualified to do:—That plumber wanted to become a lawyer, but he was advised to stick to his last.

stick up rob at the point of a gun, hold up:—The man who had been beaten and robbed said that his assailant had leveled a gun at him, crying: "Stick 'em up."

stick-up a robbery:—Many recent stick-ups have been the work of teenagers.

stick, make it stick enforce or confirm an order or directive:—I can fire that lazy employee and make it stick.

stick up for See also **stand** up for.

stick, take a stick to whip, punish, chastise with a stick:—Bill's mother threatened to take a stick to him if he ever lied to her again.

stick-in-the-mud one who is unadventurous, unenterprising, conservative:—Mrs. Forbes likes to be active and to do things, but her husband is an old stick-in-the-mud.

stick See also **neck**, stick one's neck out.

sticks, in the sticks in the country or suburbs, away from the culture and excitement of a metropolis:—That family lives in the sticks and never sees a play or goes to a concert.

sticky difficult, unpleasant:—To have both a husband and his wife working for you when they are contemplating divorce is a sticky situation.

still life a term used by artists to describe a motionless, inanimate composition such as a bowl of fruit, a vase of flowers, etc.:—One of Van Gogh's most famous paintings is a still life showing a vase of yellow flowers on a small table.

stir up incite, provoke, cause:—There are groups in many parts of the world that are committed to stirring up trouble.

stir, make a stir cause a sensation, provoke comment or activity:—The first landing of the American astronauts on the moon made a tremendous stir all over the world.

stitch, not a stitch on naked:—There the baby stood without a stitch on.

stock in trade that in which one customarily deals, the materials which one sells or offers:—Anecdotes are often an after-dinner speaker's stock in trade.

stock still completely still, motionless:—At his master's command, the dog stood stock still.

stock up buy up, lay in a good supply of:—During the early part of the war many householders tried to stock up on scarce items.

stock, take (put) stock in trust, have faith in, place credence in:—She always tends to exaggerate, so if I were you, I wouldn't take any stock in what she says.

stock, take stock of evaluate, consider, take an inventory of:—In starting out to look for work, a man should take stock of his particular training and qualifications.

stomach (v.) endure, tolerate:—He is so unkempt in his appearance that sometimes I can hardly stomach talking with him.

stone broke See **broke.**

stone deaf completely deaf:—Poor fellow, he is stone deaf, and therefore does not go to the theater.

stone's throw, within a stone's throw within a very short distance:—They live within a stone's throw of us.

stooge an agent, professional assistant:—Many comedians have stooges to make up jokes for them or to be the butt of their jokes.

stool-pigeon a criminal who informs on his associates:—The detective was able to solve the crime mainly through information obtained from a stool-pigeon.

stop by pass by, visit:—We'll stop by at about eight o'clock and pick you up.

stop in one's tracks stop completely, stop dead, check something in its very beginning:—We were stopped in our tracks right in front of our house, where a fire had broken out.

stop off to stop for a short time en route:—Mother asked me to stop off at the bake shop and get some rolls for dinner.

stop over remain for a short period at a certain place during the course of a longer trip:—On our way to Florida we plan to stop over for a few days in Washington.

stop short stop suddenly:—He stopped short when he heard his name called, but there was no one in sight.

stop the show elicit such applause from the audience as to interrupt the normal course of the show:—Carter's dancing in the third act always stops the show.

stop up close, block:—The first thing you must do if you wish to avoid having mice is to stop up those two holes in the floor.

stop up one's ears cover one's ears, refuse to listen:—When Jim told a dirty joke, Alice stopped up her ears.

stop, dead stop See **dead**.

stop See also **dime,** stop on a dime; **put a stop to**; **whistle** stop.

store teeth artificial or false teeth:—One advantage of store teeth is that they never ache.

store up accumulate, set aside:—During the summer months squirrels store up nuts to eat during the winter.

store, in store for about to befall one, destined for:—If he had known what was in store for him, he probably never would have moved to such a severe climate.

store, set store by value highly, place great confidence in:—Our science teacher was such a brilliant man that we set great store by whatever he said.

store See also **mind** the store.

storm in a teacup great excitement over some inconsequential matter:—All that argument about who was going to mow the lawn seemed to me just a storm in a teacup.

storm See also **port,** any port in a storm; **take** by storm; **weather** the storm.

story, as the story goes as they tell the story:—As the story goes, she left him as soon as she discovered that he had no money.

story, what's the story on meaning: what has happened to, what has been the disposition of, etc.:—Those books I ordered haven't come yet. What's the story on them?

story See also **cock-and-bull** story; **dirty** story.

straight away (off) immediately, without hesitation, directly:—He told me straight away that he had no intention of vacating the house before October.

straight from the horse's mouth from a seemingly reliable source:—She doubted the information, but I told her I had gotten it straight from the horse's mouth.

straight ticket the complete ballot of one political party:—My father always voted the straight Republican ticket.

straight, give it to one straight be frank, direct:—I asked the doctor to give it to me straight and tell me exactly what my daughter's condition was.

straight, keep a straight face maintain a sober expression, conceal one's merriment or real emotions. Often expressed as **with a straight face**:— I had a difficult time keeping a straight face when I told him that ridiculous story.

straight See also **set** one straight; **shoulder,** straight from the shoulder.

straw in the wind an indication of future developments:—Their frequent requests for peace talks can well be interpreted as straws in the wind.

straw vote a sampling of the electorate, an unofficial or test balloting:—Several of the leading newspapers conduct their own straw votes before each national election.

straw, the last straw that which constitutes the final limit of endurance:—When, in addition to his indifferent ability, we discovered that he was also dishonest, that was the last straw.

streak of luck a temporary run of good fortune:—Toward the end of the card party, Tom had a sudden streak of luck and kept winning steadily.

stretch a point strain a rule, make an exception, go beyond normal or legal limits:—The landlord said he would stretch a point and let us occupy the apartment two weeks before the beginning of our lease.

stretch out extend, make do:—Though there was really only enough food for four, I had to stretch it out to feed the six of us.

stretch, at a stretch at one time, during a single period:—He would often stay away from work for three or four days at a stretch.

stretch, do a stretch serve time in prison:—That forger did a stretch of ten years at the state penitentiary.

stride, hit one's stride reach one's best capacity or speed:—The Yankees never really hit their stride until about the middle of the season.

stride See also **take** in one's stride.

strike (v.) seem, appear to one, occur to one:—It strikes me that he is more interested in his profession than in anything else.

strike a bargain arrive at a price agreeable to buyer and seller:—After a great deal of haggling they managed to strike a bargain.

strike a happy medium arrive at a compromise, avoid extremes:—Since Jackson loathes the country and his wife dislikes New York, they struck a happy medium by settling in a suburban city.

strike a match ignite a match, cause a match to burn by striking:—It was so dark that Bill had to strike a match in order to see his watch.

strike-breaker one who takes the place of workers on strike, or one who recruits such men:—The striking workers threw bricks at the strike-breakers.

strike home See **hit** home.

strike it rich become suddenly wealthy:—He certainly struck it rich when that land he had bought in Texas was found to contain oil.

strike oil find something valuable:—After months of research, that scholar struck oil when he came upon some unknown documents concerning Shakespeare.

strike one's fancy appeal to one, please one's fancy:—The tie happened to strike my fancy, so I bought it.

strike out (1) cancel, expunge:—The judge ordered the court stenographer to strike out the witness's last remarks. (2) start an enterprise, venture out on one's own:—After working as an employee for many years, Bill suddenly decided to strike out and open his own shop. (3) putting a batter out of the game—a baseball term:—During the course of the game the pitcher struck out ten opposing batters. (4) start in the direction of:—We could see from the distance that the swimmer was very tired and was striking out for shore. (5) fail:—Bill tried to get a promotion, but he struck out.

strike speechless cause to become speechless, amaze:—We were struck speechless when the front door banged and we heard a sudden crash of glass.

strike the hour mark or toll the hour—as with a clock or bell:—We heard the village clock strike the hour of five.

strike up start playing:—When the President appeared, the band struck up "Hail to the Chief."

strike up an acquaintance make one's acquaintance without an introduction, come to know a stranger:—While on his trip to the West, Bill struck up an acquaintance with the man who later became his partner.

strike while the iron is hot act while an opportunity exists:—Let's strike while the iron is hot and ask for a salary increase now, when business is so good.

strike See also **snag,** strike a snag.

strikes, have two strikes against one:—be deeply in disfavor, in danger of losing one's job, etc.:—Our secretary already has two strikes against her: she is always late and she misplaces important papers.

string along deceive, toy with, delude:—Although she had no intention of marrying him, she kept stringing him along for almost a year.

string along with cooperate with, follow:—She wasn't very happy on the trip, but she had no other recourse than to string along with the group.

string out extend, stretch out in a line:—Special policemen were strung out all along the picket lines.

string, have on the string have power over, manipulate at will:—Helen always has three or four admirers on the string at one time.

string, with a string attached with some special proviso or condition regarded as a handicap:—He inherited a large fortune—but with a string attached: the money was to be his, only so long as he remained unmarried.

strings, have two strings to one's bow (rhymes with low) have an alternative or choice:—Oscar has two strings to his bow—he can teach or he can write.

strings, no strings attached unconditionally, without any special terms or reservations:—He was ready to sell the business for five thousand dollars with absolutely no strings attached.

string See also **pull** strings; **tied** to someone's apron strings.

strip (v.) undress, remove one's clothing:—The doctor told me to strip to the waist.

strong-arm (v.) use force or persuasion:—My buddy tried to strong-arm me into joining his fraternity.

strong language swearing, cursing:—Fortunately he never uses such strong language in front of the children.

strong, come in strong said of a radio or television whose signals are very distinct:—After fiddling with the dials, I finally got the station I wanted to come in strong.

strong See also **going** strong.

stuck on (sl.) attracted by, enamored of:—He has been stuck on her ever since they went to high school together.

stuck-up conceited:—She is very pretty, but that is hardly sufficient reason for her to be so stuck-up.

stuck, get stuck (1) become so involved or entrapped as to be unable to get out:—Our car got stuck in the ditch, and we had to get a tow-car to pull us out. (2) be victimized, cheated:—That couple certainly got stuck when they bought that antique; it turned out to be a fraud.

stuffed shirt a pompous, empty person, a pretentious bore:—Tom tells me that several members of the board of directors are just stuffed shirts who prevent the others from making progress.

stuffed up blocked, impeded:—My head is all stuffed up with a cold.

stuffing, knock the stuffing out of beat badly, chastise mercilessly:—I told him plainly that if he ever said such a thing again, I would knock the stuffing out of him.

stumble upon (on) chance upon, come upon by accident:—Fleming stumbled upon the discovery of penicillin while working in his laboratory with cultures of bread molds.

sucker a dupe, one who is easily exploited:—He was a sucker to pay so much for a business that was on the verge of bankruptcy.

sudden See also **all.**

suit, bring suit bring legal action against:—He intends to bring suit against them for misrepresenting the merchandise they sold him.

suited, be suited be well matched, well adjusted:—They should make a happy couple because they are well suited in many ways.

suit See also **follow** suit.

sum up review briefly, summarize:—At the end of his talk, he summed up the various points of his program.

summit conference a conference among or between heads of state:—The American President agreed to a summit conference with the Soviet head of state.

sun, under the sun in the whole world, anywhere:—His mother said he was the best boy under the sun.

supposed, be supposed to be expected to:—He is supposed to arrive on the five o'clock train.

sure enough in accordance with what was to be expected:—He said he would be back within two days, and sure enough he arrived Thursday night.

sure-fire effective, bringing actual results, without fail:—The only sure-fire way to get votes is to go out and greet the voters personally.

sure, for sure definitely, without fail:—He said he would give us his decision for sure by Wednesday.

sure See also **make sure**.

suspense, keep in suspense maintain in a state of anxiety pending the outcome:—It's the kind of movie that keeps you in suspense right up until the final scene.

swallow (v.) accept as true, prove gullible:—She seemed to swallow everything the man told her.

swallow up engulf, absorb, do away with:—My expenses are so great that they simply swallow up my small salary.

swamped overwhelmed with the size or quantity thereof:—We are always swamped with business at this particular season of the year.

swan song a last or farewell appearance:—Due to retire on July 1, Briggs's attendance at the executive meeting on June 29 was his swan song.

swear by be disposed to uphold under oath, have great faith and confidence in:—There wasn't a soldier in our whole outfit who wouldn't have sworn by Captain Johnson.

swear in induct into office by oath:—The newly elected President was sworn in by the Chief Justice of the Supreme Court.

swear off eschew, give up, resolve to refrain from using:—He has promised to swear off smoking for six months.

swear out a warrant issue a warrant for someone's arrest:—As soon as the loss was discovered, a warrant was sworn out for the embezzler's arrest.

swear to secrecy exact a pledge of secrecy:—Holmes insisted on swearing us to secrecy before he gave us the plans.

sweat out bear, endure uncomfortably until the end:—I had already had two interviews with the inspector; now I was going to have to sweat out a third.

sweep off one's feet overwhelm by one's sudden force, magnetism, or artistry:—His performance swept even the critics off their feet.

sweep out of leave in an impressive, majestic manner:—Indignant at John's remark, Helen swept out of the room with her head high in the air.

sweep the country (city, nation, world, etc.) gain great attention or popularity throughout the country:—No music in recent years has swept the country like rock and roll.

sweep, make a clean sweep of (1) eliminate completely and thoroughly:—The new cabinet minister is expected to make a clean sweep of all the old administrative personnel. (2) achieve a complete victory:—In the 1972 election Nixon made a clean sweep of all the states except Massachusetts.

sweet on very fond of, amorous about:—Harry is very sweet on Mary.

sweet talk loving words, flattery:—Despite his sweet talk, Harry was unable to get Helene to marry him. "You can't sweet talk me out of buying a fur coat," said the wife to her husband.

sweet tooth, have a sweet tooth have a great liking or weakness for sweets:—Jane has such a sweet tooth that she never refuses candy.

swell (adj.) good, fine, excellent (colloq.): —He is a swell chap, one of the nicest you will ever meet.

swelled head conceit:—Jack has gotten such a swelled head since his promotion that he is insufferable.

swim, in the swim participating in and aware of what is going on, particularly socially:—Though they haven't lived in New York very long, they are already in the social swim and are constantly receiving and extending invitations.

swing for be hanged as a punishment for: —If convicted of that murder, he will certainly swing for it.

swing something manage, arrange, carry out, afford:—I plan to buy that farm next year if I can swing it.

swing, get into the swing of things get adjusted, used to:—It takes several weeks for a new employee to get into the swing of things.

swing, in full swing See **full,** in full swing.

swinger (n.) a person who likes to have a good lively time, who frequently goes places for entertainment:—Henry is a real swinger when he goes out at night. Henry has become a real swinger since he moved out of his parents' home.

swipe (v.) steal:—Somebody has swiped my fountain pen.

switch on (off) turn on—said particularly of electric current:—As he entered the dark basement, he switched on the light.

T

T, to a T exactly, perfectly:—That house they bought in the country suits them to a T.

table-hop keep going from one table to another—said of a restaurant patron wishing to speak to different people at different tables:—I didn't enjoy my lunch with that actor very much, because he was constantly table-hopping.

tack on add, append:—We were ready to sign the contract, when we discovered that the lawyer had tacked on a clause that we could not approve.

tail end final or concluding part:—We arrived so late that we saw only the tail end of the show.

tail-light the rear red lights of an automobile:—I was fined five dollars for driving at night without tail-lights.

tail, with one's tail between one's legs completely cowed and frightened:—Jim is usually very self-confident, but ever since that talk with the boss, he's been walking around with his tail between his legs.

tail See also **head,** neither head nor tail.

take (1) be affected by, bear up under: —How did he take the bad news? (2) board a vehicle or train:—We took the wrong bus and had to transfer to another. (3) subscribe to:—We take Newsweek. (4) rent, lease:—We plan to take a house in the country for the summer. (5) accept, receive:—He refused to take anything for fixing the watch. (6) conduct, lead:—John will take you to the station. (7) study, undertake a course: —I plan to take both French and Spanish this term. (8) wear, use as one's size:—He takes a size nine shoe. (9) assume:—I take it you are satisfied with the work. (10) tolerate, suffer:—He has been subjected to some very unfair treatment, and I doubt whether he can take it much longer.

take a back seat accept an inferior position, remain in the background:—Recent changes in our ogranization have made it necessary for Jim to take a back seat.

take a break stop for a brief rest or intermission:—We've been working steadily for three hours; I think it's about time we took a break.

take a good (bad) picture photograph well, be a good subject for photography, be photogenic:—She is really quite pretty and takes a very good picture.

take a hand in participate in, assist in the direction of:—The women's clubs decided to take a hand in the fund-raising drive for needy children.

take a joke accept in good spirit laughter directed at oneself:—Frank has a good sense of humor, but he isn't able to take a joke.

take a liking (dislike) to begin to like, enjoy, or appreciate:—We felt instinctively that he had taken a liking to our family.

take a load off one's feet sit down:—Take a load off your feet and look over this treasurer's report with me.

take a shine to be attracted by, begin to like or be enamored of:—It was amusing to notice the way Henry and Ellen took a shine to each other immediately.

take a stand declare one's position, assert one's point of view:—It was the majority opinion at our recent meeting that the organization as a whole should take a definite stand against some of those unfair practices.

take after (1) resemble:—In his cheerful and easygoing nature, Jim takes after his father rather than his mother. (2) run after, pursue:—We took after the two boys who had run off with the children's ball.

take apart disassemble:—It is easy to take a watch apart but difficult to put it together again.

take at a disadvantage catch unprepared: —Had I had time to think it over I would have refused him the permission, but the suddenness of his request took me at a disadvantage.

take at one's word believe, accept one's statement or promise:—When he said that he would pay us by the first of the month, I naturally took him at his word.

take back (1) return:—They told me at the store that if the merchandise proved unsatisfactory in any way I could take it back. (2) recant, withdraw a statement:—Bill asked us to take back what we had said about Bob being stingy. (3) carry one backward in time:—That song takes me back twenty years to the time I sang in the high school glee club.

take by storm, capture by overpowering:—Our troops took the town by storm.

take by surprise catch unprepared, surprise:—Our cook's sudden announcement that she was leaving took us quite by surprise, as she had been with us for many years.

take care be careful, watchful:—Take care that you don't catch cold after becoming so overheated.

take care of (1) watch over, protect, assume charge of:—The neighbors have promised to take care of our dog while we are away. (2) pay:—Let me have the dinner check. I'll take care of it. (3) do, care for, repair, etc:—That handyman takes care of our summer cottage.

take charge of assume control or direction of:—Mr. Flanagan will take charge of the office while the regular office manager is away on his vacation.

take cold catch cold, become sick with a cold:—I think I took cold last evening, when I went out without my coat.

take cover seek shelter or protection:—The rain came down so suddenly and violently that we had to take cover in an abandoned barn.

take down (1) remove, dismantle:—I must take down those curtains and send them to be cleaned. (2) make a record in writing, or in shorthand, of someone's spoken words:—Part of Helen's duties are to take down the minutes of the directors' meetings. (3) See **peg**, take down a peg.

take effect operate, happen:—It was nearly a half hour before the medicine took effect and relieved her pain.

take exception to object to, have some objection against:—We didn't blame her for taking exception to his unflattering remarks.

take for judge someone or something to be, sometimes mistakenly:—From his manner of speaking I took him for an Italian.

take for granted assume as true without further investigation:—He spoke English so well that I took it for granted that he was an American.

take heart be encouraged, find encouragement:—We had been very depressed over Mother's prolonged illness, but the doctor told us to take heart and said that she would improve steadily from now on.

take hold of grasp:—She tried to stop herself from falling, but there was no railing or anything else to take hold of.

take-home pay wages actually received by an employee after tax deductions have been made:—Alice earns $100 dollars a week, but her take-home pay is only $87.00.

take in (1) attend:—Let's have dinner in town tonight and later take in a movie. (2) deceive:—We were all taken in by his smooth manners and polished way of talking. (3) absorb, understand:—The news came as such a shock that for several minutes I could not take it in. (4) receive into one's house, accept:—In order to help support the family, their mother took in roomers for many years.

take in one's stride accept calmly, meet imperturbably:—Carlson took his losses in his stride and was soon on his feet again.

take in tow lead, conduct, take charge of:—We took a group of children in tow when we went to see the circus.

take into account (consideration) consider, weigh the importance of:—In sentencing the criminal, the judge took into account the fact that it was his first offense.

take into one's head decide, conceive the idea:—I can't understand why he took it into his head to drive the car on such a stormy night.

take issue dispute, contest, argue, debate with:—The speaker took issue with those who claimed that better housing for our citizens depended entirely on the government.

take it all in listen attentively, absorb completely:—Though he didn't seem to pay much attention, he was nevertheless taking it all in when they were having a dispute.

take it easy relax, take one's time, stop exerting oneself:—I had been working so hard for several weeks that I decided to take it easy and relax over the weekend.

take it or leave it make up your mind either to accept the offer or decline it:—Twenty dollars is my lowest price for that second-hand typewriter. Take it or leave it.

take it out of exhaust, tire greatly:—I find that the hot weather takes a great deal out of me.

take liberties with be free with, abuse, treat too familiarly:—Mary told her friend that she resigned her position because some of the men had tried to take liberties with her.

take lying down accept without protest or defense:—To take such abuse lying down would only encourage more of it.

take measures initiate some action, take the necessary steps:—It was decided to take immediate measures to avoid the recurrence of such an accident.

take note of observe, notice:—Did you take note of the clever way in which the television set is concealed in the wall?

take notes write down notes on something being said, record:—Since there was no textbook for the course, his students had to take notes on everything the professor said.

take off (1) remove—said particularly of clothes:—He took off his hat and bowed politely as she passed. (2) depart—said particularly of airplanes:—The plane took off at exactly eight o'clock. (3) mimic another:—Harry does a perfect take-off of his French teacher. (4) deduct:—In computing the income tax, one is allowed to take off six hundred dollars for each dependent.

take off one's hands relieve another of, buy:—He offered to take the horse off my hands for two hundred dollars.

take offense become angry, indignant:—It was silly of Grace to take offense at our innocent remarks.

take on (1) employ:—All the department stores take on additional help for the Christmas season. (2) make an emotional display, lament:—She took on terribly when her sister was so badly hurt. (3) undertake:—Albert takes on additional work in the evenings.

take one wrong misinterpret, misunderstand someone:—Don't take me wrong, I'm not trying to defend Communism; I am simply trying to point out that it may have some advantages.

take one's fancy appeal to one:—The suit didn't fit her very well, but she bought it because it took her fancy.

take one's own life commit suicide:—Unable to face the consequences of his act, the embezzler took his own life.

take one's word accept or believe someone's promise:—They took his word for it when he agreed to return the money within a week.

take orders follow instructions, prove obedient:—In the army one of the most important things the new recruit must learn is to take orders.

take out (1) accompany, escort:—Whom is Jack taking out tonight? (2) remove, extract from a pocket, etc.:—The stranger took out his wallet and gave the beggar a dollar bill. (3) purchase, contract for:—We must take out additional fire insurance on our home. (4) vent one's feeling upon, get revenge upon. See **take** something out on someone.

take over assume charge of:—Mr. Collins will take over my duties a week after I leave.

take place happen, occur:—Where did the accident take place?

take possession of occupy:—We have already purchased the house but won't be able to take possession of it until the present tenants move out.

take root become established, begin to grow:—It is interesting to note what curious folkways have taken root among mountain people.

take shape assume form, materialize:—Our long-cherished plans for a home in the country are finally beginning to take shape.

take sick become ill:—He took sick while on the trip.

take sides be partial to one side as against the other:—We were advised not to take sides until we heard all the facts.

take something out on someone vent one's feeling upon, gain revenge upon:—Why should Margaret take it out on Jack for not coming to her party, when she knows he was out of town then?

take the cake, carry off the prize, prove superior to:—There were some excellent stories told, but Frank's took the cake. Also used ironically: If John's stupidity doesn't take the cake!

take the day off stay away from one's job or profession for a particular day:—It was such lovely autumn weather that Briggs took the day off and drove out in the country to see the fall foliage.

take the floor rise to one's feet in order to address officially a meeting or public gathering:—As soon as the Russian delegate took the floor, a hush fell over the audience.

take a load off one's feet sit down (sl.):—He looked so tired that I asked him to draw up a chair and take a load off his feet.

take the offensive (defensive) make oneself the attacking party:—It took months of preparation, but at last the liberating army was ready to take the offensive.

take the rap pay the penalty for another's crime or misdeed:—Marcia's boss expected her to take the rap for any mistakes made by the typists working for her.

take the stand take one's position in the witness box:—The judge asked the defendant to take the stand.

take the words out of one's mouth say what someone else was just about to say:—You took the words right out of my mouth when you told him he was exaggerating.

take time proceed slowly, leisurely:—Since there was no need to hurry, we took our time leaving.

take time off remain away from work:—All the men in our office took time off to go to the ball game.

take time out interrupt one's work for a short interval:—I usually take time out during the afternoon for a cup of tea.

take to drink begin to drink heavily of intoxicants, become a drunkard:—He took to drink shortly after his wife died.

take to one develop a liking for someone, feel partial towards:—She was very quiet and retiring, but somehow I took to her at once.

take to one's bed go to bed as a result of illness:—He took to his bed in March and remained there for three months.

take to task criticize, reprimand:—My mother took me to task for neglecting my household duties.

take up (1) study, undertake as a course of study:—What is your son taking up in college? (2) shorten:—That skirt is long; you'd better take it up a little. (3) adopt, begin, go in for:—His doctor advised him to take up golf. (4) occupy, make use of:—Our dog is quite large and takes up as much room in the car as a normal person. (5) utilize, absorb:—Simply watching over her three young children takes up a good part of Mrs. Smith's time.

take up with (1) consult, go to someone higher in position or authority:—If you want a raise, you will have to take it up with the personnel manager. (2) become friendly or familiar with:—Our friends, the Phelpses, have recently taken up with the country club crowd, so that we rarely see them now.

take upon oneself assume the burden or responsibility of:—She took it upon herself to register a complaint about the service.

take—Note the following expressions which, while not exactly idiomatic, always require use of the verb **take**. a) She **takes a bath** every morning. b) Let's **take a walk** through the park. c) Don't **take a chance** going out in this weather without an umbrella. d) The star of the play **took a bow** and then left the stage. e) I asked him to come in and **take a seat**. f) We are going to take **a trip** to Florida this winter. g) Harry wants to **take a picture** of us. h) I held such poor cards that I hardly **took a trick** all evening.

take See also **advantage**, take advantage of; **arms**, take up arms; **book**, take a leaf out of someone's book; **bread**, take the bread out of someone's mouth; **breath**, take one's breath away; **drop**, take a drop; **edge**, take the edge off; **French**, take French leave; **give** and take; **heart**, take heart; **heart**, take to heart; **heels**, take to one's heels; **horns**, take the bull by the horns; **lead**, take the lead; **leave**, take leave of; **medicine**, take one's own medicine; **name**, take someone's name; **occasion**, take the occasion; **pains**, take pains; **part**, take in good part; **part**, take part in; **part**, take the part of; **peg**, take down a peg; **pity**, take pity on; **pledge**, take the pledge; **plunge**, take the plunge; **pride**, take pride in; **ride**, take for a ride; **salt**, take with a grain of salt; **steps**, take steps; **stick**, take a stick to; **stock**, take stock in; **stock**, take stock of; **turns**, take turns; **wind**, take the wind out of someone's sails.

taken aback disconcerted, shocked, embarrassed:—On opening the door, she was quite taken aback to see John standing there.

taken in See take in (2).

taken with (by) impressed by, intrigued by:—I was much taken with the charm and simplicity of her manners.

taken, get taken be cheated or overcharged:—We certainly got taken at that motel. They charged us $30 a night.

takes, to have what it takes to have persistence and ability to accomplish a certain task:—Get Jones to write that editorial. He has what it takes.

talent scout someone employed by a large organization such as a moving-picture company or model agency to seek out new and promising talent:—Many of the movie stars of today were originally discovered by talent scouts.

talk back answer rudely or insolently:—Ruth was disciplined at school for talking back to the teacher.

talk big brag, boast, exaggerate:—He likes to talk big as though he were a very important person.

talk down (1) overwhelm, silence by superior loudness or force of argument:—The lawyer, armed with a briefcase full of facts and figures, had little difficulty in talking down his opponent. (2) minimize the significance of, belittle:—The hostile newspapers talked down the importance of the Minister's arrival here. (3) treat in a condescending, superior manner:—He claimed that his success as a columnist was due to the fact that he never talked down to his readers.

talk into persuade:—We finally talked father into buying a new car.

talk of discuss, consider as a possible course of action:—They are talking of moving to Florida.

talk of the town something which has become very popular or gained great prominence:—Recent nudity on the New York stage has been the talk of the town. Not long ago pop art and op art were the talk of the town.

talk out of dissuade, cause one to change his idea or plan. See **talk into**:—Jack was all for punching the fellow in the face, but we managed to talk him out of it.

talk out of turn See **speak** out of turn.

talk over discuss:—He wants to talk it over with his lawyer before he makes a final decision.

talk through one's hat speak ignorantly, make inaccurate statements, bluff:—He is talking through his hat when he says that there is basically no difference between the Latin and Anglo-Saxon temperaments.

talk turkey speak frankly and forcefully to:—I really talked turkey to Frank and told him that he could not go on ignoring his family obligations.

talk up praise, arouse enthusiasm for:—If you really believe in the product you are selling, then you should not hesitate to talk it up.

talk, make something talk said of an expert musician and his ability to play beautifully on his instrument:—That virtuoso pianist can certainly make his piano talk.

talking to, give one a talking to scold, lecture:—Mary's mother gave her a talking to for not washing the dishes.

talk. See also **tall** talk.

talk See also **back** talk; **double** talk; **shop,** talk shop; **small** talk; **sweet** talk.

tall order a demand or request difficult to fulfill:—The manufacturers maintained that to expect them to double their output within three months was a tall order.

tall story an exaggerated tale, difficult to believe:—Only two small children believed his tall stories about trapping elephants in Africa.

tall talk boasting, bragging:—In spite of all that tall talk about his connections on Wall Street, Eric was unable to make any money in the stock market.

tangle with contest or fight with, become involved with:—We warned our boys not to tangle with that group of tough boys from the other side of town.

tap, on tap available, ready:—We always keep a good supply of food and liquor on tap in case guests arrive unexpectedly.

taper down reduce, decrease:—He has tapered down his smoking from two to one package of cigarettes a day.

teach to do something (iron.) chastise, punish:—When I catch that boy, I'll teach him to tell lies about me.

team up with join with:—I prefer to go into business alone rather than to team up with someone whom I might not be able to get along with.

tear around dash about, be constantly on the go:—How she manages to tear around from one social function to another and take care of her family at the same time is more than I can understand.

tear down demolish, pull down:—They are tearing down that old building in order to build a new apartment house.

tear into attack vigorously:—The famished man tore into the steak as though he hadn't eaten in a week.

tear oneself away leave reluctantly, force oneself to leave:—All of the exhibits were so interesting that we had to tear ourselves away.

tear up destroy by tearing into small pieces:—He tore up the letter angrily and threw it into the wastepaper basket.

tear, go on a tear dissipate, go off on a spree:—Every once in a while he goes off on a tear and drinks for three days without stopping.

tears, crocodile tears artificial tears concealing the fact that one is not really feeling tearful, hypocritical tears:—She was really shedding crocodile tears when she heard of Bill's leaving, because we all knew that she was glad to be rid of him.

tear-jerker a movie or play with a sentimental, maudlin theme:—That movie we saw last evening was a regular tearjerker; we cried even though we realized that the theme was paltry.

tee-off (1) a golf term; to drive the ball from the first tee or starting point:—As soon as it stopped raining, we teed off. (2) start a long conversation:—As soon as my aunt heard about the scandal, she teed off.

teenagers youths in their teens (13 to 19 years of age):—There are magazines designed to appeal mainly to teenagers.

teeth, get one's teeth into enter into, familiarize oneself with, get deeply into:—Wait till you get your teeth into the work; you'll find it very interesting.

teeth, in the teeth of against the strong opposition of, in defiance of:—The bill was passed by a narrow margin in the teeth of strong opposition.

teeth, put teeth into make really effective and enforceable:—The legislature put teeth into the traffic law by increasing the penalties and appropriating money for its proper enforcement.

teeth, set one's teeth on edge annoy, irritate by the stridency or disagreeableness of its sound:—The scraping of chalk on a blackboard always sets my teeth on edge.

teeth See also **pick** one's teeth; **show** one's teeth; **skin**, by the skin of one's teeth; **store** teeth.

tell apart distinguish between:—The two brothers look so much alike that it is difficult to tell them apart.

tell it to the (Horse) Marines since there is no such thing as Horse Marines, this phrase means: tell it to a non-existent body because the story is so ridiculous or incredible that no one is going to believe it anyway:—When he started boasting about his fabulous earnings, I couldn't help suggesting that he tell it to the Marines.

tell off speak plainly, to censure, give someone a clear self-description, indicate the limits to which one's faults may go:—The head of our department had been so rude and overbearing that we were glad when the boss finally told him off.

tell on (1) disclose, inform against:—Jackie hid the dish he had broken, but his little sister told on him. (2) have a noticeably bad effect on:—All those years of worry and hard work are beginning to tell on Bob.

tell tales out of school disclose confidential information:—I don't think it was loyal to talk about our company's policies to a stranger; that was really telling tales out of school.

tell time able to read a clock:—Although Ernest is only four years old, he is already able to tell time.

tell where to get off See **tell off.**

tell See also **fortune,** tell someone's fortune; **beads,** tell one's **beads.**

temper, lose one's temper become angry, lose one's self-control:—I am afraid that I lost my temper and said several things for which I am very sorry now.

tempest in a teapot See **storm** in a teacup.

ten to one ten chances to one chance for or against something happening:—Ten to one he doesn't even bother to telephone us.

terms, be on good (bad) terms with enjoy friendly (hostile) relations with:—We have always been on good terms with our neighbors, the Smiths.

terms, bring to terms cause to surrender, force to accept the conditions imposed:—Hitler thought that by the ceaseless bombings over England he would bring the English to terms, but he was mistaken.

terms, come to terms reach an agreement:—After weeks of arbitration, the owners and the union leaders have finally come to terms on the question of sick benefits.

terms See also **easy** terms.

thank, will thank you to a form of rather stern reproach:—I'll thank you not to interfere any further in my affairs.

thanks to because of:—Thanks to his strong constitution, Henry was able to pull through his recent serious illness. Thanks to Jim's carelessness, we had a fire in our apartment.

then sometimes used with the meaning of "in that case," "under those circumstances":—a) If you say that you saw him, then it must be true. b) How, then, do you account for the fact that there was no one home at the time?

thick, be thick with be intimate with, on familiar terms with:—She has been thick with that family for years.

thick, in the thick of in the heaviest or most intense part of:—In the event of a brawl, you could always be sure to find Henry in the thick of it.

thick, through thick and thin unchanging in devotion through good times and bad:—His wife stuck faithfully to him through thick and thin.

thick See also **lay** it on thick.

thin out reduce in number, make less crowded:—I want to thin out those tomato plants since they are growing too close together.

thing, a thing or two a considerable amount, a lot:—Why don't you ask Jenkins that question? He knows a thing or two about sports.

thing, do one's thing do what one is supposed to, or prepared, or wants to do, especially referring to one's plan for a career :—Jill always wanted to become an actress, and hard work and a lucky break aided her in doing her thing.

thing, just the thing the fashionably correct or desirable thing:—Short skirts are just the thing again this year.

thing, to have a thing about to have a pet aversion for or specific fear about something:—Susan has a thing about flying, and won't ever get in an airplane.

thing See **not** the thing; **quite** the thing; **run**, get the run of things.

things, take off one's things remove one's outer garments such as an overcoat or topcoat:—Why don't you take off your things and sit down for a few minutes?

think a lot of have a high opinion of, be very fond of, love:—His friends think a lot of Bob.

think better of change one's mind for the better, alter a decision:—Margaret was going to write them a letter of complaint, but she thought better of it and decided to wait a few days.

think fit consider proper or advisable:—Apparently he thought fit not to follow our advice in the matter.

think highly of have a high opinion of, respect greatly:—The boss seems to think highly of your work.

think much of usually expressed in negative form with the meaning: not to have a high opinion of:—He said he didn't think much of him as a teacher.

think nothing (little) of consider unimportant, treat casually:—She thinks nothing of buying new clothes all the time.

think of (1) have an opinion of:—What do you think of Hemingway's first novel? (2) remember, recall:—I can't think of the word for "sky" in Spanish. (3) consider, intend:—We are thinking of painting our living room walls a light green. (4) consider, dream of, usually used in the negative:—I wouldn't think of disturbing the family at this hour of the night.

think out work out, devise, elaborate:—We must think out some way of making better use of our floor space.

think over consider carefully, delay making a decision upon:—We'll think over your offer and give you our answer in the morning.

think twice about consider carefully, wait before making a decision which might be imprudent:—If I were you, I'd think twice before investing my money in that business.

think up devise, invent, discover:—I wish I could think up some way of convincing them of their mistake.

third degree a method of severe grilling, used to extract information from an arrested suspect:—When the suspected murderer refused to talk, the police gave him the third degree.

thought, give thought to consider, think about:—Have you given any thought to the question of how you are going to dispose of the property?

thrash out confer about until a decision is reached, discuss fully:—We met to thrash out our differences, so that we could come to some decision as to what to do.

thread, lose the thread of suddenly forget:—In the debate the younger debater seemed to lose the thread of the argument and his rival won.

three sheets to the wind intoxicated:—Don't give him anything more to drink; he's already three sheets to the wind.

through and through completely:—Nelson is a Democrat through and through.

through train a direct train necessitating no changes:—Is this a through train to Chicago, or do I have to change at Buffalo?

through, be through (1) to have completed something, to have terminated:—I won't be through today until about six o'clock. (2) ready to quit or abandon:—He's had enough of married life. He's through.

through, be through with to have finished with. Same as **be through:**—He said I could read the book after he was through with it.

through See also **get** through; **squeak** through.

throw a fit See **fit,** throw a fit.

throw a party give a party:—They insist on throwing a party for us before we leave for Europe.

throw a race or game purposely lose a race or game by prior arrangement or bribe:—The jockey was paid a sizable sum of money to throw the race.

throw away discard:—Don't throw away those magazines yet; I still haven't read some of them.

throw cold water on discourage, dampen enthusiasm for:—I felt very discouraged when he threw cold water on my idea.

throw in add as a premium or something extra:—The shop advertised that with every suit of clothes they would throw in a pair of leather gloves.

throw in (up) the sponge give up in defeat, surrender:—Clark realized he couldn't win and so he threw in the sponge and left the poker game before it broke up.

throw off get rid of:—I can't seem to throw off this cold.

throw off the track mislead, confuse, divert:—It was unfortunate that the police were thrown off the track by the man's seemingly excellent alibi.

throw one's weight around exercise one's power, domineer:—He's a very capable manager, but none of us like the way he throws his weight around.

throw out (1) eject:—The shopkeeper was very polite, but he was forced to throw out the man who behaved so abusively and caused such a disturbance. (2) discard:—Once a month we throw out all our old magazines. (3) offer, speak:—Burns threw out the suggestion that we adopt a pension plan.

throw over desert, abandon:—He threw Agnes over, but then later on, Jean threw him over.

throw the boot at exact or impose the maximum penalty:—Angered by the increase in drunken drivers, the judge threw the book at the defendant and sentenced him to six months in jail.

throw together cause two persons of kindred interests to meet:—Because she entertained a lot, that widow was able to throw her niece and an eligible bachelor together a good deal.

throw up (1) retch, vomit:—Something he ate disagreed with him, and George suddenly began to throw up all over the place. (2) resign, give up:—George got disgusted and threw up his job last week. (3) confront with, irritate by reference to:—That's the third time this week you have thrown that mistake up to me.

throw up one's hands give up in despair:— After countless attempts to explain the point, our teacher threw up his hands in disgust.

throw See **curve,** throw a curve; **light,** throw light upon; **sponge,** throw in the sponge; **stone,** within a stone's throw; **weight,** throw one's weight around.

thumb a ride solicit or beg a ride from a motorist who is a stranger:—Max thumbed his way to the coast in just twelve days.

thumb through read or look through by turning the pages with the thumb, examine cursorily:—I always enjoy thumbing through a mail-order catalogue.

thumb, under one's thumb under one's domination:—Janet has her husband right under her thumb.

thumbs down the gesture of negation or rejection used in ancient Rome to indicate the death of a gladiator:—It became quite clear to us that it would be thumbs down on our proposal.

thumbs, all thumbs clumsy, awkward in the use of the hands or fingers:—Whenever a man is required to do a little sewing, he seems to be all thumbs.

thumb See also **green,** have a green thumb.

thunder by (in, out, down, etc.) pass with a great roar and pounding:—Those huge trucks thunder down the highway day and night.

thunder See also **steal** one's thunder.

tick, make one tick motivate:—What makes Frank tick? He doesn't care for wine, women, or song.

tick, on tick on credit:—We generally trade in the store on the corner because we can buy on tick there.

tickled very pleased. Often expressed as **tickled to death** or **tickled pink:**—I am sure that Sarah will be tickled to death with her present.

tide over bridge over a difficult period, help along:—I need ten dollars to tide me over until pay day.

tie down limit or restrict one's movement or activities:—The care of the baby naturally ties Jane down so that she is not so active socially as before.

tie one on (sl.) get drunk:—When he lost his job, Bill tied one on and had to be taken home.

tie up (1) secure with string, rope, etc. Intensive form of **tie:**—We tied up both packages well with heavy cord. (2) delay, stall:—The accident tied up all traffic along the highway for more than an hour. (3) engage, cause to be busy, detain:—Jack was tied up at the office until seven o'clock and was late for dinner.

tied to someone's apron strings strongly influenced or dominated by a wife or mother:—That boy is shy because he has been tied to his mother's apron strings.

tied up busy, engaged:—Murray wanted to take his wife out to lunch, but she was tied up at the hairdresser's.

tight (1) intoxicated:—He is one of those persons who can get tight on two or three glasses of beer. (2) stingy:—He saves almost every penny he earns and is one of the tightest persons I know. (3) difficult—as used particularly in such expressions as **tight spot, tight place, tight corner,** etc.:—Smith was certainly in a tight spot, having to meet all those obligations when business was not too good.

tight, hold tight grasp firmly, hold strongly to:—Hold tight to the railing or you may slip and fall.

tilt, at full tilt at full speed:—The painting showed two mounted horsemen charging at each other at full tilt.

time after time repeatedly:—I have asked him time after time not to leave confidential letters on his desk over night.

time and again Same as **time after time.**

time and a half wage payments of fifty percent over the regular rates for overtime:—If that carpenter works more than eight hours a day, he gets time and a half.

time of day the hour of the day:—I asked him the time of day, but he replied that he didn't have a watch.

time off a period of release from work:—If I had some time off this afternoon, I'd like to go shopping.

time is up the allotted period of time has passed or terminated:—At the end of the intermission period the referee blew his whistle, indicating that the time was up.

time, against time with a definite limit of time, with little time left to prevent something unfavorable:—The rescuers dug frantically against time to reach the buried miners.

time, all in good time within a reasonable time, not at once:—Alan plays the piano with a heavy touch, but he will improve all in good time.

time, do time serve a sentence in prison:—Wallace had done time in the State Penitentiary.

time, for the time being for the present:—For the time being you will have to share this room with another person.

time, from time to time occasionally, infrequently:—I see Hicks at the library from time to time.

time, have quite a time doing something encounter some difficulty in doing something:—I had quite a time locating your office.

time, have time on one's hands be idle, have nothing to do, also expressed as **have time hanging on one's hands:**—Now that it is June and school is over, Frances will have a lot of time on her hands.

time, in time within or before a fixed time, by a certain date or hour:—I hope to get downtown in time to visit one or two stores before they close.

time, on time exactly at a fixed or pre-arranged time, punctually:—The train, which was due at four o'clock, arrived exactly on time.

time, save time arrange one's trip or busi-ness so that it is done quicker, more quickly than as originally scheduled:—Let's buy all of our groceries at the supermarket and save time.

time See **ahead** of time; **at** times; **behind** the times; **beat** time; **good** time; **high** time; **keep** good time; **keep** time; **kill** time; **make** good time; **mark** time; **nick** of time; **once** upon a time; **pass** the time; **serve** time; **take** one's time; **tell** time; **work** against time.

tinker with play with, amuse oneself with, attempt to adjust in an amateur-ish way:—Her father's hobby is tinker-ing with old clocks and other mech-anisms.

tip off warn, give advance information about:—Apparently the gang had been tipped off, because when the police ar-rived, there was no sign of the stolen loot.

tip the scales (1) weigh:—Marie tips the scales at 120 pounds. (2) effect the bal-ance in favor of one person or group as against another:—It may well be that the speech he made tipped the scales in their favor.

tire, flat tire a dull person, one who is boring:—Everybody at the party seemed to be enjoying himself except that flat tire Carl.

tired out very tired, exhausted:—After shopping all day we were both tired out.

toe the mark (line) adhere strictly to regulations:—The new Mayor is expect-ed to make everybody in the city gov-ernment toe the mark in the perform-ance of his duties.

toes, be on one's toes alert, active:—We need several more salesmen who not only know the business, but are on their toes.

toll bridge See **bridge,** toll bridge.

toll call a long-distance telephone call, one having toll charges:—There were several toll calls on our last month's telephone bill.

Tom, Dick, and Harry the average or typ-ical man:—He says he doesn't want to dress exactly like every Tom, Dick, and Harry.

tone down moderate in intensity, lessen the vigor of:—We noticed that in its recent editorials, the newspaper toned down its attack on the President's veto of the tax reform bill.

tongue in (one's) cheek in an ironic or insincere manner:—When the Congressman from our district said he wasn't going to run for office anymore, he said it tongue in cheek.

tongued-tied slow of speech because of bashfulness, nervousness, or some physical malformation:—She was so nervous when she was introduced to the famous actress that she was tongue-tied.

tongue twister a word or group of words difficult to pronounce:—Many of the long Indian names given to our lakes and mountains are tongue twisters for the person learning English.

tongue, hold one's tongue remain silent, uncommunicative:—Unless you think he can hold his tongue, don't mention anything about this to Jenkins.

tongue, on the tip of one's tongue about to be uttered or spoken, not quite within recall of memory:—His name was on the tip of my tongue, but for the life of me I couldn't remember it.

tongue See also **slip** of the tongue.

tooth and nail furiously, fiercely:—Naturally the inhabitants fought tooth and nail to protect their homes.

top banana (sl.) the chief person in a group:—Phil has always been the top banana in our club.

top dollar the highest rate or price:—That car lot pays top dollar for used cars.

top-drawer (adj.) of the highest importance or quality:—The acting in "Hamlet" last night was absolutely top-drawer.

topless waitress a waitress in a restaurant who wears nothing above the waist:—The police banned topless waitresses in that city.

top notch (top flight, top drawer, etc.) of the highest quality or category:—His performance of Hamlet was top notch.

top off finish off, complete with a flourish or in some special manner:—We decided to be extravagant and top off the meal with the richest dessert on the menu.

top secret a very important secret closely held by the highest officials:—That Ambassador was sent to a neighboring country on a top-secret mission.

toss a coin throw a coin up in the air to decide in the favor of one of two persons:—I'll toss a coin, and heads, you win; tails, I win.

toss off do or drink something rapidly, drain at one draught:—Helen tossed off three martinis, one right after the other.

toss, a toss up an even chance, a matter of complete uncertainty:—It was a toss up, in the race, between the holder of the title and the younger, unknown contestant.

toss See also **hat,** toss one's hat in the ring.

touch and go critical, likely to go in either direction:—At first it was touch and go whether the heart patient would live or not, but within a few days he was much improved.

touch off set off, ignite, explode:—The danger lies in the fact that some slight incident may touch off a major war.

touch to the quick offend, injure deeply the feelings of:—Your remarks about his lack of education touched him to the quick.

touch up repair, restore, improve:—It was easy to see that the painting had been touched up in several places.

touch upon (on) mention, make reference to:—In her remarks on child care, she touched upon the importance of nutrition.

touch, get in touch with communicate with:—He promised to get in touch with us as soon as he returned from Europe.

touch, lose one's touch lose an ability or skill:—I used to be able to grow flowers, but I think I've lost my touch.

touch, make a touch borrow or seek to borrow money:—Jones tried to make another touch yesterday, but I had to refuse him.

touch See also **keep** in touch with; **out** of touch with; **bottom,** touch bottom.

tow, in tow accompanied by:—In swept the guest of honor with her husband and children in tow.

town, go to town do completely, thoroughly:—As soon as we got the O.K., we went to town on the sales campaign.

town, on the town (sl.) go for an evening's entertainment:—Those delegates to the New York Convention went on the town after the closing of the afternoon meetings.

track down follow, chase, pursue until captured:—I read a story last evening about how a detective, through some very clever maneuvering, tracked down a criminal.

track up leave tracks or marks upon, soil:—Wipe your feet well because I don't want you to track up my new rug.

track, beaten track an established main route or routine:—We bought that antique chair in a little shop that is far off the beaten track.

track See also **keep** track of; **side** track; **inside,** have an inside track; **wrong** side of the tracks.

trade in exchange one's old car for a new or newer one:—Bob traded in his old Chevy for a new model and was allowed a $400 trade in.

trail off decrease in intensity, disappear gradually:—When she saw that her pleas were disregarded, her voice trailed off in sobs.

trailer park an open area where persons having trailers can park and hook up with plumbing and electrical facilities:—On our vacation by trailer we stopped at two trailer parks.

trick or treat a saying by children on Halloween, which means treat us with money, candy, etc., or we'll play tricks on you:—When the children came to the door and cried "Trick or treat," we gave them some cookies and apples.

trick, do the trick do the job, accomplish the task:—If that key doesn't fit the lock, I think this one will do the trick.

trim one's sails restrict one's activities, economize:—The Robinsons are not as wealthy as formerly; in fact, they have had to trim their sails and give up such luxuries as going to the theater every week.

trip up cause to fall, confuse, catch in error:—Jack had memorized his table of chemical equivalents so thoroughly that it was impossible to trip him up.

trot out display, bring out for inspection:—Don't mention anything about stamp collecting or Tinker is sure to trot out his entire collection for everyone to examine.

truck, have no truck with (sl.) have nothing to do with, avoid:—After the way Phil mistreated his wife, she will have no truck with him.

true, be true to oneself adhere to one's principles or ideals:—John felt that he could not be true to himself as a serious painter, and go on working as a commercial artist.

true See also **come** true; **hold** true; **ring** true.

trump card a winning card or move, a decisive resource:—The government held one trump card over the strikers, namely, the law under which it could invoke the sixty-day cooling-off period.

trump up fabricate or invent some story or excuse:—It became clear, during the trial, that most of the charges against the defendant were trumped up.

try on test, put on a garment or other article of clothing to test its size and appearance:—I tried on at least a half-dozen suits before finding one I really liked.

try out test, use for a trial period:—This time I plan to try out several makes of cars before making a final choice.

try See also **hand,** try one's hand; **nice** try.

tuck in (1) place the bedclothes carefully in position around a person in bed:—I remember that when I was a child, my mother used to come and tuck me into bed every night. (2) place the edges of the bedclothes beneath the mattress:—On such cold nights, it is best to tuck the covers in carefully before getting into bed.

tumble to learn, find out, discover:—It was a long time before Jones tumbled to the fact that his trusted employee was stealing money from Jones's store.

tumble, give another a tumble notice, be pleasant to, affable, receptive:—John admires Marcia very much, but she won't give him a tumble.

tune in adjust or synchronize—a radio or television term:—Some nights I can tune in that station easily; other nights I can't tune it in at all.

tune, carry a tune be able to hum or sing a simple piece of music:—Tim is tone-deaf and can't carry a tune.

tune, change one's tune reverse one's previous position or point of view:—He had not been very polite to us, but when he found out that we were the owners of that property, he quickly changed his tune.

tune, to the tune of to the large extent of, at the great cost or loss of:—The bank had to refuse them the loan, because they had already borrowed to the tune of ten thousand dollars.

turn a pretty penny make a good profit. Also expressed as **turn an honest penny:** —That real estate operator must have turned a pretty penny in selling that whole block of buildings to the city.

turn against develop an aversion to, change from a friendly to an unfriendly attitude:—Many of his former associates turned against him when it became known how he had abused his position of trust.

turn away reject, refuse admittance, dismiss:—Hundreds of people were turned away from the concert.

turn back return, retrace one's steps:—We drove up to their house, but they were not in and we had to turn back.

turn color change color, blush, or become pale:—Each time we mentioned Bill's name, Helen turned colors.

turn down (1) reject:—Henry tried to join the army but was turned down because of a weak heart. (2) lessen in intensity:—That radio is pretty loud. Can't you turn it down a little?

turn down a bed partly pull down and fold back the covers:—In most first-class hotels a maid comes to the room each night and turns down the bed.

turn in (1) submit, deliver:—Each student has to turn in a composition to the teacher once a week. (2) go to bed, retire for the night:—I want to turn in early tonight and get a good night's rest.

turn off stop, close, shut off:—Be sure to turn off the lights when you leave the room.

turn on (1) open, begin—the opposite of **turn off**:—The plumbers turned on every faucet in the house. (2) turn against, swing from friendship to enmity:—The dog is very vicious and has even turned on its master several times.

turn on one's heel turn about, leave abruptly in displeasure:—Apparently Fred took offense at what I said, because he suddenly turned on his heel and left the room.

turn one on (off) appeal to (repel) one, interest greatly:—Wyeth's paintings certainly turn me on.

turn one's hand to See **put** one's hand to.

turn one's stomach cause one to become sick at the stomach, nauseate:—It turned my stomach to see that poor dog lying wounded in the street.

turn out (1) result, develop:—Though it looked like rain this morning, it has turned out to be a nice day. (2) produce:—That factory can turn out about 3,000 cars a month. (3) eject, evict:—The owner of the building threatened to turn out his tenants if they continued to ignore the fire prevention laws. (4) appear:—Very few people turned out for the rally.

turn over (1) overturn, turn so that the upper and lower positions of an object are reversed:—The car swerved from the road, turned over twice, and landed in the ditch. (2) hand over to, deliver:—To whom should we turn over the keys when we vacate the apartment?

turn over a new leaf reform, start afresh: —The judge did not sentence the man, but admonished him to go back to his family and turn over a new leaf.

turn over in one's mind consider carefully:—After turning the offer over in my mind several days, I finally decided to accept it.

turn pale become white in the face:—At the news of the plane crash Mrs. Smith turned pale.

turn tail reverse, run off:—Upon the appearance of the large police dog, both little poodles turned tail and disappeared.

turn the other cheek permit the repetition of some indignity, blow, or attack:— When struck upon one cheek, the true Christian, according to the teachings of Christ, should turn the other cheek.

turn the tables reverse the situation:— They beat us badly at bridge last night, but tonight we hope to turn the tables on them.

turn the tide cause events to take a new direction:—What turned the tide in the battle was the arrival of fresh reinforcements.

turn to seek and obtain help from:— Frank assured me that if I ever needed financial help I could always turn to him.

turn to account utilize, profit by:—It is expected that the new Ambassador will turn to good account his knowledge of the European military situation.

turn turtle overturn, turn over on its back: —After colliding, both cars turned turtle.

turn up (1) appear:—Only a few faculty members turned up for the meeting. (2) increase in intensity. See **turn** down:— Turn the radio up a little. I can scarcely hear the program.

turn up one's nose at look with scorn upon, reject:—The meal seemed adequate to most of us, but Gertrude, who was accustomed to more elaborate service, turned up her nose at it.

turn upon See **turn** on (2)

turn, do a good (bad) turn perform a good deed:—Every Boy Scout pledges to do at least one good turn every day.

turn, take a turn go for a walk:—It was such a nice day that we decided to take a turn through the park.

turn, take a turn for the better (worse) change for the better, improve:—The doctor told us that the sick man had taken a turn for the better.

turn, to a turn cooked to just the proper degree:—The roast had been cooked to a turn and was extremely delicious.

turns, by turns singly, alternating one with the other:—Jack and I agreed to work at the office on Saturdays by turns, he on the first Saturday, I on the second, etc.

turns, take turns alternate:—Since we took turns driving, we did not find the trip too tiring.

turn See also **back,** turn one's back on; **head,** turn one's head; **speak** out of turn; **talk** out of turn.

two bits twenty-five cents:—The beggar seemed surprised when I gave him two bits, but as it happened, I had no other small change at the moment.

two-time (v.) secretly go out with another man or woman other than one's husband or wife:—Ralph is divorcing his two-timing wife.

U

ugly duckling an ill-favored or unprepossessing child in an otherwise attractive family:—Grace, originally the ugly duckling of the family, turned out to be quite an attractive young woman.

ugly customer a dangerous, quarrelsome man:—That burglar who tried to break into our apartment was certainly an ugly customer.

unbosom oneself disclose private information to a confidante, confess one's personal thoughts or feelings:—Having at last a receptive listener, Mrs. Frank unbosomed herself of all her troubles.

uncalled for said of a tactless, impolite, savage remark or action that should not have been made:—In scolding his secretary, his reference to her private life was uncalled for.

under (1) sometimes has the force of "subject to" as in the expressions **under** fire, **under** orders, **under** protest, **under** oath, etc.:—He swore under oath never to attempt to leave the country again. (2) in its usual meaning of "below" or "in a position lower than" it combines with various nouns and verbs to form many useful compounds. Note the following: **underact, underbid, undercharge, underdone, underexposure, undergraduate, underground, underhand, underline, undermanned, undermine, underpay, underrate, undersell, undersized, understate, undervalue,** etc.

under one's breath in a whisper:—She said something to him under her breath which I did not hear.

under the table secretly:—The price-fixed rental of that apartment was $150 a month, but the tenant was supposed to give the landlord something extra under the table.

under the weather in bad health or spirits:—Jack is not coming to the office today; he phoned to say that he is feeling somewhat under the weather.

under the wire within a narrow time limit:—Jenkins, who is 38 years old, got into the Navy just under the wire because a few days later they lowered the age limit to 36.

under way in motion, in progress. Sometimes spelled **under weigh:**—The yearly campaign to raise funds for the Red Cross is already under way.

under, go under fail, become bankrupt:—During the 1929 depression, many heavy investors went under.

under See also **out** from under.

up a tree confused, perplexed, in a predicament:—The news that no hotel accommodations were obtainable at that resort left me rather up a tree as to my vacation plans.

up and about (around) in good health again after an illness, recovered and able to move about:—Tom was ill for several weeks but is now up and about again.

up-and-coming ambitious, progressive, bound toward success:—The newly elected state representative is an up-and-coming young man who is expected to go far in politics.

up in arms See also **arms.**

up-tight hostile, annoyed, uncooperative:—You needn't get so up-tight about my living alone. Everybody does.

up-to-date modern:—The building, after being remodeled, will be completely new and up-to-date.

up to one's neck See **neck.**

up to scratch See **scratch.**

up, be all up with finished, hopeless as regards any chance of escape or recovery:—It is believed that unless the rescuers reach the entrapped miner within the next few hours, it will be all up with him.

up, be up (1) having arisen from bed:—Mary got up about an hour ago, but Helen isn't up yet. (2) terminated:—Even so hardened a criminal as he was realized that the game was up when the police closed in on him. See **time** is up.

up, be up against confronted with:—In that type of business you will naturally be up against very stiff competition.

up, be up against it in poor financial condition:—Though they still seem to live well, it is rumored that the Smiths have been up against it for some time.

up, be up to (1) dependent upon, depending upon the decision of:—He said it was up to us to choose where we should go for our vacation. (2) physically capable of. Sometimes expressed as **feel up to:**—I'm sorry, but I am so tired that I am really not up to going to the theater with you tonight.

up, be up to something involved in some dubious, mischievous, or evil act; plotting something:—The boys had been quiet for so long that we began to wonder if they were up to something.

up, on the up and up honest, legal, reliable:—Don't be afraid to take a job with that organization. It's very much on the up and up.

up, what's up what is going on, what's taking place:—When I saw him busily cleaning out his desk, I asked him what was up.

upper crust the upper social class:—Newport used to be famous as the summer gathering place of the upper crust.

ups and downs changes in fortune, alternating between good and bad periods:—Though he is now successful and well-established, Smith, like many others, had his ups and downs when he first went into business.

upset the applecart See **applecart.**

upset, be upset be disturbed, worried:—I explained to her that her son's injury was a very minor one and that there was no reason for her to be so upset.

use up use, consume completely:—As soon as their money was used up, they came back home.

use, have no use for (1) have no need for:—Do you want my old lawn-mower? I'm moving to an apartment and have no further use for it. (2) dislike, scorn:—She has had no use for Dan ever since he broke a date with her.

use, make use of utilize, use, employ:—On your trip to Mexico you will be able to make good use of your knowledge of Spanish.

used to have continued doing over an extended period of time in the past, to have had the habit of doing:—I used to buy my clothes at Black's; now I buy them at White's.

V

vain, in vain without result, futilely:—We tried to persuade him not to go swimming, but in vain.

vain See also **name,** take someone's name in vain.

vicious circle a situation in which an evil event leads to the next evil event, in a kind of circular or chain reaction:—Raising wages to meet higher prices during a period of inflation only results in a vicious circle.

view, in view of in consideration of, considering:—In view of his stern opposition, no other course remained to us but to give up the whole idea.

view, with a view to with the purpose of:—He bought the land with a view to building a summer home there.

virtue, by virtue of by reason of, as a consequence of:—He got the job by virtue of his superior qualifications.

vote down vote against, defeat:—Perkins moved to adjourn, but was voted down by the opposition group.

W

wade through read through something long and laborious:—It took me at least two months to wade through The Decline of the West.

wagon, go (be) on the wagon give up drinking, embark on a period of abstinence from alcohol:—Carter says that he is really serious this time about going on the wagon.

wait on (upon) serve, attend:—The clerk asked me whether I had been waited on.

wait on (upon) hand and foot be constantly in attendance upon, serve in a slavish manner:—She spoils her children by waiting on them hand and foot.

wait up postpone going to bed until another's return:—Ruth told her parents not to wait up for her since she might not get home until very late.

wait See also **lie** in wait.

waiting room a receiving room, as in a doctor's office or bus station:—I'll meet you at 2 o'clock in the waiting room at Grand Central Station.

walk all over someone dominate, abuse, take advantage of:—I have little respect for any man who lets his wife walk all over him.

walk away with See **walk** off with.

walk of life social status, income group, occupation:—As a doctor in a hospital he had come in contact with people from all walks of life.

walk off with take, steal:—It looks as though someone has walked off with my new fountain pen.

walk on air be in ecstasy, be thrilled:—When Mary agreed to be his wife, John walked on air for the rest of the week.

walk out on desert (v.):—That poor woman had to seek public assistance because her husband walked out on her and the kids.

walking, give someone his walking papers dismiss summarily, send away:—As soon as she found someone she liked better, she gave George his walking papers.

walk-up an apartment without an elevator:—The Browns live in a six-story walk-up.

wallflower one who is forced to sit out dances because no one invites her to dance:—Since she had no desire to be a wallflower all evening, Doris refused to go to the dance alone.

wall See also **drive** to the wall; **go** to the wall; **back,** have one's back to the wall; **handwriting** on the wall.

wane, on the wane losing popularity, waning:—The latest fashion news indicates that short skirts are not yet on the wane.

want-ad a small advertisement on a special page of a newspaper which offers employment opportunities and merchandise:—Karl got his job through a want-ad which he placed in last Sunday's Times.

want in (or out) wish to be associated (or disassociated) with an enterprise or a person:—Two of my partners have decided to stay in the business despite a bad year, but my third partner and I want out.

want, in want needy, destitute:—In China there are reported to be millions of people in want.

ward off avert, deflect, fend off:—Mother was certain that the cod-liver oil which she made us take each winter helped us to ward off colds.

war-paint cosmetics: — After getting dressed for the party, Ellen put on all her war-paint.

warm reception (iron.) a severe counterattack to an assault:—You may be sure our troops gave the enemy a very warm reception when they dared to attack our well-fortified positions.

warm up (1) become warmer:—It was very cold this morning, but it seems to be warming up. (2) heat, cause to become warm or hot:—As soon as I warm up this soup, we will have a little lunch. (3) become more friendly:—At first he was rather distant with me, but later, when we discovered that we had several mutual acquaintances, he began to warm up.

warm up to develop more interest or enthusiasm in, become more animated:—When the speaker finally warmed up to his subject, his lecture became very interesting.

warm, get warmed up (1) become comfortably warm:—When we reached the cabin, we had to build a fire immediately in order to get warmed up. (2) become physically fit and skilled:—A pitcher must always throw several practice balls in order to get warmed up before starting a game. (3) become angry:—They both got warmed up in their dispute over the merits of the two candidates.

warm, get warmer approach closer and closer to something which one is searching for:—In playing hide-and-seek, children always shout "warm" or "you're getting warmer" whenever the child who is searching approaches the vicinity of the child who is hiding.

warpath, on the warpath in an angry or warlike mood:—Jackson has been on the warpath ever since he saw that unflattering cartoon Bob made of him.

wash one's dirty linen in public violate good taste by revealing personal matters publicly rather than privately:—We all felt that Mrs. Stern should have more pride than to wash her dirty linen in public.

wash one's hands of reject, disclaim all responsibility for:—He stalked out of the meeting and said he was washing his hands of the whole problem.

wash out disappear through washing:— Do you think this stain will wash out?

wash, come out in the wash be learned, work out, get settled:—Don't worry about the solutions to our management problems. They will all come out in the wash.

washout a dismal failure:—Our camp leader proved to be a washout as far as sports was concerned.

wash up wash completely—intensive form of wash:—I'll be with you just as soon as I wash up.

wash out pale, listless in appearance:— No wonder Henry looks so washed out; he has just recovered from a serious illness.

washed, all washed up finished, no longer serviceable, a failure:—He can perhaps work as a coach for one of the teams, but as a pitcher, he is all washed up.

waste away diminish in strength and size, grow weaker:—One of the chief characteristics of the disease is that the patient loses weight and gradually wastes away.

waste one's breath lose one's time and effort arguing:—Why do you waste your breath on a person who is so stubborn and so set in his views as Harris?

waste See also **lay** waste.

watch one's step exercise prudence, tact, and care; mend one's ways:—The teacher advised Jim to watch his step or he might fail the course.

watch out for be on the alert for:—Special troops were garrisoned all along the coast to watch out for enemy airplanes.

watch over take care of, guard:—The farmers of that section use specially trained dogs to watch over their sheep at night.

water off a duck's back that which has little result or effect. Sometimes expressed as **pour water over a duck's back:**—The more I tried to dissuade her, the more determined she became, so

that I felt my arguments were just water off a duck's back.

water under the bridge that which is past and unchangeable. Sometimes expressed as **water over the dam:**—He started to discuss all the difficulties we had been through, but I told him it was just so much water under the bridge and that it would be best to forget.

water wagon See **wagon,** go one the wagon.

water, be in deep water be in difficulties, beyond one's capabilities:—When Nelson started to discuss law with a real lawyer, he found himself in deep water.

water, make one's mouth water stimulate desire or envy:—The appetizing roast set in the center of the table was enough to make anyone's mouth water.

water, of the first water of highest quality:—The critics immediately acclaimed him as a novelist of first water.

water See also **fish** out of water; **hold** water; **hot,** be in hot water; **head,** keep one's head above water; **throw** cold water on.

watered down weakened, diluted:—The play was a watered-down version of Shakespeare's Macbeth.

wave on direct a motorist to proceed by giving him a wave of the arm:—We had to stop on account of a collision ahead of us, but soon afterwards a state policeman waved us on.

waves, make waves upset a rather placid situation or agreement:—After we had all agreed on the contract, one of the vice-presidents began to make waves.

way off a great distance from a particular point, said of an estimate:—We were way off in our calculations, with the result that the house cost us twice as much to build as we had originally planned.

way out radically different, said of some styles in clothes, decoration, art, etc.:— That artist's style of painting is way out.

way, be in the way be an obstruction, cause inconvenience:—Although he thought he was helping us prepare the dinner, he was only in the way.

way, have a way with have an attractive and appealing manner, exert an influence over:—Jack is certainly not handsome, but he seems to have a way with the women.

way, have one's own way do as one wishes, especially against advice or admonitions to the contrary:—The child is rather spoiled because his mother has always let him have his own way.

way, in a way to a certain extent, in one sense:—He predicted I would lose money on the deal, and in a way he was right.

way, well on one's way having covered a sizable portion of one's journey, or having come close to a higher step in one's career:—He is well on his way to becoming an officer of the company.

way See also **by** the way; **feel** one's way; **give** way; **go** out of one's way; **Great White Way**; **know** one's way around; **make** one's way; **make** way for; **meet** half-way; **no** two ways about it; **other,** just the other way around; **out** of the way; **pave** the way; **pay** one's own way; **pick** one's way; **put** someone out of the way; **rub** one the wrong way; **see** one's way; **set,** be set in one's ways; **under** way.

wear and tear deterioration through use:—It was by no means a new car and showed evidence of a good deal of wear and tear.

wear away disappear gradually through wear:—The sign was no longer legible because much of the lettering had worn away.

wear down (1) lessen in size or height through wear:—I need new heels on these shoes; the present ones are all worn down. (2) manage by insistence or constant pressure:—I wasn't going to let her wear my gold bracelet, but she begged so hard that she finally wore me down and I let her have it.

wear off pass off, disappear gradually:—The effects of the drug naturally wear off within a few hours.

wear on pass slowly in time:—The hours spent in waiting for the attack to begin wore on slowly.

wear out (1) become useless or unpresentable from wear:—It looks as though you need a new suit. The one you are wearing is almost worn out. (2) tire greatly:—Every time she goes shopping she comes home completely worn out.

wear See also **welcome,** wear out one's welcome.

weather the storm survive some disaster:—When we started the business, we had very little money and had a hard time getting credit, but in a year we had weathered the storm.

weather, be under the weather See **under.**

weave through (in, out, along, etc.) pass through in an indirect or weaving manner:—Jack weaving his way skillfully through the crowd, was one of the few who managed to get a good view of the President.

weed out sort out, select and discard:—We had to weed out most of the applications, until we were left with about a dozen from which we could make our choice.

week of Sundays a long time, literally seven weeks:—I haven't seen Bill in a week of Sundays.

weep one's eyes out See **cry** one's heart (eyes) out.

weigh anchor hoist the anchor, set sail:—After a week in Marseilles we weighed anchor and sailed in the direction of Alexandria.

weigh one's words speak with care, avoid inaccurate statements:—It was a situation requiring great tact, and I advised her to weigh her words carefully before making the complaint.

weigh upon be a burden upon:—His guilt weighed heavily upon him.

weight, throw one's weight around use dictatorial pressure to get results:—She disliked her supervisor because he was always throwing his weight around.

welcome wagon a truck sponsored by local merchants that calls on a new resident with free samples of merchandise and information about the locality:—When we moved to Buffalo, we were visited by the welcome wagon and its hostess.

welcome, wear out one's welcome stay too late or too long as a guest:—By the fifth day the Allen's guest had worn out his welcome.

well-heeled See **heeled.**

well off (1) rich, having more than adequate means:—They may not be millionaires, but they are sufficiently well off to be able to spend each winter in Florida. (2) in good condition, free of problems or difficulties:—Why does he want to invest in still another business? Doesn't he know when he is well off?

well-to-do wealthy:—Only the well-to-do can afford to own homes in that exclusive suburb.

wet blanket See **blanket.**

wet one's whistle appease one's thirst:—I was getting thirstier by the minute and suggested to Bill that we stop at the first roadside tavern and wet our whistles.

what with considering:—What with rising prices and higher taxes the average family man is hard pressed to make both ends meet.

what, and what not almost anything else, nearly everything, and so forth:—They will sell you food, supplies, and what not by direct mail.

what, or what have you and so forth:—Their attic is filled with old broken-down furniture, old clothing, and what have you.

what, know what's what See **know.**

what's more in addition, furthermore:—I don't like her manner of working and what's more I intend to tell her so.

what's up? what's going on, happening:—Everybody in the office is so gloomy today. What's up? Are we all getting fired?

wheelhorse a reliable and industrious worker, one upon whom others depend to do the heavy work:—In getting out the vote Calder has always been the wheelhorse of the local Republican club.

wheel See also **shoulder,** put one's shoulder to the wheel.

while away pass the time (days, hours) agreeably:—The weather was too bad for us to go out, so we whiled away the afternoon playing bridge.

while, give it a while allow enough time for something to get adjusted:—The action of that new piano is a little stiff. Give it a while to ease up.

while See also **once** in a while; **worthwhile.**

whip up prepare quickly:—Mary is very skillfull in whipping up a meal at a moment's notice.

whiphand, hold (have) the whiphand over dominate, control:—Ellen is a lovely girl, but we all feel sorry for her, because her rich aunt, with whom she lives, holds a whiphand over her.

whistle-stop a small town where the trains stop only on signal:—President Truman made excellent use of the whistle-stop during his 1948 campaign for the presidency.

whistle See also **wet** one's whistle.

white-collar workers workers employed in offices and at desks as opposed to those who work as manual workers:—It is a well-known fact that white-collar workers are not nearly so well organized or unionized as the manual worker.

white elephant a useless or unmanageable gifts, something proving to be a burden which one cannot dispose of:—We finally realized that that large house my father left us in the country was really a white elephant, because it was too expensive to run and we couldn't find a purchaser.

white trash See **poor** white.

white See also **lie,** white lie.

whodunit a mystery tale or novel:—Jenkins regularly reads four or five whodunits every week.

whole, on the whole in general, taking all things into consideration:—He is, on the whole, a satisfactory student.

whole See also **go** the whole hog; **swallow** whole.

wide awake (1) completely awake:—The coffee I drank before going to bed kept me wide awake almost all night. (2) alert:—He is a wide-awake young man who should go far in this business.

wide of the mark far from the target, inaccurate:—When you estimated that the trip would cost two hundred dollars, you were wide of the mark, because it cost almost twice as much.

wide, give someone a wide berth avoid someone, stay as far away from as possible:—Brooks is such a bore that I give him a wide berth whenever I meet him at the club.

wild goose chase an absurd and completely futile errand:—The young reporter told his editor that he had been sent on a wild goose chase when he was assigned to get the facts about a man who, it later developed, had never really existed.

win hands down win conclusively:—The opposition proved so feeble, that Jones won the election hands down.

win out win after a rather protracted struggle:—That lawsuit lasted a long time because many of the witnesses had disappeared or had moved to distant parts of the country, but we finally won out.

win over convert to one's position or point of view, win to one's cause:—The Democrats offered him a Cabinet position, and in this way won him over to their side.

wind up (1) tighten the spring of a watch or clock:—My watch has stopped. I must have forgotten to wind it up. (2) terminate, conclude:—The party tonight will wind up our entertainment program for this season. (3) end up, finish in:—We started for Radio City but wound up at a little night club in Greenwich Village.

wind, get wind of hear of, learn of, get information about:—Somehow, the children got wind of the fact that there was going to be ice cream for dessert.

wind, in the wind existing as a possibility, rumored imminent:—It was in the wind that there was going to be a shift in the Cabinet.

wind, take the wind out of someone's sails disconcert, deflate, embarrass:—His failure to get that scholarship certainly has taken the wind out of Perkins' sails.

windbag a talkative, boring person, one given to exaggerated and foolish talk:—I was warned not to take too seriously what Evans said because he was such a windbag.

windfall an unexpected gain or gift of sizable proportions:—That check Jane's father sent her just as she was so low in funds proved a happy windfall.

window dressing an elaborate exterior sometimes designed to conceal one's real motives, facade:—Jack warned me that those invitations were just so much window dressing; that what the Smiths really wanted was an introduction to my influential brother.

window See also **shopping**, window shopping.

wing, take under one's wing treat as a protege:—He didn't know many people when he came to the community, and the family took him under their wing.

wing, take wing flee, hasten away:—When they heard a policeman approaching, the thieves took wing.

wink at pretend not to notice, overlook:—Her employer winks at her late arrivals at work because he values her services highly.

wink, not to sleep a wink not to sleep at all, not to close the eyes:—I didn't sleep a wink all night.

wipe out obliterate, destroy:—The atomic bomb wiped out Hiroshima.

wire (v.) to telegraph:—We'll wire you as soon as we get to Chicago.

wire See also **live** wire; **pull** strings (wires) ; **under** the wire.

wise guy a fresh, cynical, and frequently impudent person; one who parades his knowledge; a smart aleck:—He had been such a wise guy that all of us felt he deserved his punishment.

wise up inform or become informed:—It's about time he wised up to the fact that no one in the office likes him.

wise, get wise to learn about, become informed about:—It was months before he got wise to the fact that they were training someone else for the position.

wise, put wise (to) inform, make aware of:—Apparently someone had put the police wise, because they were there when the robbers arrived.

wisecrack a joke or witty remark—generally at someone else's expense:—The two comedians kept up such a rapid fire of wisecracks that we were unable to control our laughter.

wise See also **penny** wise; **word** to the wise.

wish off on get rid of by delegating to another:—I'd like to know who wished off this messy job on me.

with, are you with me? are you following what I am saying?:—First you factor the number, then you extract the square root, and then—are you with me?

with, get with it get organized, get in step, involve oneself, etc.:—You're not cooperating with the other members of the staff. Get with it!

wits, keep (have) one's wits about one be alert, remain calm:—Fred was the only one who kept his wits about him when the fire broke out.

wolf in sheep's clothing one who deceives by his attractive and guileless exterior:—Helen resisted George's attentions because she suspected that he was a wolf in sheep's clothing.

wolf, keep the wolf from the door stave off hunger, avert starvation:—With a wife and six children to support, Jones had all he could do to keep the wolf from the door.

wolf See also **cry** wolf.

wonder, for a wonder as an exception, surprisingly:—Ames arrived, for a wonder, almost sober.

wonder, no wonder See also **no.**

woods, out of the woods out of danger, in the clear, having emerged from some problem or difficulty:—They were in serious financial difficulty for several days, but now are out of the woods.

word for word literally, verbatim:—I will give you the story word for word as it was told to me.

word of mouth communication by oral rather than written means:—The merchant told us that the best customers he had were recommended to him by word of mouth.

word to the wise advice or warning which the intelligent person is expected to follow:—I had spoken to him about his tardiness earlier, and assumed that a word to the wise was sufficient.

word, as good as one's word reliable, dependable:—I am certain that David will do the job on time, because he is as good as his word.

word, give one's word pledge, give one's promise:—He gave us his word that he would repay us next week.

word, give the word give the signal, indicate:—Any time you need any additional help just give us the word.

word, have a word with talk with, discuss, speak briefly with:—The personnel manager said he wanted to have a word with me.

word, keep one's word keep or fulfill one's promise:—He kept his word and paid us the money before the first of the month, as he had promised.

words, have words with quarrel:—Every time the two of them get together they have words.

words, in other words to express the aforementioned idea in another form:—He became, in other words, a great hero.

word See also **break** one's word; **eat** one's words; **leave** word; **man** of his word; **put** in a word for; **take** one's word; **take** the words out of one's mouth.

work a change cause a change, effect a difference:—The fact that he is now crippled has naturally worked a change in his living habits.

work against time See **time,** against time.

work in find a place or time for:—I'll be busy all day tomorrow, but if I can possibly work it in I'd like to attend that lecture with you.

work on (upon) bring gradually increasing pressure upon, influence:—The two girls worked on their father and finally got him to agree to take them to Europe this summer.

work one over assault, injure, pummel:—When the storekeeper refused to open his safe, the robbers worked him over and left him unconscious.

work one's way (1) earn one's expenses while studying, or engaged in some other unremunerative pursuit:—Jack plans to work his way through college (2) penetrate gradually:—The needle had slowly worked its way through the child's stomach and entered the liver.

work out (1) turn out, develop:—I am sure that she will work out well in that type of job. (2) train, undergo regular physical exercise as a form of training:—Both boxers work out every day in Stillman's gymnasium on 8th Avenue. (3) exhaust through working or exploiting:—The area was dotted with iron mines which had been worked out years ago and were now abandoned.

workout strenuous physical exercise, usually undertaken as a physical conditioner. See **work** out:—Since I had not played in a long time, the three sets of tennis proved to be quite a workout for me.

work up (1) ascend gradually to a higher position through working:—Starting as office boy, he worked up to the position of vice-president. (2) develop, prepare:—The professor spent the summer working up a new series of lectures to deliver to his fall classes. (3) advance gradually toward:—We couldn't tell until the end just what the speaker was working up to. (4) excite, cause to become gradually more nervous and emotional:—There was no reason for her to get so worked up over such an innocent remark.

work wonders have miraculous results:—I assure you that this medicine will work wonders for your cold.

works, give one the works beat up, punish, scold:—When the collared suspect tried to wriggle away from the policeman's grasp, the latter gave him the works.

works, shoot the works act without limitation or restraint, use one's total resources at one time:—We were scheduled to visit only two countries, but when we reached Europe, we decided to shoot the works and stay longer and see the whole Continent.

works, the works the whole thing, the complete procedure:—I wanted to look particularly well that evening, so I told the barber to give me the works: shave, haircut, shampoo, tonic, etc.

world to come the future world, heaven:—Their philosophy being materialistic and hedonistic, they scoffed at any thoughts of the world to come.

world, a world of a great deal of:—We've had a world of pleasure out of that old car.

world, for all the world exactly completely, in every detail:—She looked for all the world like her twin sister.

world, for the world for anything, for the greatest possible reward:—I wouldn't for the world go into that deserted house at this time of night.

world, give the world to give anything in order to achieve an objective:—I'd give the world to know what they are talking about.

world, out of this world, exceptional, remarkable, wonderful:—Patsy's cooking is really out of this world.

world, what in the world what, among all things existent, an intensive form of "what":—What in the world does he think he will gain by such conduct?

worm in penetrate gradually, insinuate oneself:—By cultivating the friendship of a few of the prominent men, Mr. Parvenue had hoped to worm his way into that exclusive country club.

worm may turn even the meek will ultimately react to abusive treatment:—He may think that he can continue indefinitely to mistreat his wife, but knowing her, I should say that some day the worm may turn.

worm out draw out from, learn through persistent questioning: — I finally wormed out of her the reason she broke off her engagement to Jim.

worry along get along or survive despite obstacles:—We have been through worse difficulties than this, and for the present, we'll just worry along for a while.

worship the ground someone walks on love or admire greatly:—She worships the ground her son walks on.

worst, at worst in the worst possible eventuality:—At worst, we cannot lose very much on the deal.

worst, do one's worst do one's utmost by resorting to every foul means possible:—Out of sheer revenge, he did his worst to blacken her character and ruin her reputation.

worst, if (the) worst comes to (the) worst if the worst happens:—If the worst comes to the worst, we can always ask Dad to help us out.

worthwhile adequate in payment or advantage for the time or money spent. Sometimes expressed as **worth one's while**:—I'd like to begin studying Spanish, but with so little time to give to it, I wonder whether it would be worthwhile.

worth See also **money**, one's money's worth; **salt**, not to be worth one's salt.

would-be aspiring:—The Broadway casting offices are always crowded with would-be actors.

wrapped up in enthralled by, completely absorbed by:—He is all wrapped up in his scientific studies.

wrinkle, a new wrinkle an original or novel approach, a new idea:—The manufacturers of women's clothing are always looking for some new wrinkle to change the current fashion and stimulate buying.

write down make a note of:—Just a moment. Let me write down your name and address.

write out write fully in detail:—He sat down and wrote me out a check for the entire amount.

write-up a published account of some person or event:—There was an interesting write-up of the President's goodwill tour abroad in last week's issue of Time magazine.

writing on the wall a sign of impending trouble or disaster. See **handwriting** on the wall.

wrong side of the tracks the less socially desirable section of a town:—Her wealthy parents were unalterably opposed to her marrying a boy from the wrong side of the tracks.

wrong, be in the wrong be at fault, in error:—The taxi driver was obviously in the wrong in going ahead against the red light.

wrong, get in wrong come into disfavor, incur the anger or dislike of:—Though he means well, Frank is always getting in wrong with someone or other because of his complete lack of tact.

wrong, get one wrong misunderstand someone, misinterpret:—Don't get me wrong. I wasn't trying to criticize you.

Y

year in and year out regularly, over a long period:—He goes to church every Sunday year in and year out.

year round the entire year:—I like Florida, but I wouldn't want to live there the year round.

yellow cowardly. Sometimes expressed as **yellow-livered**:—Bruce resented being called yellow and immediately started to fight.

yellow journal a cheap and sensational newspaper:—Yellow journals generally feature crime and scandals rather than legitimate news.

Yellow Pages a classified business telephone directory:—I found the name of a nearby taxidermist in the Yellow Pages.

yeoman service help in time of need, good and serviceable assistance:—Frank did yeoman service in organizing our yearly fund-raising campaign.

yes-man a subordinate who always agrees with his chief, one who assents to everything proposed or stated:—After only a few days on his new job, Jim realized that his boss did not like a yes-man.

yesterday See **born** yesterday.

young ones children, those still dependent upon their parents for protection and support:—We would like to take a trip this summer, but we don't know what to do about the young ones.

Z

zero in on attack rapidly, confront, reprimand:—When Rhoda was rude to her mother, her father zeroed in on her and sent her to bed.